I Want to
Stay Married,
But How?

I WANT TO STAY MARRIED, BUT HOW?

EMPOWERING CHRISTIAN WOMEN IN MARRIAGE

KATHY SCHOENBORN, MS, LPC

WinePressPublishing
Great Books, Defined.

ISBN 13: 978-1-4141-1842-0
ISBN 10: 1-4141-1842-2
Library of Congress Catalog Card Number: 2010908074

To my dearest Phil, I am glad that we stuck with our
marriage through better and worse and better,
through poorer and richer, and beyond its near death.
May we always praise the One who saved us,
and may our love be blessed as we grow
old hand in hand.

To Warren and Donna, who will continue to
encourage me to faithful and joyful living until
I join them in heaven.

CONTENTS

INTRODUCTION: MOVIN' OUT, MOVIN' IN, MOVIN' ON

Movin' Out

*You can't solve a problem with the same
level of thinking that created it.*[1]
—*Albert Einstein*

Movin' In

*You were taught, with regard to your former way of life, to put off
your old self, which is being corrupted by its deceitful desires; to
be made new in the attitude of your minds; and to put on the new
self, created to be like God in true righteousness and holiness.*
—*Ephesians 4:22-24*

Movin' On

*God does not give us overcoming life—
He gives us life as we overcome.*[2]
—*Oswald Chambers*

*S*ALDAGE IS A Portuguese word that I learned from our Brazilian exchange student. It fits many situations and means "happy, but sad." It describes the mixed feelings that I have for the hurting women who will find this book. I am sad for the pain and heartache and loneliness that you feel as a woman in a challenging marriage. But I am also happy that you have found this resource.

- You can rekindle hope.
- You are not alone.
- You can be stronger.
- You will be encouraged.
- You can do a lot to improve your life.

Being both an experienced professional counselor and a woman who has struggled in her marriage, I have had the privilege of walking alongside hurting women through counseling at my office, at church, and in the classroom. As I teach and walk with other women being challenged spiritually and emotionally, I am encouraged as well. Their courage and strength as they grow in personal understanding continue to empower me to be my best alongside them.

Early on in my career, as I attempted to apply my skills and counseling expertise to my husband and our marriage, the outcome was less than satisfying. For some odd reason, my husband had not signed up to be my client to be analyzed and "encouraged" according to my assessment of his personal flaws. His understandable resistance to my efforts and my resistance to looking at myself contributed mightily to our marriage struggles and made solutions more elusive.

Finding help in the church for my own dying marriage was difficult. I *am* a believer, I *do* have faith, I *have* prayed for my marriage, I *have* gone to counseling and classes and have worked with pastors, but none of these avenues provided the healing I needed. Often feeling alone, shamed and defective, I cried out to God and pastors, women mentors and members of my church women's groups.

My stubbornness paid off for once as I doggedly and desperately searched for solutions that would help me and my marriage. In the process of doing my own work, I became a student of what theologians, marriage researchers, and "therapy types" thought would work as well. As mentors they reflected the wisdom, truth, hope, and love of God to me. They facilitated my spiritual and emotional transformation and healing and pulled me out of the mire and sludge of my difficult marriage.

I pray that God will reach out to each of you in your pain and do a healing work in your heart and your life. I pray that you will live out 1 Corinthians 16:13 as you become empowered, learn to be on your guard, stand firm in the faith and in love, and become strong women of courage.

MOVIN' OUT

There are various habits that we need to *move away* from for self-transformation. The first is our denial of relational dysfunction and our role in it. In denial, we magically think that doing nothing or blaming others will have a positive relational outcome. When it doesn't, we become more fearful and overwhelmed in knowing what to do. The definition of insanity is doing the same thing over and over while expecting different results. Albert Einstein obviously agrees by saying, "We can't solve a problem with the same level of thinking that created it." We need to push past the facade that denial is a helpful or safe place and to move ahead with the plethora of hope-filled alternatives. Freud has the final word here by saying, "Pain does not decompose when we bury it."

> "Pain does not decompose when we bury it."

The second habit we need to *move out* of is our tireless work of changing and blaming our husbands. Both of these choices lock us out of ever experiencing solutions to our problems. I have been a super "fix him up" wife. As long as I was pointing the finger at him, I didn't have to look at me. I thought I knew best how to make a family. I wanted to have *my* way. Sometimes I didn't want to make waves with truth telling. Other times I just didn't know what to do or how to do marriage. The first and immediate action for any hope of salvaging our marriages is to accept that we are powerless to change our husbands. We need to acknowledge that past strategies have been ineffective and have even blocked our own emotional, intellectual, and spiritual growth. Marsha Means quotes Christian marriage counselor Mark Luciano, saying:

> The obsessive searchlight trained on your spouse will be refocused to look at what is within your power to change, namely yourself. The energy spent worrying and fretting over what your spouse will do next is more effectively used to fulfill your own needs. As you implement each new step, you will find you have recovered more and more of your life's energy.[3]

As a hurting woman, the thought of recovering my life energy is very appealing, and I imagine it is for you too. We move out of old patterns and into new hope as we focus on our own growth and get smarter about how we do marriage.

Movin' In

After we move beyond denial and changing our husbands, we can begin to *move into* a real place of change *within* ourselves. This book will provide many opportunities to change the way you think about yourself, God, and marriage. These often counterintuitive thoughts are called *paradigm shifts*, and they have the potential to have monumental effects for life transformation. A paradigm shift is a way of reframing or looking at the same unchanging situation in a totally different way. We might shift the meaning of a problem, we might change the way we view marriage, we might challenge unmet expectations, or we might refocus our attentions. Learning skills is important, but making small, meaningful shifts in our thinking has the potential for much more powerful and permanent change in our lives and marriages.

Another internal shift that can help us be more relationally healthy is what I call "walking the line." This phrase from a Johnny Cash song relates to a precarious line we need to walk in our marriages. We need to confront difficulties to prevent ourselves from becoming bitter and angry, and we need to do it with respect. Two parts of walking the line include speaking the truth and confronting our spouse respectfully.

When we speak the truth we:

- Care enough for ourselves and partners to move out of denial.
- Learn to speak up respectfully regarding our hurts and needs.
- Be assertive to set boundaries against wrongs.
- Seek prayer and wise counsel for ourselves to help us decide what to do and what we need.

Terry Real, a therapist and marriage researcher of intimacy differences, discusses the struggle and risk that women have with truthful speaking up. Women often fear that when they speak up and ask to have their needs met, they risk losing their marriage. It is a real catch-22, because if they back away from full disclosure, they will risk becoming resentful, which kills passion and authenticity. Dr. Real observed that women who deny themselves will eventually get to the point where they either *explode* or *corrode* due to buried resentment. He acknowledges that it *is* a danger to speak up, but *more* dangerous not to. He encourages women to grow out of learned accommodation and indirectness and give up the "good girls don't make waves" mantra. He explains the great paradox of intimacy: in order to sustain passionate connection, one must be willing to "go to the mats"—from time to time to risk being truthful against fears of the unknown outcome.[4] We need to become strong and courageous, warrior women, in the fight for our families.

The second imperative skill for walking the line is learning to confront respectfully. In her book for women whose spouses have sexual addictions, Marsha Means says that women need to confront so that they aren't enabling sin. She says confrontation motivates change, and love demands it. Respectful confrontation helps women not become victims in relationships.[5] Means recommends that we do not confront alone or without education, prayer, and support. We are told in Matthew 18:15-17 to confront our brother who sins. Our confrontation requires setting limits and needs to be motivated by love.

So, what does respectful confrontation look like?

- We make sure our motivation is to do what is right, not to change, fix, or blame our spouse.
- We learn to separate our spouse's value as a person from his unacceptable behaviors.
- We hold ourselves and our spouse accountable to God's standards.
- We extract ourselves from our spouse's dysfunction by letting him experience consequences.
- We do not enable or tolerate abuse or addictions of any kind by setting boundaries.

In his classic Christian bestseller, *Caring Enough to Confront*, David Augsburger calls this difficult but necessary skill *care-fronting*. He defines care-fronting as a genuine caring that bids another to grow, the uniting of love and power. It is a way to communicate truth with impact and respect.[6]

Moving out of denial and confronting what is wrong in our lives and marriages are expressions of caring for ourselves, our partner, and our marriage, and it also honors God. As we confront what is wrong, we learn to do it in the way that best facilitates change. There is no guarantee that as we learn to walk the line, the outcome will be a "happily ever after" ending. Even though we usually hope that our marriage will be redeemed, we are "care-fronting" and speaking the truth in love out of obedience, not because of promises of marital reconciliation. This takes courage. The promises in Deuteronomy 31:6 encourage us to be strong and courageous, not afraid. The Lord our God *will* go with us, he will *never* leave us or forsake us.

LIVING STRONG AND COURAGEOUS

In most of the chapters to follow you'll find a section titled "Living Strong," which features examples of real women who have faced their fears. They have found God totally faithful in never leaving them and in giving them the strength, courage, and peace that He promises, regardless of the variable outcomes for their marriages.

- Lynn walked the line by getting stronger and saying no to her husband's sexual addictions.
- Molly walked the line by getting stronger and in spite of fear, courageously said "no more" to her husband's verbally abusive and controlling ways.
- Jan walked the line by getting stronger in her faith and finding her calling, reducing the impact of her husband's pornography addiction on her life.
- Kerri walked the line by getting healthy and confronting her husband's alcohol abuse and his verbally abusive treatment through a controlled marital separation.
- Karen walked the line while asking for the space and support she needed to address and heal from her childhood sexual abuse.

All of these sisters faced their challenging situations from a submitted and educated position of strength, not out of neediness, impulsiveness, or manipulation.

Dr. James Dobson wrote a classic book about this version of tough love in which he states that genuine love demands this type of toughness. Passivity does not invite a person to change, and does not ask him or her to respect you.[7]

MOVIN' ON

It's not easy to walk the line through old patterns and fear of change, risks, and unknown outcomes. Both "movin' out" of blame and denial and "movin' in" toward self-growth require a degree of strength beyond our human selves. We need to be well-protected Warrior Women, facing the emotional, spiritual, and relational battle for our families. We need to be armed with the full armor of

God for this battle (Ephesians 6:10-18). It is not a battle we can face alone.

Gary Smalley defines *courage* as "The inner commitment to pursue a worthwhile goal without giving up hope."[8] He guides his readers to be proactive at building a better marriage. Although we are intelligent women, it is not always clear how to go about doing that.

- Sometimes being courageous means saying, "I really cannot go on pretending everything is OK."
- Sometimes being courageous means accepting we will get healthy no matter what our spouse decides to do.
- Sometimes being courageous means being the first one to say, "This is not the marriage I expected."
- Sometimes being courageous means learning about and setting up firm boundaries against what I call "Triple Threats" of abuse, addictions, and adultery. (See Appendix C.)

We need courage to step back from our understandable reactive emotional tensions in a struggling marriage to assess our situation. We can then respond thoughtfully, rather than having a knee-jerk reaction that we may regret. That is what Laura Munson did when her "midlife crisis" husband of twenty years said he didn't think he loved her anymore and was not sure he ever did. She told him, "I'm not buying it." She controlled herself from fully expressing her anger and hurt with him. She made a conscious decision not to get caught up in his struggles. She periodically asked him, "What do I have to do to give you the distance you need without hurting the family?" She accepted that his problem was not hers to solve, and what she needed to do was get out of the way. She did not allow it to become a marital issue so that he could turn around and blame her for it. She acknowledges that this was very difficult and against

> Stepping back from our emotions helps us assess our situation thoughtfully.

reason at times. She walked the line of truth and accountability that is recorded in her book, *This Is Not The Story You Think It Is*. She describes her book to her husband by saying:

> It is really not about our family. It's more about my process. It's about not taking things personally, even when you feel the world is crumbling around you. It's about choosing happiness over suffering. It's about retraining the way we think.[9]

MISSION POSSIBLE

This mission is possible. You *too* can refuse to buy into the sociological mandate for entitlement, the cultural trend for easy divorce, the unrealistic expectations, the fallacy that our husbands and marriages are responsible for our personal happiness. Enter at your own risk into this danger zone that will introduce you to new ways of thinking and doing marriage. Expect to be strengthened and empowered with hope as you learn to work much smarter at marriage. If you choose to accept this mission, you will discover that one person equipped with spiritual armor and courage from God and with skills from experts and mentors can be transformed, experience renewed hope, and positively impact her marriage!

Will you join me in movin' out, movin' in, and movin' on toward a healthier life, to turn your valley of trouble into a door of hope?

"I will make the valley of Achor (trouble) a door of hope."
—Hosea 2:15

NOTES

1. http://www.great-quotes.com/cgi-bin/viewquotes.cgi?keyword=solve+a+problem&action=search

2. Oswald Chambers, *My Utmost for His Highest*, (Nashville: Thomas Nelson, 1992), February 16 Devotion, Accessed September 11, 2007.

3. Marsha Means, *Living with Your Husband's Secret Wars*, quoting Luciano (Grand Rapids: Revell, 1999), 52.

4. Terrence Real, *How Can I Get Through to You?* (New York: Fireside, 2002), 53-56.

5. Means, *Living with Your Husband's Secret Wars*, 64.

6. David Augsburger, *Caring Enough to Confront* (Ventura, CA: Regal Books, 1973, 1981), 10.

7. James Dobson, *Love Must Be Tough* (Dallas: Word, 1996).

8. Gary Smalley, "A Woman's Call to Courage," in www.dnaofrelationships.com, 1/8/2007.

9. Laura Munson, *This Is Not the Story You Think It Is* (New York: Penguin, 2010), 334.

CHAPTER 1

FROM THERE TO HERE

For I know the plans I have for you, declares the Lord,
plans to prosper you and not to harm you,
plans to give you hope and a future.
—Jeremiah 29:11

"I QUIT!"

SOMETIME IN 1997, I was once again fed up and ready to quit my marriage. It only brought me pain and heartache. God knew that over the past twenty-six years I had prayed, waited, and attended enough counseling with pastors and professionals to fix my marriage, if it was even fixable. One day I approached a pastor at church, looking red-eyed, bedraggled, and desperate. In a quavering voice, I asked, "If God hates divorce, and I don't want to divorce, where can I go in the church to save my marriage?"

The pastor glibly replied, "Well, what would you have us provide?"

I crumbled inside as I shouted to myself, "If I knew that, I wouldn't be asking you. After all, you're the pastor!" I felt crushed, rejected, and angry. Little did I know that this cold and seemingly hurtful reply would put me on the path to becoming the answer to my own question.

Of course, the difficulties in my marriage began long before I thought of being married…

LITTLE KATHY, LITTLE PHIL

I have this specially framed picture of "little kathy" and "little phil" when we were about seven years old. I framed them to provide encouragement at a time when I was struggling with letting go of past pain and habits.

"Little kathy" grew up innocently in a house with a mom and dad who loved her, but they had minimal ability or experience in knowing how to love, nurture, and teach her about relationships. Mom's father died when she was ten, which she attributed to her becoming a vulnerable, emotionally needy young woman with a tendency for depression. Outwardly Dad was a typical 1950s' dad who worked hard, was successful, and led his family with strength and confidence. Behind the mask and in our home was a different story. He was a controlling authoritarian who was verbally abusive and threatening as he medicated his secret pains with alcohol. Dad acted out his inner pain with the outer bravado of dominance and

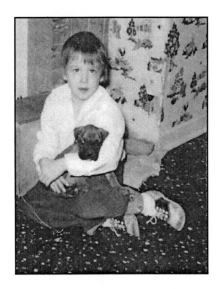

yelling, fueled by alcohol. Mom was increasingly lost as she seemed to cry away her identity, absorbing the lies of abuse.

On July 5, 1965, our family life went from bad to worse. My seventeen-year-old sister, Jill, was suddenly killed in a car accident. I remember hearing the siren that day but not giving it much thought until I realized the ear-piercing noise took Jill away and changed our family forever. As was "normal" for our family, we didn't talk, feel, or grieve Jill's loss. Mom and Dad did "more of the same" pulling away from us and each other. Mom retreated in tears to her room and Dad went in silence to his bottle and its accompanying lies, blackouts, and deception. I was fourteen and I remember wondering if I died, would they never say my name again and not acknowledge that I had ever existed, like they have done with Jill? Is that how much I am loved as well? I certainly didn't know the answer to the questions, and I knew not to ask. Jill's death exacerbated the slow, torturous decline of my parents' marriage, which ended bitterly sixteen years later.

My coping mechanism for this family pain was to develop a protective shell and to set out to prove my worth and earn the love I desired. In my intimate relationship, my unconscious mind "chose" the dominant and controlling position over the passive dependency of my mother. The truth of the matter, which I didn't realize until years later, was that they were opposite sides of the same dysfunctional coin. My two sisters, younger brother, and I learned the three tenets of the alcoholic family: don't talk, don't trust, and don't feel. They "worked" to get us through our upbringing, but caused problems in our relationships. I shut down emotionally and looked for fulfillment in all the wrong places, becoming sexually active at fifteen. I also worked hard for acceptance through my performance in school and sports. I started experimenting with drinking at eighteen, and happily ran off to college to get away from the hurt and emptiness at home.

"Little phil" grew up under a passive-aggressive authoritarian, alcoholic father and the emotionally vague love of his mother. He believed the lies that he was unworthy and unlovable. His functional childlike response was to close down and build big, thick walls around himself. He told himself, "No one will ever get close enough to hurt me again." That attitude got him through his teenage years, but not surprisingly became ineffective in the intimacies of marriage.

Today my picture of "little kathy" and "little phil" still helps me to remember that our intentions are not to hurt each other as we continue to outgrow the dysfunctional dance of our families of origin. We match up in such perfect imperfect ways. In his excellent book, *Getting the Love You Want*, Dr. Harville Hendrix proposes that God's very purpose for marriage is that we marry a person who, by confronting us with the same hurts of our childhoods, allows us the "opportunity" to grow up and out of our past dysfunctions, by God's grace alone![1]

HOPES TO FEARS, SAVING EACH OTHER?

Phil was my first real love, and at fifteen and sixteen years old we had fun going on dates to the drive-in, homecoming, and prom. We wrote love notes and experienced high school jealousies. Phil was a wrestler and I was his queen. We "dragged the ave" (avenue), ate McDonald's fish sandwiches, paid twenty-five cents a gallon for gas, and kissed in the driveway. Phil and I have fond memories of high school.

The "rest of the story," as Paul Harvey used to say, is of a relationship built primarily on sex and clinging to each other out of unmet needs. There were intense arguments, pouting, tears, breakups and make-ups, pregnancy fears, disappointment, and lots of confusion.

Marrying at the tender, "know-it-all" ages of twenty and twenty-one, "little kathy and little phil" embarked on some kind of journey! Little did they know the rough road ahead of them when they said "I do." It's not a surprise to me now that the roles and rules of our troubled upbringings brought the same repetitive pain and discord to us as adults, and later to our little family of four.

His Story in Me!

I lived in denial for five to seven years, and then I worked unsuccessfully to blame and "fix up" Phil for about the same length of time. I was thirty-three years old before I came to the end of myself. Living the American dream on the outside, I was still the hurting, angry, protective, stubborn little girl on the inside that I'd always been. Inwardly I cried out the same questions over and over:

- "Why am I so unhappy?"
- "Is this all there is?"
- "What is missing in my life?"

- "What is wrong with me?"
- "Does anyone love me?"
- "Will I ever be good enough?"

I had many questions and nowhere to turn.

And then God in His mercy entered my world through a TV evangelist. He seemed to speak directly to my needs as he asked, "Do you have all that the world says should make you happy but you're not?" "Do you feel like something is missing but don't know what it is?" "Are you empty inside and lack peace?" I was riveted to the TV as he said, "What you need is a personal relationship with Jesus Christ." I knew without a doubt in my heart that *was* what I needed. I fell to my knees and asked Christ into my life.

My excitement quickly turned to major disappointment as my pain and problems did not automatically disappear. Little did I know then how long it would really take. It took me some time to find a good church and begin to learn more about how to heal and become the woman God wanted me to be. For once in my life I wasn't pushy and domineering as I grew in my newfound faith. My husband also gave his life to the Lord within the next year.

God is good. This became the first of many "God incidences" of my life. God has allowed circumstances to provide me opportunities to grow and know Him more deeply. God has used these strong, periodic, clear directions from Him to keep me faithful to Him and to remain in a marriage that I often wanted to leave.

HAITI

The next significant God incidence in my life was when Phil and I and our two sons went on a four-month short-term mission trip to Haiti. Circumstances led us to believe that God had an important plan for us in going. Even as new believers, we felt strongly led to go. The trip caused us both to want to enter long-term mission work. Knowing that our marriage was shaky, we came home from Haiti for a "little counseling" to prepare to fulfill God's calling on our lives. Little did we know how unhealthy, resistant, and stubborn we both were!

After three-plus years of counseling with little progress, we separated to reassess if we wanted to remain married. Following the guidelines of our pastor, we both decided after six months that we did not want to give up on our marriage and family. At alternating points one or the other of us would say, "I give up. This marriage is not going to work. I need to get out. Let's just end the pain and get divorced." When one of us was weak, God allowed the other to be strong. The reply of the  strong one was, "No, God would not have brought us to himself and given us this common missionary vision without healing our marriage. I will not give up on God." This bantering went back and forth for years. When I was in the giving up mode, I was very frustrated and even angry at the times that Phil refused to quit.

Today, I am so thankful to God for putting this pattern in our lives. A verse that kept me going was Ephesians 2:14: "He himself is our peace, who has made the two one and has destroyed the barrier, the dividing wall of hostility." I often prayed, "Dear God, destroy these barriers, get rid of this hostility, I want to be one with my husband!" I needed this verse. God is good.

We continued to work on our marriage, seeing counselors together and separately. We attended Bible studies, met with pastors, went to sex therapists, attended a Retrouvaille™ Catholic marriage retreat and various marriage conferences, and yet we still struggled.

Sadly, I received the most encouragement at church to get divorced rather than persevere in this difficult marriage. I observed that women in painful marriages in church (these were not easy to find!) seemed to adopt one of three options:

- Some got divorced.
- Some stayed and became bitter and angry.
- Others got stronger and loved and served the Lord in spite of their difficult marital situation.

I determined that I would follow the third path, and actively sought out women who could become my mentors. At an intensive sex therapy retreat, I admitted to Phil for the first time that I'd had a brief affair. The affair was long over by then and Phil said he understood why I had done it. He graciously forgave me and accepted my confession of guilt and deep remorse. As we processed it with the therapist and each other, I learned that another man was not the answer to my problems, and felt immense relief that my sin was finally behind us. God is good.

Walk-Away Wife

I continued to struggle for years, and realized that I had what Michelle Weiner Davis calls the "Walk-away wife syndrome" in her book, *The Divorce Remedy*.[2] I carried this attitude for the last years that my two sons were in high school, separating emotionally from my husband and my marriage. I planned to take care of myself, get healthy, grow in the Lord, and become economically self-sufficient. When my youngest son graduated, I was prepared emotionally, spiritually, and financially to divorce my husband and go on and live happily ever after. It was not a God-honoring motive, but as it so often happens, God graciously used this time in my life to grow me up. I'm glad He didn't give up on me.

Although these years continued to be painful and uncertain, when I quit trying to "fix" my husband, God finally had a chance to work in his life without my interference. It may have been the first time in our marriage that Phil didn't have to spend the majority of his energies defending himself from my misplaced intentions. He had the freedom to take his first honest look at himself.

Today I grieve my former aggressive and selfish ways, but am thankful that God held us together in spite of ourselves. Often I wanted to pretend the part like our parents did, yet I also desired to heal and to pass on a healthier, godly heritage to our children. We had many good family times during these years with kids—sports, church activities, camping, and mission trips. I was involved in serving at church as a Bible study teacher, counselor, and missions team trainer. I also grew as a believer through going on numerous short-term mission trips with my husband's support.

When my four years of being a "walk-away wife" were behind me, I was shocked as I looked at my husband and our marriage, and said to myself, "This isn't (and he isn't) as bad as I thought." I no longer needed to leave and my loving feelings for my husband were beginning to grow. As I healed more and grew in my faith, God enabled me to have a more mature outlook on my husband and our marriage. God is waaaaaaaay good!

Working Together

After that I had moved beyond the "walk-away wife" syndrome, God moved us into a new endeavor that has grown us some more. In midlife my husband began to desire owning his own veterinary business. I was supportive, and he asked if I would partner with him to get it going. We envisioned that, even though it didn't look like we would be going on the mission field full-time, maybe if we had our own business we could do regular short-term mission work in our retirement. Working together turned out to be the challenge of the century. It was fortunate that no human blood was shed! But because I had felt clearly that God had led me to support Phil, I stuck it out for the Lord when I didn't always feel like sticking it out for us. Sound familiar?

As we worked side by side all day, every day in the planning, remodeling, and developing of a veterinary practice, an interesting thing happened. For the first time in our twenty-five-year marriage, I developed a respect for my husband that I'd never had. To me, he had always been the husband who doesn't help at home, the husband

9

who refuses to love me in the way I want, the husband who refuses to heal from his alcoholic upbringing. Now, through God's plan  and timing, I began to see him as the man who was gentle and compassionate with customers, the vet who carried around little kitties in his shirt. He was the calm, patient diagnostician, the doctor who was so wise and practical in his care of sick pets. He was the business-man who knew where each penny was, and the boss who wanted the best for his employees.

We both developed a new appreciation and acceptance of each other as partners in work. For the first time in our lives, we appreciated our different complimentary gifts. We discovered that *together* we could create something of value that neither one of us could ever do alone. What a wonderful gift from the Lord this has been. I am confident that if we had not been obedient in the big step of going into business together, I may not have developed enough respect for my husband to stay in the marriage.

RE-ENTER KATHY AND THE PASTOR

So, how did I follow up on my discouraging, maddening encounter with the pastor who said, "Well, what would you have us provide?"

For the next few years I ranted and raved in my journal and wrote, "I would have *You* provide this and I would have *You* provide that." "The group should be positive, hope filled, and practical, providing concrete skills for how to be a better wife. And it should be Christ centered"...and it should be this, and it should be that.

As He so often does, God in His graciousness took my immature, wrongly focused efforts and turned them into something beautiful for Him. It became scarily and clearly evident that *I* was the one being tapped on the shoulder to develop this group. The verses that have become the fuel for me in this ministry are 2 Corinthians 1:3-7:

> Praise be to the God and Father of our Lord Jesus Christ, the Father of compassion and the God of all comfort, who comforts us in all our troubles, so that we can comfort those in any trouble with the comfort we ourselves have received from God. For just as the sufferings of Christ flow over into our lives, so also through Christ our comfort overflows. If we are distressed, it is for your comfort, which produces in you patient endurance of the same sufferings we suffer. And our hope for you is firm, because we know that just as you share in our sufferings, so also you share in our comfort.

God had been my Savior and comforter so that I could endure trouble, He was calling me to be the same for my fellow sister strugglers. Being able to encourage other women who are struggling in the way that I have struggled redeems my pain, allowing it to be used for His good. God is good!

I have had pain from my upbringing and my parents' divorce. I have experienced the near end of my marriage and have struggled with being stubborn and selfish. As I have begun to grow into the woman God created me to be, these experiences have molded who I am today. God in His graciousness has allowed my sometimes difficult character traits to be channeled into beneficial use for His kingdom.

I am angry at the lies we hear from society about marriage and self-promotion. I am frustrated about how we are often encouraged to "pretend" in our churches about the real struggles we experience in our marriages instead of talking about them. It saddens me that the divorce rate in the church is the same as in the world. I am confident that God wants to make a difference in our lives and marriages, and wants us to fight for our families. I am irritated that hurting people can be shamed into hanging out in the dark corners of the church, rather than being affirmed and loved and encouraged to grow in wisdom and awareness and truth. God is ready to tell us what to do so we can be motivated to learn *how* to grow spiritually, emotionally, and relationally. I hope to encourage our growth with this book. We need God—and we need skills.

Full Circle

In the last few years, Phil and I have had the opportunity to go on numerous short-term mission trips and we continue to seek God's direction in missions. We have been able to give testimony to God's grace in our marriage, and we have encouraged others not give up on their marriages. In the last few years we have been involved in facilitating marriage workshops in the church, *together*. This is

a miracle! This is a mission field, and it is sweeeeeeet. We represent so many hurting people in the church today. During our own time of hurt and uncertainty, we loved each other and desperately wanted to stay married, yet we didn't know how. We were confused about hurtful patterns and how to stop them. This most desperate dilemma doesn't always have a clear solution. However, the one promoted most by society, friends, and even the church is to end the pain with divorce.

We all know that divorce commonly does not bring the results expected and that some who divorce will keep making the same well-intentioned mistakes over and over again. In the meantime, the very fabric of our society is disintegrating in front of our eyes.

I am mad! We just don't have to sit by and watch the destruction of lives, marriages, children, families, and our society! God can make a difference; He can heal the pain from the past and we can learn to love again.

I have had quite a ride. There were years when I didn't like my husband, and thinking about getting old with him made me physically sick. But I can tell you as I healed, as we have grown, I can honestly say my love for him is stronger now than ever, and I can't imagine growing old with anyone else. God is good!

God has been there all along in the story of my life. He made me a feisty fighter, a rebellious dissident, a verbal gymnast. All of these characteristics were my survival tools in childhood, but they became the curse of my difficult marriage. They have now become the fuel and fire of the plan of redemption that God had in mind all along. He didn't want my pain and struggle to be wasted. He wanted my suffering to be redeemed through comforting and encouraging other women and couples.

Even today, there are times when I ask myself is it worth it? Should marriage and ministry be so hard and challenging at times? Where is this work going? Should I persevere through this or that roadblock?

Then the phone often rings, and a woman with a quavering voice, sounding familiarly desperate says, "I heard you have a group to help women who have problems in their marriages." I hear myself in those words and know that God is good, all the time.

Will you join me on the journey to become strong and courageous?

NOTES

1. Harville Hendrix, *Getting the Love You Want* (New York: Henry Holt, 1988).
2. Michele Weiner Davis, *The Divorce Remedy* (New York: Simon & Schuster, 2001), 39.

CHAPTER 2

I KNOW HE CAN!

*May the God of hope fill you with all joy and peace
as you trust in Him, so that you may overflow
with hope by the power of the Holy Spirit.*
—Romans 15:13

Hope is giving people a vision to go beyond what they see.
—Author unknown

*C*HUG, CHUG, CHUG. Puff, puff, puff. Ding-dong, ding-dong." *The beloved story by Watty Piper tells about a happy little train that needed to get over the mountain with its big load of toys, animals, and goodies for kids to eat. The small engine tired under its heavy load and soon stalled. When the big passenger engine came by, it was much too shiny and new to help the little train. Next came the large steam engine, but it was too important to pull the small train of toys. The dingy old freight train was so tired it couldn't even think of helping the little engine get over the hill. Finally, a little blue switch engine came chugging happily along the tracks. Although it had never been over the mountain it succumbed to the tears and pleas of the toys as it thought of the empty-handed children waiting on the other side. She merrily hitched herself to the little train with her "I think I can, I think I can" attitude. Slowly, slowly, they started off. Puff, puff, chug, chug, I think I can, I think I can, I think I can. The little blue engine moved up and up, working harder and harder, finally reaching the top of the mountain. The little blue engine smiled as she puffed down the other side and said, "I thought I could, I thought I could."[1]*

The Little Engine That Could was one of my favorite stories to read to my children when they were little. I read it regularly and with great enthusiasm, hoping to instill a sense of "I think I can" and "I thought I could" in the mom as well as the kids. It speaks to me of my great human desire for hope. Yet I quickly remember that life doesn't always bring us the happy outcomes of the little train story. Fortunately we have a great big and all-knowing God who loves us, sustains us, guides us, and promises never to leave us, no matter what life brings our way. God promised the Old Testament hero Joshua, "I will never leave you nor forsake you" (Josh. 1:5b). Now, that is *real hope*!

CHOOSING TO HOPE

Man's Search for Meaning discusses the incredibly powerful possibility that we can choose to find meaning in the midst of even the most hopeless of circumstances. Viktor Frankl gives his account of being held in a concentration camp, where he and his fellow prisoners had absolutely no choice over any part of their daily lives, except their thoughts. In spite of this dire situation, Frankl observed that those who were able to find meaning in their tragedy literally experienced the difference of life over death! We certainly do not have such extreme examples of powerlessness in our modern lives, but it is an inspiring message from some who found life-sustaining meaning through their chosen interpretation of hopeless surroundings.

The men of faith spoken about in Hebrews 11 are revered biblical examples of those who held on to a higher hope. Hebrews 11:1-3 talks about faith being *sure* of what we hope for and *certain* of what we do not see. And yet these awesome, faithful men and women did not see the fruit of their hopes in their lifetimes. This is the substance of faith. Romans 8:24-25 says that hope that we can see is no hope at all. But we wait patiently in hope for what we do not have. No small task. Luckily we have a big God. We often expend tremendous energy attempting to escape our difficulties and tough circumstances. I want to challenge you to imitate these people of faith who developed strength from their weaknesses and chose to find meaning in their struggles, which resulted in a hope not dependent on circumstances.

> Now faith is being sure of what we hope for and certain of what we do not see. This is what the ancients were commended for. By faith we understand that the universe was formed at God's command, so that what is seen was not made out of what was visible.
> —Hebrews 11:1-3

> All these people were still living by faith when they died. They did not receive the things promised; they only saw them and welcomed them from a distance.
> —Hebrews 11:13

CHOOSING WHERE TO PLACE MY HOPE

In our modern American world we tend to put our hope in many things—a good job and education, children, financial success, family, beauty, a good husband, perfection, a nice home, and lots of stuff. When I was thirty-two years old, and I had many things of the world that I had been erroneously led to believe would make me whole and happy. I was despairing and empty when I finally fell on my knees and gave my life to God. Little did I know that my transfer of hope from the things of the world to the things of God was a process that would take years. I believe that my poor examples, bad habits, selfishness, and stubbornness contributed to this slow transfer. I pray that you could be more efficient in the exchange of your human hopes to eternal hope in God!

When we put our hope in the common things of the world based on our circumstances, we set ourselves up for huge and repeated disappointment. Trusting Christ with our lives moves us into a new birth, which is the start of having the living hope referred to in 1 Peter 1:3:

> Praise be to the God and Father of our Lord Jesus Christ! In his great mercy he has given us new birth into a living hope through the resurrection of Jesus Christ from the dead.

Then we begin the process of transferring our human hopes into the ultimate and true hope in God. As we grow in the Lord, we experience more of the peace, love, contentment, and satisfaction that we seek.

Hope is one of those ephemeral entities that can ebb and flow from our lives like the gradual changing of seasons. Sometimes it departs suddenly with circumstances out of our control. The hopelessness in a difficult marriage often occurs gradually and is especially tormenting as we sense our Cinderella dreams slipping through our fingers. Most newlyweds have the following hopes:

> Hoping in the things of the world always bring disappointment.

- All the good things I want, I will find with you.
- All the good things I have had, I will keep.
- All bad things that have ever happened to me will never happen with you.[2]

Application Questions:

1. What are some of the things you have placed your hope in?
2. Which of the above hopes did you have early in your marriage?

As the shiny newness of marriage begins to fade, we have all wondered, "What in the world have I gotten myself in to?" "How could I have so misjudged this relationship?" "Did I make a mistake?" "Is there any hope for us?" We often sit alone in our growing anguish, especially in the church, where it seems every other couple is the perfect model of what I'm not! So who do I even talk to or be honest with? Will I have to hide out in the recesses of the sanctuary with my fake face forever? Will I have to live out this slow and torturous death alone?

Our newlywed hopes turn to fears as we face the reality of life together:

- All the good things I ever wanted are not happening with you.
- All the good things I ever had, I am losing.
- All the bad things that have happened to me will happen again with you.[3]

It is imperative that we understand that the switch from our dreamy hopes of early marriage to the despairing fears of hopelessness is a totally normal process of marriage for many people. It is usually a very premature injustice to jump to the conclusion that this marriage should end. The movement from hopes to fears signifies instead, a need to dig deep to heal and do the real work of learning skills for effective marriage and mature love. "In every marriage over a week old, there are grounds for divorce. The trick is, to find and continue to find the grounds for marriage."[4]

Hope can be sneaky at times. After I had been a believer for quite a few years, I had the hope that our marriage would glorify the Lord. Sounds like a really good and spiritual desire, doesn't it? However, this hope of mine almost drove me crazy! The problem was, this seemingly righteous hope included *two* people, one of whom I had no control over. When I adjusted my desire to be what I wanted to be—a woman and wife who glorified the Lord—the craziness and pressure I had inflicted on myself and my husband diminished. My peace and joy increased substantially. Hope can be misplaced, even when it sounds good.

FINDING STRENGTH IN EXAMPLES OF HOPE

We have many biblical examples of strong and faithful men and women. Job, Jeremiah, Joseph, Mary, and Naomi were real people. I sometimes struggle with being able to relate to their examples. After all, they are in the Bible! I know that God chooses normal, doubting, and inferior humans for His work, but they seem so distant from my life. Yet the stories of their lives exude attitudes of perseverance, undying faith, strength, and courage, and do draw me to more faithful and hopeful living.

I have been inspired as I have read of famous individuals who overcame insurmountable obstacles and came out with hope and faith. Some favorites include:

- **Corrie ten Boom** who showed great courage as she hid Jews during the war and survived a concentration camp. She later traveled the world with minimal comforts, as a "Tramp for the Lord," humbly telling of His work and forgiveness in her life.[5]
- **Charles Spurgeon** was a great theologian who suffered from despairing depressive episodes in the midst of his inspiring and world-famous preaching.
- **Gladys Aylward** overcame gender bias to follow her call to become a missionary to China for God's glory, and mission agencies' dismay![6]

Some current-day heroes in the field of living hope include:

- **Candy Lightner**, who organized Mothers Against Drunk Drivers after the death of her thirteen-year-old daughter from a drunk driver (http://www.madd.org). She formed a very successful grassroots campaign for change. She began as an enraged and grieving mother and became a tireless crusader, obsessed to change a pattern that contributed to so many senseless deaths.
- **Joni Eareckson Tada** dove into the water at seventeen, became a quadriplegic, and went on to develop and lead an international Christian organization that advocates for disabled people around the world. (http://www.joniand-friends.org)
- **Dave Dravecky** was a professional baseball player who eventually had to retire due to cancer and amputation of his pitching arm and shoulder. Dave has gone on to write books, become a Christian motivational speaker and develop a ministry for others with cancer, called Outreach of Hope. (http://www.endurance.org)

My very favorite stories of hope are those I see closest to home:

- **Pam** struggled in her marriage to a resistant alcoholic. She went into treatment for three weeks for her own codependency. She came out with a plan and some skills for being healthy no matter what her husband decided to do. She lived with joy in the Lord in spite of her circumstances. Her five children thank her for that today. God is good!
- My neighbor **Delores** raised a mentally handicapped son because of a drunk doctor who delayed his delivery. Russell was without oxygen too long and lived with his parents until he was in his 50s and they were in their 80s. She still wept when she spoke of it, but lived at peace and with joy in spite of it. God is good!

- **Lynn** persevered faithfully in her very difficult marriage. She grew in her faith and out of her dysfunctional patterns into a strong woman of God. In spite of her choices, her husband continued with addictions to pornography and prostitution, leading her to end the marriage. She came out strong and able to continue to be a healthy role model for her four children and many other young wives. Lynn was one who was fortunate to survive heartbreak because she took what Dag Hammarskjold referred to as "the longest journey, the journey inward." God is good!

- **Sarah** came from an abusive, drug-addicted, and broken family. She was sexually abused and dabbled in promiscuity and drugs, had an abortion, and gave a child up for adoption. Since coming to the Lord she has become a nurse and a missionary and ministers today to any and all women who have suffered with a deep compassion that heals. God is good!

- **Gail** had done her best to be a good, submissive Christian wife to her husband of twelve years. When she began to get stronger and encouraged him to move beyond his relational deadness, he said he didn't love her and wanted a divorce. She didn't fight his leaving. Because of her strong faith and assurance from God, she weathered the breakup. A few years later, God brought her into another marriage with a strong, loving Christian man. God is good!

I am sure that many of us know additional stories of women who found unimaginable strength against all odds. What is the key for these biblical, historical, current, or everyday heroes of hope? They did not set themselves up for huge disappointment by depending on their health, or circumstances, or their money or fame for the hope they desired. They found strength and hope as they chose to seek meaning within their challenging circumstances, rather than running away from them. They were able to do this because they were anchored in the hope of the living God.

Living Strong

Sara has come to know living hope through her struggles in the last years of her twenty-year marriage. Early on she felt alone and misunderstood, and thought the marriage could be better. Their disconnection continued to grow even though they took a marriage class after he had an emotional affair seven years of marriage. When her husband became depressed four years ago, Sara's concern grew and so did her faith. She prayed that God would expose the problem. She soon discovered her husband's relationship with another woman. Sara confronted him and kicked him out of the house. Regretting her impulsive reaction, she asked him to return home the next day. Even though he was remorseful, they entered a long, tormenting period in their marriage.

Sara grew tremendously with the Lord as her husband struggled with shame, yet continued to be drawn to the other woman. He repeatedly left home for days or weeks without warning. She realized that she had been selfish, wanted things to go her way and expecting her husband to make her happy. She saw that she had some growing up to do and knew it would come from her deepening dependence on God.

Sara and her husband sought help in a variety of ways, but none provided the depth then needed to get to the core of their issues. She asked for a separation and began to lose hope as her husband admitted to sexual intimacy with another and ongoing confusion. Sara finally let go of her husband and his choices, but continued to pray for marital restoration. After four months apart they reunited. Sara's uneasiness returned when her husband once again sunk into a pattern of depression, drinking, and leaving home. When confronted, he left for three months. Knowing her husband was wounded, shamed, insecure, and tenderhearted, she resisted a harsh confrontation.

Many individuals in and out of the church were quick to judge them both and encouraged her to dump him. She was able to walk by faith, always waiting for the "go ahead" from God about establishing appropriate boundaries and confrontation. Her tough love included mandatory counseling, changing the locks, kicking him out, confronting him with evidence, and asking hard questions.

Sara did many things that improved the chances for a good outcome for her marriage:

- She primarily pursued the Lord's will in making decisions.
- She never let others' counsel supersede the Lord's leading.
- She looked at herself and was willing to grow out of her dysfunctional attitudes and behaviors, which hurt herself and her marriage.
- She refused to give up easily on her husband or the family that she dearly loved. This determination was not dependent on what he did.
- She continued to hold her husband accountable for his behavior with tough love.

Sara sees the Lord's gracious timing in the pilgrimage that she and her family have been on for the last four to five years. Each hurt, each lie, the rejection and betrayal were revealed slowly, allowing her to process them gradually. She cried and wrestled with God during what she describes as the hardest but best time in her spiritual life. When Sara said that she was done being the only one trying to restore the marriage, her husband came home, broken again. He opened up more than ever before and stayed. When their daughter had their first grandchild, a son, Sara's husband was convicted of the legacy he would leave this child if he continued to run. When he lost his job and found out he had arthritis, his depression returned. But this time he responded by more fully surrendering to God. He is a changed man. Sara says he talks differently, his joy has returned, his prayers have changed, and he praises the Lord for what He has done. They praise the Lord together; they know He did it! God is good! His timing is right!

BECOMING STRONG AND COURAGEOUS

Being hopeless in a difficult marriage is a lonely place to be. It challenges us to ask big existential questions like, "Why did this happen to me? Is life worth living? What do I now believe about God, life, and happiness?" Carl Jung said that when we are challenged to reach into our innermost experience, into the very being of who we are, many of us are overcome by fright and run away. When tragedies enter our lives, it is easier to run away, and we need to face whatever big questions come our way.

> "When we are no longer able to change our situation, we are forced to change ourselves."

Viktor Frankl has said, "When we are no longer able to change our situation, we are challenged to change ourselves."[7] We need to take responsibility first, for our own healing. If we have not addressed or healed issues from our upbringing or past, we need to heal those first, before we can hope to be effective in our relationships. I came from an alcoholic family background and have struggled with depression. Until I am aware of and begin to grow out of my own dysfunctional patterns, I am unlikely to be able to positively affect my marriage.

We need to take responsibility to address our marital issues from a position of strength. Another common block to hope and growth is when we get stuck blaming the other person for our situation. Blaming another person blocks us from developing strategies or growing from our dilemma. We are not responsible for what they choose, but we can choose our reactions to their choices. This allows us to see options and have hope in spite of them.

We are not alone, and God does have a plan for us. We need to start out on our knees, turning ourselves and all the difficulties of our lives over to Him (Appendix A). We have options about where to place our hope. When we choose to look for meaning in our suffering, we are often led to have a hope way beyond ourselves which also compels us to live above our circumstances. We have tremendous examples of others who have chosen to make meaning out of tragedy. We too, have choices in spite of our disappointments. When every human freedom is snatched away, we still have the ability to choose our attitude. We can focus on growing our ability to:

- Choose God's sovereignty over our circumstances.
- Choose humility over our rights.

- Choose to be grounded in our secure faith over the frailty of our feelings.
- Choose to root ourselves in God over the "why" of our circumstances.

I am only able to make these choices as I develop my spiritual self. I can do this by being involved in a supportive community, developing spiritual disciplines such as prayer, Bible study, service, and quiet times. I need spiritual mentors and discipleship from more mature believers so that I can be challenged to grow. I need to allow sufficient time for silence and solitude so that I can listen to God's guidance for me. It is often helpful and necessary to get wise Christian counsel from a pastor or counselor when we are stuck in hopelessness.

<h2 style="text-align:center">Will you join me in growing toward
a hope that will never fail?</h2>

NOTES

1. Watty Piper, *The Little Engine That Could* (New York: Platt & Munk, 1959).
2. Lori H. Gordon and Jon Frandsen, *Passages to Intimacy* (New York: Fireside, 2000), 23.
3. Gordon and Frandsen, *Passages to Intimacy*, 24.
4. Robert Anderson, "Marriage Quotes" http://www.smartmarriages.com, accessed October 10, 2008.
5. Corrie ten Boom with John and Elizabeth Sherrill, *The Hiding Place* (New York: Bantam Books, 1971).
6. Gladys Aylward, *The Little Woman* (Chicago: Moody Bible Institute, 1970).
7. Viktor Frankl, *Man's Search for Meaning* (Boston: Beacon Press, 1959), 116.

CHAPTER 3

MIRROR, MIRROR, WHO IS THAT?

*But whenever anyone turns to the Lord, the veil is taken away.
Now the Lord is the Spirit, and where the Spirit of the Lord is,
there is freedom. And we, who with unveiled faces all reflect
the Lord's glory, are being transformed into his
likeness with ever-increasing glory, which
comes from the Lord, who is the Spirit.
—2 Corinthians 3:16-18*

*To sacrifice what you are and live without belief
is a fate more terrible than dying[1].
—Joan of Arc*

LITTLE KATHY—A Two-Act Play

IT'S A PROFOUND but simple two-act play with four characters. It is 1957, little kathy is sitting on the wood floor near the threadbare brownish rug in the living room. She has her back to the front picture window with those little hard to clean divided panes. little kathy, at seven years old, is dressed for play in her comfy blue jeans, stylishly rolled to mid-calf. She's got on her brown and white saddle shoes scuffed up from much tomboy wear. The faded T-shirt completes the ensemble over her petite but strong and tanned torso. The plain brown bandage on her knee tells of her rough and tumble neighborhood life. You can see the smooth, unworn innocence on her face with anticipation for the day. Below the surface is an insecurity paired with little-girl tenacity. You see it in those expressive coffee-brown eyes. Four levels of her log home are done. The bright green roof pieces and brown logs are scattered nearby, ready to complete the masterpiece. She is sure this is going to be her best yet. The door is off center on the long front side, and side and back windows will bring in lots of light. Her pride and excitement in this special creation will be certain to earn her the prize of her parents' approval. Her parents are in view of the project with their backs to little kathy. Their usual crossed-arms, angry stance is replaced on this day by more of a "barely there" kind of presence.

Scene 1

Little kathy's masterpiece takes shape as she begins the fifth course of logs. The windows are beginning to emerge. She clears away excess building material to show it off most effectively. She says to the mom and dad, "hey, mom, dad, look what I did, look at my neat house." It is like they can't hear her, and she repeats in her little-girl excitement, "mommy, daddy, I'm making a house, look, look…" no reply. ("do I exist? can they see me?") As a spectator in the play, it is lucky you are near the front row, because you can hardly believe your eyes. Each time little kathy pleads for the recognition she craves, the delicate pixie features of her face seem to fade. "Is it true, is this really happening?" you ask. You sit forward in your seat, barely breathing, staring intently. With increasing volume and pleading, Kathy says "Daddy! Mom! Look at my house, it has a lot of windows," and sure enough, her face fades. Nearly crying now: "Daddy, Mommy. Look—I made a house." Underneath the words, saying, "are you proud of me, do you see me, do you see what I can do, am I important, am I special and loved?" Her pleas fade in intensity as her features fade into a blank palate with her parents' stoic, statue-like non-response. little kathy fades away....

Scene 2

A man enters the room across from little kathy—the girl without a face—and walks confidently up to her. He is a big, strong man—but gentle and loving. He kneels at her side, careful not to disturb her masterpiece. He towers over her little seven-year-old self and gently places his hands on her tomboy face. She can feel warmth and love and tenderness unknown to her as he says, "I love you, little girl. You are special; you are so important to me; and your house is so cool. You are a good builder, you have good ideas, and you did a great job. I like your work but I love you for who you are. You don't even have to make houses for me to love and accept you. You are smart and strong and important." Once again, you are on the edge of your seat, but you are confident and excited, now, that you know exactly what you see. After each time this stranger speaks those life-giving words to little kathy, the features of her face return. "You are special." The little button nose first, then you can see her little sun-drenched eyebrows, as her rosy mouth also shows up. "You are loved." Then her sun-kissed cheeks are visible and you can see her eyes take shape. Without taking those warm, strong, loving hands from her cheeks, the words of life and love bring back that little pixie face. With it comes the innocent excitement of a little girl's life. As Jesus walks away from Kathy, she is content, she is happy, she is confident, and a little more certain that she *is* loved and acceptable, just for who she is.

29

This little play elucidates only one of many possible sources of our identity as women. Our views of ourselves are greatly determined by how we are treated, by what is reflected or mirrored back to us from our caretakers. We believe the verbal or non-verbal messages of our worth, value, and importance without question. After all, they are the big people, they must really know if I am valuable and lovable, right? Wrong! We live out this secondhand identity through our self-talk and self-image. Other influential sources of our identity include our experiences and personalities, society, and the church. The good news is that no matter how distorted our image has become from past input, as adults we can challenge these views and correct them according to who God says we are.

In this chapter we will seek to answer the question "Mirror, Mirror, who is that?' We will first look at the image God has of us, or the "God me." Next we will examine our "Should me," the one often imposed by family, social influences, and the church. The "Lost me" is the one who often disappears within marriage. We will then explore "Finding me," our healthy response to develop our *real* me! We have a lot to look at! Come peek in this mirror with me....

"God Me"

The best and truest image we can have of ourselves naturally comes from the Creator who made us. He knew us before we were born and knows how many hairs we have on our heads (Psalm 139:13, Matthew 10:30). He loves us unconditionally, even knowing everything we have thought and done (Psalm 139).

Wow! That is a kind of love and acceptance that is still challenging for me to grasp fully. This is the truth about me that will set me free from any other distorted images that I might have. As we learn to replace our distorted self-image with His truths, we will be able to be more fully who

> We can only fully become who God made us to be when we discard other distorted self-images.

He made us to be. We will be confident and secure, even celebrating and enjoying who He made us to be. I remember a time when I couldn't fathom even liking myself, much less celebrating who I was. I was led to believe that I wasn't anything special to celebrate. All of the imposed and fake images I had of myself crowded out His truth. It has been so freeing and peaceful and joyous to see myself more accurately (the good, the bad, and the ugly!), possible only as I put His truths into my heart. At first I just had to learn about the truths, but I didn't believe them. Then I dared to think they might be true. As I took them deep into my spirit through Scripture memory, came to know the Lord, had counsel by wise mentors or counselors, and through the passage of time, I came to believe His loving truths more and more. Appendix B is a resource called "The Image of Me." It includes Scripture references about God's love and acceptance of us. It also includes verses about how God strengthens and empowers us. This resource is an awesome starting place to get the real picture of who we are. God and His all-knowing and loving view of us needs to be the foundation to our loving and accepting our real selves. Our self-esteem, the value we place on ourselves, is most accurate when we get it from God. When we discount ourselves and do not accept who He says we are, we are not accepting His creation or His Word as truth.

"SHOULD ME"

Learning about sociological patterns helps me see how I have been influenced by expectations and trends. They describe why I sometimes act in such destructive ways toward myself. Somehow, I feel less defective when I can attribute my dysfunction to something outside myself. Mental gymnastics aside, there is a bit of truth to the reasoning. We *are* partially shaped by the world around us.

The "should me" was formed from the expectations of everybody and his cousin and by society at large, about who I need to be. So many women fall into a trap of trying to be good girls and keeping everyone happy. We are being sacrificial, submissive Christian women but at the expense of losing ourselves. We are called to be humble and sacrificial, but such an attitude becomes unhealthy when it causes us to disappear, burnout, become angry and resentful, or not care for ourselves.

I love interesting and descriptive vocabulary terms that enlighten me for growth. *De-selfing* describes what occurs when we live out our "should me" through being a people-pleasing, peacekeeping, approval-seeking, shame-based person. We can lose ourselves as we live totally for others. We do not identify or develop our God-given gifts. We are *de-selfed*.[2] This really rings true for me because I was conditioned to please others to earn approval, and I have certainly experienced the loss of me in the process.

Some examples of early-American treatment of women help me continue to understand from whence I've come. For about a century beginning in the 1700s, there were little booklets written for women in England and America called "conduct books." These books instructed women on every detail of how to keep a home and a man. The instructions were not bad in themselves, but they crossed a line in telling her who to be. She was instructed on how to earn the love and approval of her husband through most pleasing and perfect conduct. The conduct books told women: "Make yourself indispensable to this new man."[3] Early medical texts warned that women who attempted to use their brains would be risking serious malfunction of their reproductive organs.

Early-American women were primarily slaves and property to men for economic survival and childrearing. Married women, as property of their husbands, had no legal rights. It took seventy-two years of effort for women to get voting rights. Universities initially refused women admittance. Even once admitted to universities, women were banned from professions of law and medicine. Women were typically banned from involvement in church affairs.

My mother greatly influenced my view of myself as she passed on her philosophy of womanhood from a song by Sandy Posey in the mid-1960s "When You're Born a Woman". I remember her saying to me with great contempt, "You better get used to the idea—this is what it means to be born a woman." Posey spoke about a woman's place being under a man's thumb, it did not matter if they were rich or poor or smart or dumb. The message said that women were born to be hurt. They could expect to be cheated on and lied to and treated like dirt. Quite a legacy, isn't it?

My mom was suggesting to me through this song what she had learned from her experiences regarding a woman's worth. This phenomenon actually has a name. A *meme* is an inherited way of thinking passed from one generation to another through the process of imitation. It is to the brain what a gene is to our bodies. Memes have power to affect our thinking and consciousness. We take in these memes to imitate through books, music, and patterns of our ancestors. The subtle and not so subtle patriarchal structures also influence us, as do those old conduct books. Until our old memes are actively replaced by rival memes, they do not go away, but instead circle round and round in our mental and emotional circuitry. Memes help explain why many intelligent and capable women today still struggle with losing their identity in marriage.[4]

LIVING STRONG

Lynne Hybels' testimony is a classic and all too common representation of women who have lost themselves to societal expectations of who they "should" be. Lynne is the wife of Bill Hybels, pastor of Willow Creek Community Church, a Chicago area mega-church. She tells her story in her book, *"Nice Girls Don't Change the World."*[5] Lynne is quick to say that her self-sacrificing, nice-girl attitude for most of her life had little to do with demands or expectations from her husband. The primary source of her de-selfing was her embrace and practice of the messages of society and childhood that emphasized being a nice girl. Lynne describes herself as obedient, polite, socially accept-able, and possibly a bit restrained. She was a people pleaser to the max, but lived life by going through the motions of others' expectations and for their happiness. She was motivated to earn the love of God and everyone else but at the expense of not finding herself. To her own admission, she had one of those classic Christian woman smiles permanently planted on her face as she was dying inside.

Many women like her have found that they can only keep up that routine so long before they run out of energy and tire of the "fakeness." I so appreciate this godly woman being vulnerable about her struggles without getting stuck in anger and bitterness. But that is not where it ends—she tells us about her answer to this lost "nice girl." She talks about trading in the safe, passive, people-pleasing niceness for the opposing strength and maturity of the world-changing, empowered power and passion of what she calls "the good woman" as delineated below.

- The *good woman's* life is grounded in the love of God that drowns out the false voices of the "should me." Being deeply embraced by God's love changes who we are.
- The *good woman* knows that her unique life matters to God. She no longer sees her calling as enhancing her husbands' life. She asks for help and seeks to discover her unique gifts. She steps out in faith to fully live out the dreams God has instilled in her very marrow.

> Receiving God's embrace changes who we are.

- A *good woman* faces her fears, not allowing them to hide the truth and magnify her weakness. She pushes past fear of failure and fear of telling people she needs to live to her full potential. She learns to get comfortable honoring her own dreams, needs, and desires.[6]

I want to be a "good woman." Don't you? Lynne's testimony shows how women get trapped in the approval, performance, shame, and blame traps. Remaining trapped results in a life half lived for others and never fulfilling the full potential of God's expectations for us.

Application Questions:

1. Which aspects of Lynne Hybels' testimony about being a nice girl do you relate to?

2. What appeals to you most and scares you most about becoming a good woman instead?

"LOST ME"

The "lost me" is a subgroup of the "should me" in terms of what women can lose through marriage. I had the erroneous expectation that as I sacrificed endlessly for my husband and children, over time it would be my turn to be loved in return. In hindsight I was really trying to earn love. By the time I reached forty (I am a slow learner) I began to realize the long-sought-after love was not forthcoming. Duuuuhhhhh! I had set myself up for this disappointment and spent a good portion of my life trying to earn love, and all I got was angry and tired! Not to mention that I *lost* who I was.

Women have been culturally conditioned in many ways to lose ourselves through being over-accommodating to others. We have been discouraged from being assertive, competitive, and expressive of our opinions. We have been labeled as the "weaker sex" with encouragement to "play dumb" or to "let men win." Attitudes like these not only keep us in a weaker position, but they protect men from feeling anything less than strong or dominant. Our accommodating becomes entrenched and we fear displeasing our husbands. We may protect them from tasks that they don't like to do, adjust our work to fit their desires, and not excel in areas that he does so we don't appear competitive or more skilled. We go out of our way to keep their lives undisturbed, protecting them from the normal dilemmas that plague any two people living together! We excuse our accommodation by saying things like "It's not worth the fight to change" or "I didn't really want to do that anyway."

In *The Dance of Anger*, Harriet Goldhor Lerner says that our de-selfing is at the heart of our most serious anger problems and makes us prone to depression.[7] Carol Gilligan connects our de-selfing tendencies with the core of our identity development as little girls in her book, *In a Different Voice*. She claims that much of our feminine identity depends on our level of connectedness and intimacy with others. Little boys' identities, in contrast, are strengthened by being independent. Women are defined by attachment and threatened by separation. Men are defined by separateness and threatened by connection.[8] These differences obviously cause relational struggles. You can see how these characteristics cause a problem. Our identities are tied up in relationship, but are also threatened when we give too much of ourselves away.

Matrimorphosis is a term Dalma Heyn uses to represent the subtle and largely misunderstood loss of themselves women experience as they become wives.[9] Not every wife experiences this loss and many have nothing to do with pressure or expectations from husbands. These wifely "shoulds" are unwritten, seldom-discussed secrets of becoming good wives as we evolve into being a poor and disappearing version of ourselves. We become the overseer of the marriage and home. We withhold our views so as to not offend. We carefully monitor our words. In many ways we are still adopting principles from those dusty conduct books. We give over our personal needs and desires to the marriage. We do most of this subconsciously and unwittingly. I recall being so frustrated with my husband that he could so easily do something at home that was totally just for himself. It was a difficult thing for me to do. After all, the "good wife" is not selfish, she *always* puts the needs of the family and home before herself! Blah, Blah, Blah....

Why is it so hard for me to be different? I don't want to sacrifice myself totally to "the fam," especially knowing it hurts everyone. Dalma Heyn states that married women experience an internal war with differing voices telling them what to do. One is from societal "shoulds" and memes, and the other is the oft-underdeveloped authentic voice of ourselves. She claims that we have particular difficulty with these warring voices at adolescence, marriage, after childbirth, or at other times of significant transition in any woman's life. Heyn states, "She decides on such a deep level, that she can handle swallowing her authentic words more easily than her husband can handle hearing them." She says we edge into "compliant relatedness." Our false face usurps our honest voice, swallowing authenticity for compliance.[10]

The solution for this war is not to blame the spouse or become a nun, or run away and change our names (I have considered all). We have to learn to honor, listen to, and grow our authentic truthful voice. We start by first knowing and embracing ourselves as God sees us. As my grandson says, "This is wreally, wreally scearry."

This great chasm with an unknown outcome *is* scary for a woman who does not know herself. Much like me, Lynne Hybels, and so many other sisters, come to the end of the war when we are finally too tired to go on with the battle. We have lost our real self to our fake self. One day we finally sit down with God, and say, "OK, God, I have had enough. I'm tired, I want to find *me*, I want to know the real me."

BECOMING STRONG AND COURAGEOUS: "FINDING ME"

Our first step in finding our true selves is to fully surrender to God, allowing Him to peel away what is false to uncover what is real. Benner says, "It is by losing our self to God that we discover our true identity."[11] Allowing God in to accept me just as I am helps me do the same. We need to spend the time and energy it takes to excavate our real self. We must be willing to walk through the fear of learning about ourselves and moving into uncomfortable but rewarding territory (see Appendix A).

When confronted with losing ourselves to "win" at love, or losing love to find ourselves, we may be tempted to think that we would be better off not being married. This decision needs to be individually discerned. First of all, we are not necessarily going to find our identity just because we divorce; in most cases *we* are the ones holding ourselves back. Our first task, then, needs to be taking full responsibility for our views of ourselves. Second, most of us desire marriage and are healthier for it. Our society has changed dramatically in the last century but our skills and

relational dynamics have not kept up. The answer to these dilemmas is usually not divorce, no matter how appealing it might be at
times! (Remember, abusive relationships may be exceptions; see
Appendix C). Generally, the preferable reaction to this situation is
not divorce, or acceptance of being lost, but getting smarter and
skilled at growing out of these troublesome patterns within the
context of marriage.

There are some within the Christian community who have
problems with the topic of self-esteem. They believe the focusing on
building ourselves up is selfish and not living out the sacrificial and
submissive life that God commands. Biblically speaking self-love is
commanded, second only to God's love and necessary in our ability
to love others as we are called to love others as we love ourselves
(Matt. 22:37-39). In *Healing for Damaged Emotions*, David Seamands
explains how Satan capitalizes on our low self-esteem to defeat and
disable us as Christians. He identifies sources of our self-esteem as
being our inner and outer world, Satan and evil, and God and His
Word. We can make choices regarding which sources of self-esteem
we feed and which ones we starve out.[12] Of course, it *is* possible
to be selfish and love our self too much. This personality disorder
is called *narcissism* in psychological terms. The answer is to have
a balance, to love ourselves in the way God loves us, so we can
properly reach out and love others.

Self-care is the key to finding and loving yourself, no matter
how you have lost *you*. It needs to start, as I said in the introduction
to this book, with knowing and connecting on a deep level with
who God says we are. We can start by identifying those "should"
messages we have received from others and then challenging and
replacing them with God's truths. We do have power in ourselves.
Eleanor Roosevelt said, "No one can make you feel inferior without
your permission."[13]

I like what Gary Smalley talks about in *The DNA of Relationships*.
He believes we need to have a relationship with ourselves. He
acknowledges at first blush that this may seem like a self-centered
position to take. Yet how else would we begin to heal from our
past and find our own true self unless it comes from us? We can

exert what he calls the "power of one" as we take responsibility for ourselves, stop expecting others to make us happy, and take control of our thoughts, feelings, and actions. When we have a healthy relationship with ourselves, we are able to say no to others and take good care of our spiritual, physical, and emotional self, and quit trying to get gas from an empty tank. Dr. Smalley discusses three parts to healthy and balanced self-care:

- Receive from God and others.
- Attend to our legitimate needs and feelings.
- Give to others in relationship out of our own self-care.[14]

More suggestions for finding ourselves are made by Cheryl Jarvis in *The Marriage Sabbatical*.[15] She logically suggests that if we have lost ourselves in marriage, we need to take proactive steps to find our true selves. Within the ivory towers of institutions of higher learning, sabbaticals are given to professors every so often so that they can be removed from their everyday environment to stimulate creativity and self-development. When they come back to their routines, they are refreshed and renewed.

It is most important to note that Ms. Jarvis is not recommending sabbaticals for marriage in order to punish our husbands or as a prelude to leaving the marriage. It has to do with finding ourselves. She recommends a customized sabbatical for each woman's needs. She tells stories of women taking a job in another locale as a sabbatical. Some go away for varying lengths of time for study or a class. Some go away to write or travel or explore. Some sabbaticals are within our own community, taking a class once a week. I have taken brief sabbaticals by going camping by myself, taking a workshop or class for a week or a few days, and going on a mission trip for up to three weeks. I am pretty typical of the stories told in this book in that I have come back a better person. I bring a more authentic me to the marriage. I have stories to tell, I know myself more, and I see my husband and marriage differently. I become stronger and more confident in who I am, and I like myself more as I step out and know myself and God more intimately.

It is easy to get the wrong idea about women taking a sabbatical from their marriages. It can look like running away or abandoning the family. A true sabbatical, though, allows us as women to discover who we are in our deepest selves by stepping outside the structure that gets so much of us. The purpose of this exercise is to preserve the marriage and ourselves within it. It can be particularly helpful for those of us who married young. As women, we can be so easily influenced and changed by those around us, that a time away gives us a chance to think, feel, rest, and become our true self, the self we often have lost a part of in marriage. A sabbatical can be as simple as a quiet bath alone, a special spot in the house that is just for me, a short trip out with a friend for coffee, a regular time of serving the Lord, alone.

Even though our need for a sabbatical may be misunderstood, I think we would all agree that a little discomfort is preferable to allowing ourselves to be so totally suffocated within a marriage that we see divorce as our only option. Unhappiness in our marriages can often be a result of unhappiness in ourselves and will improve most effectively with investment in ourselves.

Joan Anderson writes extensively about her sabbatical in her book, *A Year by the Sea: Thoughts of an Unfinished Woman.* It is a revealing account of the fear and courage of her journey to find herself and re-create her life. Her goal was to revitalize herself, rediscover her potential, and return to renew and renegotiate her marriage.

The process of identifying and correcting our distorted identities is usually not a snap-your-fingers, magical, pray, and you're out of it one-time event. It is a process that goes on for a lifetime. It starts when we get to the "I can't do this anymore" stage and we become motivated to negotiate our lives and marriages on different terms. We get the power and courage to radically resist our "shoulds" as we start to see ourselves as God does. David Benner goes as far to say that any ideas of ourselves that are not from the Lord are of our own making![16] This one and only accurate view of the "real me" is critical for having successful relationships.

We can become a leader to adjust our family values to include what is valuable for us. We need to step out in faith to become the best version of our unique selves. This spiritual transformation certainly can happen in an instant with the Lord, but it mostly happens inch by painful inch, one step forward and two back. The good news is this: you are not alone—and you are well worth the effort.

Will you join me in Lynne Hybels' challenge to be dangerous women?

May we be dangerous women.
May we be women who acknowledge our power to change,
and grow, and be radically alive for God.
May we be healers of wounds and righters of wrongs.
May we weep with those who weep and speak for those who
cannot speak for themselves.
May we cherish children, embrace the elderly,
and empower the poor.
May we pray deeply and teach wisely.
May we be strong and gentle leaders.
May we sing songs of joy and talk down fear.
May we never hesitate to let passion push us, conviction
compel us, and righteous anger energize us.
May we strike fear into all that is unjust and evil in the world.
May we dismantle abusive systems and silence lies with truth.
May we shine like stars in a darkened generation.
May we overflow with goodness in the name of God and by
the power of Jesus.
And in that name, and by that power, may we change the world.
Dear God, please make us dangerous women, Amen[17]

Notes

1. http://www.brainyquote.com/quotes/authors/j/joan_of_arc. html, accessed January 20, 2008.
2. Harriet Goldhor Lerner, *The Dance of Anger* (New York: Harper & Row, 1985), 20.
3. Dalma Heyn, *Marriage Shock: The Transformation of Women into Wives* (New York: Random House, 1997), 64.
4. Heyn, *Marriage Shock*, 80.
5. Lynne Hybels, *Nice Girls Don't Change the World* (Grand Rapids, MI: Zondervan, 2005).
6. Hybels, *Nice Girls Don't Change the World*, 21-80.
7. Lerner, *The Dance of Anger*, 20.
8. Carol Gilligan, *In a Different Voice* (Cambridge, MA: Harvard University Press, 1982), 8-9.
9. Heyn, *Marriage Shock*, 3.
10. Heyn, *Marriage Shock*, 120.
11. David G. Benner, *The Gift of Being Yourself* (Downers Grove, IL: IVP Books, 2004), 92.
12. David Seamands, *Healing for Damaged Emotions* (Wheaton, IL: Victor Books, 1981), 48.
13. http://www.brainyquote.com/quotes/authors/e/eleanor_roos-evelt_2.html
14. Gary Smalley, *The DNA of Relationship* (Wheaton, IL: Tyndale House, 2004), 124.
15. Cheryl Jarvis, *The Marriage Sabbatical* (New York: Broadway Books, 2001).
16. Benner, *The Gift of Being Yourself*, 48.
17. Hybels, *Nice Girls Don't Change the World*, 89.

CHAPTER 4

BE RIGHT OR BE MARRIED

*Disillusionment means having no more misconceptions, false
impressions, and false judgments in life; it means being free from
these deceptions. However, though no longer deceived, our experience of disillusionment may actually leave us cynical and overly
critical in our judgment of others. But the disillusionment that
comes from God brings us to the point where we see people as they
really are, yet without any cynicism or any stinging and bitter
criticism. Many of the things in life that inflict the greatest injury,
grief, or pain stem from the fact that we suffer from illusions. We
are not true to one another as facts, seeing each other as we really
are; we are only true to our misconceived ideas of one another.
According to our thinking, everything is either delightful and
good, or it is evil, malicious, and cowardly.*
—Oswald Chambers[1]

*F*RIENDLY TOWN" GOT us so excited. We had spent the first eight years of marriage as college and professional students. We scored off the charts in the life change assessment, but were excited to finally begin our grown-up life together. We had our diplomas, one baby, one dog, our VW Rabbit, and a full measure of naïve anticipation. That's why we thought it a perfect fit as we drove in to "friendly town" for our first interview. It was such a cute little farm town. The downtown area covered three blocks and had all we needed. Friendly Town listed 300 individuals on its sign. The people were so friendly; all waving as we passed with our young, wide-eyed stares. After waiting the token time, we accepted our first full-time position as a young family, moving from a busy metropolis to the calm, friendly farm town. Little did we know, though the waving continued, a deeper level of friendship would be slow to come.

I was ecstatic to meet my first local friend. Then I found out that whatever I told her was shared with many others, she being the town gossip! I was clearly not befriended by my husband's boss's wife. She was a busy local with family and children and no time or interest in the newcomer. So Friendly Town soon became Frustrating Town and Rejection Town and Depression Town. We had seen signs of "friendly" but probably out of our neediness, we had misinterpreted what it would mean in our lives. But we were so sure…but we were so excited… but it seemed so real…yet it was such a disappointment, so shallow, and different from what we'd expected.

Does this sound familiar, like what often happens in marriage? Kind of a "setup" in a way. The friendly waving sort of sucked us in to thinking and hoping that it would mean more. We so wanted it to mean more, we needed it to mean more, yet that did not make it so.

An illusion is a *misleading* image, a perception is an *individual comprehension* of an observation, an expectation is an *anticipated* outcome. All of these definitions are terms that reflect subjective rather than factual truth. Like our Friendly Town story, trusting illusions, perceptions, or expectations *always* brings disappointment and frustration. We commonly make things even worse as we blame another party for our failed and typically unexpressed expectations. It was not the fault of the townsfolk that we did not experience the deep, warm, and friendly acceptance that we had expected. It was not their fault that we thought their friendly waves meant deep friendships would form quickly. Individuals involved in our expectations are typically blind regarding how their actions or responses disappoint us. We set ourselves up to be hurt by our expectations, and are the *only* ones who can take responsibility for our disappointment and be more realistic in the future. "Setups" like this occur on many levels in marriage and challenge our ability to adjust and last in lifetime marriages.

In this chapter, we are going to look at broad historical and sociological changes that affect marital expectations. Then we will examine our individual and personal expectations. Our marriages will be healthier as we closely examine and reduce the ways we set ourselves up for hurt and disappointment.

Historical and cultural changes in American society have changed the nature of the marriage union. Our society has promoted many lies and distortions regarding marriage. These unrealistic expectations have set us up for increased frustration and failure. The role of marriage in society has changed, as have the roles of husbands and wives. It is imperative that we be informed of these trends, so we can realistically check out our expectations from the context of these changing realities. We don't tend to stop long enough to examine trends of change or personal expectations regarding marriage. Thus, our ability to make realistic adjustments is limited. Failed expectations are a major contributor to the high rate of divorces after only seven years of marriage. We all start marriage with ideas of how it should work. We usually get more adamant about the "rightness" of our personal expectations over time. This chapter will help us examine if our ideas about marriage have been realistic in the context of personal and social systems. We need to get much smarter about marriage and what we expect of it. Much like exercise, this work is uncomfortable and not fun. But after we do it, we are stronger and prepared to cope more effectively with life.

> We need to get much smarter about our expectations of marriage.

HISTORICAL/CULTURAL "SETUPS"

- God's plan was that we not be alone, and that marriage would provide a place of protection and nurture for children. The purpose of American marriage in the 1800's through the early 1900's was survival. Women, still seen as property, were dependent on the economic partnership of marriage. In these early years, and still true in many countries, both men and women expected much less personal satisfaction as they worked primarily just to survive.

- As recently as the early 1900's both men and women had a life expectancy of forty-seven years. One or the other typically died at the peak of their struggle to survive and raise children. Families were supported by extended family and pro-marriage social, religious, moral, and legal systems. By contrast, today our lack of family support and a longer lifespan have dramatically changed the landscape regarding the efforts necessary for lasting marriage. Being married for thirty to sixty years or even more, through the "empty nest" and retirement years, requires new and renewed skills previously unnecessary.

- As society moved from farming roots to the industrial then post-industrial era the need for large families for economic survival was reduced. Women started to become economically self-sufficient as they began to work during World War II. Family needs were met in differing ways such as insurance, social security, unemployment, welfare, retirement programs, and other forms of aid. These factors contributed to marriage becoming more dispensable than ever before.

- Women sought equality on many levels with the women's movement of the 1960s and '70s. We grew in economic and personal power, depending less on men and marriage. The power shift that resulted challenged the old rules for marriage and is still an issue today. Marriage was not the same, but healthy adaptive standards have been difficult to establish.

- Relational alternatives currently abound in the United States. Actions that are no longer held in check by moral stigmas include premarital sexual activity, teen pregnancy, permissive sex education, condom and birth control use, sexual freedom, and abortion. These cultural changes have had a confusing and detrimental effect on the age, rate, and success of marriage.

- Cohabitation has grown in the United States from 500,000 couples in 1970 to approximately 5 million opposite sex couples currently. Almost 50 percent of married couples have cohabited. Many people view cohabitation as a "trial marriage" and think it increases marital success. Statistically it leads to a two times greater chance of divorce for the small twenty percent who end up marrying. Couples who cohabit often have a fear of commitment, less satisfaction, more arguing, and poorer communication. This complicated scenario involves shared expenses and problems, fuzzy future plans, pressure to marry, fear of marrying, and marrying out of guilt. Cohabitation contributes to the growing number of children born to unwed parents. The outcomes for cohabiting couples who are engaged are better than those who cohabit more from convenience. Cohabitation has affected marriage.[2]

- Thomas Jefferson is the person who introduced the entitlement mentality of "life, liberty, and the pursuit of happiness." These ideals have encouraged our drive for individualism and personal happiness. Frank Pittman, a marriage researcher, responds to this quest by saying, "Marriage is not supposed to make you happy; it is supposed to make you married."[3] Marriage is still highly sought after—with 94 percent of college students hoping to marry, 90 percent of them will. We have an expectation that our purpose in life and within marriage is to be happy and personally fulfilled. When a group of women from a developing country were asked if marriage made them happy, they stared incredulously at the researchers, hesitating briefly before they laughed in disbelief at the prospect.[4]

- The American personal entitlement attitude has contributed to legal and counseling professionals being supportive of divorce and downplaying its effect on children. We have terminology such as "starter marriage," "first marriage," and "serial marriages." We have divorce parties and cards reflecting societal acceptance of divorce. Recent studies have shown that those who adopt a favorable attitude about divorce experience a lower quality of marriage, increased conflict, and reduced happiness. As divorce becomes easier, more common and acceptable, marital happiness decreases. As more divorces occur, the young people hurt deeply by their parents' divorces are more fearful and less committed or interested in marriage.

- The no-fault divorce law was initially proposed by the professional bar association in the 1970s. Secondary gain aside, its members thought divorce should be easier. They were successful, one state at a time, in making the marriage contract unenforceable. It now takes two people to enter into a marriage contract and only one to end it. The law sides with the one who wants out, making marriage much less secure and more risky. Women in particular are often driven to work more and be less engaged in their relationship for fear of financial and emotional ruin should they be divorced down the road. The fear of potential unilateral divorce has become a self-fulfilling prophecy. The dilemma is summed up by Linda Waite in *The Case for Marriage*: "We cannot embrace no-fault divorce as a new social ideal without fundamentally changing the way we think about marriage in ways that turn out to be deeply hostile to our goal of building a happy marriage."[5]

- We have many current trends in the United States that undermine the security and success of marriage. Our society is moving at breakneck speed with two-career families in an age of materialism. Our role changes and power shifts have caused conflict at home and work. The little time we have is often spent supporting our child-centered society rather than doing the work to maintain the marriage. The result is that the union that was formed to give our kids much-needed security withers away. Of course, our skewed Hollywood and media view of romanticized marriage and divorce is challenging to contend with. A couples therapist, Isaiah Zimmerman, writes that much of the relational despair we have is due to our current American "have-it-all" syndrome. He describes a current compulsion to want to have everything and to feel cheated if we fall short.[6]

LIVING STRONG

Lynne is the perfect person to share her testimony regarding expectations. She represents so many caught between the past and present. She dearly wanted to be married. But growing up in the late 1980s, she only knew the liberal morality and "marriage should make me happy" mantra of the day. She came to my group at the age of only twenty-three, and having been married one year, she was the "hero wife" of the group. She was there to address difficulty early on, causing us lingerers a fair amount of admiration!

Lynne and her spiritual soul mate boyfriend had "The Plan" from early on in their relationship. They would have two to four children, he would work, she would stay home, and they would live happily ever after. They prayed together, had deep discussions, and he encouraged her to be her best. They took church premarital classes before they were engaged. Even with Bob's father's premature death before they met, they seemed to be on a path to mutual contentment.

When Bob lost his job a few months before their marriage, he could no longer deny the depression over the loss of his father and his work. The dream marriage began on rocky ground as Bob was depressed, failed to look for work, lost interest in the church, and got hooked on video games. Lynne wondered where her Prince Charming went. She only got more confused as family and friends were overly generous with their free and varied advice about what to do. Her expectations and hopes for her marriage faded as did their former social and church networks. She desperately wanted to fix her situation and get her "normal" life back. She is thankful that through these struggles and confusion their attraction and love remained strong.

When she could not fix her situation, it helped Lynne tremendously to limit her exposure to family and friends who badmouthed her husband and told her to "leave the bum." She realized after the fact that she had told too many people too much information. Another thing she did was to refocus on her own spiritual growth. When she became so fed up with his denial of the issues she left for a few days to make the point "It can't go on like this."

At that time they became much more proactive as a couple, getting lay and professional counseling. In a short period of time he got a job, they bought a house, and she became pregnant. Three months before their daughter was born, a job loss plummeted him into depression and anxiety that necessitated brief hospitalization and medication. He continues in treatment and is now able to work part time. Lynne describes them as poor and happy, and even though she is disappointed to be going to church alone, she has "let go" of trying to get him to fulfill an expected role or the infamous "Plan."

The story of Lynne's marriage is not at all what she expected. She did an awesome job of examining her expectations according to reality, connecting with the Lord, and working with what she had. Today as we met at McDonald's with her cute and much beloved daughter, she described having an inner peace and contentment in spite of her marriage struggles. She summed it up that she had expected a Disney type of life with Prince Charming as her rescuer, only to realize that with God's help, she had to become the rescuing prince to herself! Lynne and her husband are certainly examples of living this quote by Linda Miles:

All those "and they lived happily ever after" fairy tale endings need to be changed to "and they began the very hard work of making their marriages happy. "[7]

Personal Expectations

It is typical for different persons to see different images in the picture on the right of this page. I often encourage the women in my group to get into heated discussions about who is right about what they see. Are the ones who saw the duck first the right ones? Are the ones who saw the rabbit right? Obviously in this case, there is no right or wrong.

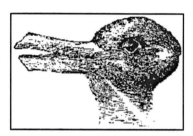

Thinking our views are right or presuming negative intention from our spouse are both deal breakers for contented marriage. The argument of "right or wrong" causes trouble in our marriages as we take issues not related to morality and dig in our heels to show our spouse that we are right. It is quite arrogant of us, actually, to think that our views and perspectives on life are right, which, by the way, would automatically make their views wrong!

I like the saying "You can either be right or you can be married!" Terry Real identifies this as a "perception battle," or a contest about meaning. He says it occurs all the time in relationships, is a huge waste of time, and is irresolvable. He says it begs the unanswerable question "Whose reality is most legitimate?"[8]

Obviously, both individuals in a marriage can't be right, but actually, we *can* both be right if we accept that there is no right or wrong, just different. That is, unless we are discussing a moral right or wrong. We take it a step further when we see ourselves as right, then presume a negative intention regarding our spouse. This really escalates defensiveness and conflict, making a compromise much less probable. To reduce relational damage we need to ask for clarification of intent if we suspect a negative motive from our partner. In the case where one of us senses we are being negatively judged, we need to respond with an assertive versus an aggressive response.

Women adopt many early marriage expectations from family, society, culture, movies, books, and friends. Our expectations are often not talked about or challenged for truthfulness. They include such ideals as:

- "He will meet my needs and make me happy."
- "I will not be hurt by my spouse because we love each other."
- "He will change after we get married."
- "My love for him will always stay the same."
- "We will never be torn apart by problems."

These early and unrealistic expectations often get turned into negative attitudes, such as:

- "I will never be happy with this spouse."
- "Our fighting shows that we are just not right for each other."
- "He is not changing, so I must have made the wrong choice in a spouse."
- "We have just fallen out of love and it can't be rekindled."
- "We can never overcome this problem."

Whether we believe the first or second set of statements regarding our marriage, they are both subjective. These self-generated beliefs often lead us to blame our spouse for the outcomes. Blaming them locks us out of a solution and disables our ability to discern the real truth.

I implore you to take the time to examine expectations about your husband, marriage, and love. Only then can you make intelligent and informed decisions based on truth, not the often-skewed perceptions of a hurting person! Remember, there is another person on the other side of the wedding rings who has expectations of his own. Ladies, we owe it to ourselves, our spouses, and our children to stop and examine these highly lethal "setups" to marital disaster.

Application Questions:

1. What are some expectations that you have or have had regarding marriage?
2. What have the outcomes been of these expectations?
3. Do you perceive your marriage expectations as "right" as compared to your husband's expectations?

The romanticism and infatuation that we all love to experience and want to last forever is another expectation setup. The purpose of our warm fuzzy feeling, "He/she is so perfect for me, we won't ever have problems. I will love him/her forever," of our early connecting phase is just that—to connect. If the hormones of early love did not deaden our sense of reasoning and engage our positive interpretations of just about everything, few of us would ever connect!

Seems rather cruel, doesn't it? Actually, where it becomes cruel is when we, others, or society in general, assume that our all too enjoyable infatuated state is supposed to, and can, last. It doesn't and it can't last. And that is OK!

I like an anonymous quote I found on the Smart Marriages. com website:

And You Wonder "Why" It Didn't Last

She married him because he was such a "strong man"
She divorced him because he was such a "dominating male."

He married her because she was so "fragile and cute."
He divorced her because she was so "weak and helpless."

She married him because "he is such a good provider."
She divorced him because "all he thinks about is business."

He married her because "she reminds me of her mother."
He divorced her because "she's getting more like
her mother every day."

She married him because he was "happy and romantic."
She divorced him because he was "shiftless and fun-loving."

He married her because she was "steady and sensible."
He divorced her because she was "boring and dull."

She married him because he was "the life of the party."
She divorced him because "he's a party boy."

Once we live with someone, not only do we see negatives we never saw before, but those once endearing characteristics become annoying (might I say *very* annoying?!?!?). As we settle in to life on a daily basis, many formerly appealing differences become a challenge as we try to accept and love each other.

The truth is, opposites attract, then attack! We do tend to match up with a partner who is different from us. We balance and compliment each other and become a whole together. The quiet one marries the enthusiastic one, the emotional one marries the calm one, the perfectionist marries the laid back one—you know the pattern. Different is not bad or wrong (I am not referring to moral right or wrong). We are blinded by our early infatuation and only grow in love as we accept that God made us different. We certainly need wisdom and strength from Him to learn to appreciate and live with those differences.

> There is no right or wrong, just different.

BECOMING STRONG AND COURAGEOUS

With growing social acceptance of liberal sexuality, out-of-wedlock pregnancy, cohabitation, and divorce, the times of Ozzie and Harriet are definitely past. Changes in traditional marriage have given more choices, but they also bring confusion and chaos to individuals, marriages, and society. These historical and social changes have weakened the bond of marriage and are propelling the United States into what is called a "post-marriage" culture. It is a sad term accurately reflective of our fifty percent failure rate. Our roles and power structure have changed and our interpersonal skills have not kept up. In the interest of being politically correct and inclusive, there has been a phenomenal reduction in external social forces in support of marriages. The former stigmas regarding sexual expression and divorce are gone. Divorce is easy and more supported than the work it takes to make a marriage work. Our disposable society seems to support the disposal of our marriages when they require work or appear broken.

The marriage researcher John Jacobs says that the glue that used to hold marriages together is gone. He sees that these social forces for marriage and stigmas against divorce have kept marriages together. Dr. Jacobs claims that we are in an era where couples now have to provide their own glue for long-term marriages. These "glue factors" are such things as accepting that marriage is work and has ups and downs.[9] We need to respect and strive for mutual satisfaction and give up the search for greener grass. Unfortunately, Christian couples follow these mainstream trends and relinquish their powerful covenant commitment of marriage for these weak and worldly options.

I invited a pastor from my church to answer tough questions from women struggling in their marriages. One of the most requested questions was, "What is realistic to expect from marriage?"

You could hear a pin drop as the question hung in the air. I remember the tightness in my stomach as he said, "Expect to be disappointed." This was not what we wanted to hear. He went on to say we *could* expect fidelity, addictionlessness, financial responsibility, and no rage. I know some would add or subtract from this list, but we cannot disagree with him also saying, "What else would you expect besides disappointment when you have two fallible sinners living together?"

I was shocked by a recent discussion with a single young man in his early thirties. He told me that single women in the church today practically expect a guy to be Jesus himself before they will consider marrying them!

Wow! That's quite a claim. Although I certainly don't think all young women have these impossibly high standards, his statement is a reflection of the unrealistic expectations of many. Lori Gottlieb explores this cultural trend in an intriguing new book called *Marry Him: The Case for Settling for Mr. Good Enough*. This initially unsettling book is creating a firestorm in the media and among "liberated" women. These groups are offended with a book that appears to set women's equality back fifty years. They are up in arms about the settling part, and who is Mr. Good Enough?

One reviewer called the book "daring and wise." The truth in the text is that women have swung so extremely far in their long list of the perfect man that they typically eliminate most options by the time they are in their mid- to late thirties. Gottlieb, a forty-two-year old single parent, has gathered an enormous amount of data for this book, starting with herself. She also got guidance from sociologists, marriage researchers, dating coaches, couples therapists, lawyers, clergy, matchmakers, and surveys of married and single men and women. Her conclusions document her contention that women have unrealistically high standards for the men in our lives. She found that as women age, they eliminate so many good men (for undeniably lame reasons) from their pool of potential husbands that by the time they are thirty-five to forty there are few eligible men left. She claims that our cultural and private fantasies create so many expectations that they destroy the possibility of finding real love.[10]

How do her conclusions relate to those of us who are married? We too, like our searching single sisters in this culture, have expectations for our husbands that are often unrealistic. We make them into idols when we expect them to be God-like. We can also destroy love and bring much disappointment and difficulties to ourselves as a result.

> Unrealistic expectations destroy real love.

My semi-feminist hackles rose again when I came across a book called *Surrender to Marriage* by Iris Krasnow. I have to admit, my early distaste became overwhelming agreement as the author discussed our need to relinquish our expectations of marriage and our spouses. I winced when she talked about her own realization that marriage was a "clipping of our wings." She said we need to give up our selfish desires to be the center of the universe.[11]

Krasnow describes three stages of surrendering:

1. *Malaise* is where our dissatisfaction begins to set in when we realize that our marriage is not meeting many of our expectations.
2. *Choice* is where we weigh options and decide to stay or go.
3. *Surrender* is when we decide to stay and work for the best outcome within this union.

I agree with Iris that when we don't give ourselves an option to leave, we respond with a certain acceptance and more relaxed attitude to the normal ups and downs of marriage. Staying in a dangerous, high-conflict marriage may be different. But two-thirds of those who divorce have low to medium conflict and can be highly influenced by staying and working. Here are some of Krasnow's major recommendations regarding surrendering to marriage:

- Let go of fantasy.
- Expect imperfection.
- Expect opposites and clashes.
- Surrender to an imperfect marriage.
- Accept that our happiness is self-generated.[12]

Even though my selfish self bristled at the premises of *Marry Him* and *Surrender to Marriage*, I could not deny their truth. They were consistent with our biblical call to truth, love, humility, acceptance, and sacrificial living.

Are you ready to discover and discard unrealistic expectations you have had for your marriage?

Notes

1. Oswald Chambers, *My Utmost for His Highest* (Nashville: Discovery House, 1992), July 30 devotion.
2. Linda J. Waite and Maggie Gallagher, *The Case for Marriage* (New York: Broadway Books, 2000).
3. Frank Pittman, www.smartmarriages.com, "Quotes" section, accessed February 22, 2009.
4. John W. Jacobs, *All You Need Is Love and Other Lies About Marriage* (New York: HarperCollins, 2004), 3.
5. Waite and Gallagher, *The Case for Marriage*, 155.
6. Quoted by Iris Krasnow, *Surrendering to Marriage* (New York: Hyperion, 2002), 40.
7. Linda Miles, "The New Marriage," http://www.smartmarriages. com, October 2009
8. Terrence Real, *How Can I Get Through to You?* (New York: Fireside, 2002), 231.
9. Jacobs, *All You Need Is Love and Other Lies About Marriage*, 7.
10 Lori Gottlieb, *Marry Him: The Case for Settling for Mr. Good Enough* (New York: Penguin, 2010).
11. Krasnow, *Surrendering to Marriage*, 11.
12. Krasnow, *Surrendering to Marriage*, 6.

CHAPTER 5

BUYER BEWARE!

To get divorced because love has died is like selling
your car when it runs out of gas.[1]
—Diane Sollee

In every marriage more than a week old, there are grounds for
divorce. The trick is to find, and continue to find,
the grounds for marriage.[2]
—Robert Anderson

People make the mistake of thinking divorce is a cure.
But marriage isn't a disease. Marriage is a relationship.
If you aren't good at relationships, divorce doesn't make you better.
You don't leave doors of divorce court and come out the other side
into the garden of perpetual bliss.[3]
—Diane Sollee

O NE OF MY *most irksome provocations is the concept of planned obsolescence. This is the purposeful intent of those in the manufacturing industry to make things that do not last long. The intent is for economic gain and to drive me crazy.*

It's working! This concept is being exploited more and more in our tight economy and is used for items large and small, from electronics, to cars, to toys and tools. My current example is the weed whacker we bought a few years ago that is now broken. It cost $100, and after inquiring about its repair, we found that no replacement parts are made for it. Planned obsolescence, Yarrrrgggggahhhh!

I'm thinking in some ways marriage is becoming an object of planned obsolescence. The sin, society, and circumstances in our lives are moving it into the "disposable and easily replaced" category. We express this in multiple ways. We call our marriages "first marriages" or "starter marriages" or "trial" marriages. Young people are not always seriously concerned about the lasting power of a marriage, because today it is possible to get divorced easily and try again without much stigma or difficulty. Not! Our definition of family is so inclusive it has become as watered down as our ability to persevere. We don't expect marriages necessarily to last, so they don't.

We can make it different as we research the "product" of marriage and be smarter about our "purchase." We can listen more intently to God's plan for our matchups. We can kick the tires and wait for the best timing. We need to be smarter in learning skills and having the deep commitment, wisdom, selflessness, and perseverance that it takes for long-term marriage. We need the guts and staying power to ride out this irreplaceable commodity for a lifetime. The good news is that we are and can be more responsible consumers of this precious commodity called marriage. We can give it a value above all else if we want to, and turn the tide of the decline of marriage today. An important place to start is to get smarter about the appeal of divorce today. We need to approach divorce with a defensive consumer attitude.

BUYER BEWARE!

This chapter's purpose is to compare our expectations with the truth about what commonly happens with divorce. It is imperative that we be accurately informed about divorce should we feel led down that path. It is common when we want to escape the pain of a difficult relationship to experience shortsightedness regarding the truth about divorce. Divorce does not commonly bring the much sought-after relief and there are many successful methods to reduce relational pain prior to divorcing. The overarching purpose of this book is to add to that education—to teach ways of avoiding divorce and have a better, smarter marriage.

I want to clarify that I am not opposed to divorce in some situations. We all know God hates divorce, but He also allowed for it under certain circumstances. Approximately one-third of the difficult marriages today that end in divorce are due to miserable circumstances of abuse and dysfunction including unrelenting addictions and serial adultery. In the cases of extreme conflict and chaos, all individuals involved are typically better off ending the marriage. If you are in this category, I hurt for you and am so sorry for your pain. The truth is, not all marriages are able to be saved. One person can only do so much to affect a two-person marriage. If your marriage is one of extreme circumstances, please read ahead with caution. I do not want you to have unnecessary pain, and much of this information may not apply to your very difficult and entrenched circumstances. (See Appendices C and D for more information.)

Two-thirds of the divorces today occur due to unhappy but low to medium conflict marriages.[4] Reasons given include personal unhappiness, unmet expectations, not being in love, wanting more out of life, difficulty communicating, and the classic "irreconcilable differences." This category of difficult marriages that I am addressing here has the best potential for resurrection into what God intended all along. All of the reasons given in the "two-thirds" category can be addressed and significantly improved by education rather than disposal!

The divorce rate in the United States is twice that of France and Germany, and three times greater than Japan. Many of our current struggles are due to living in a time of great cultural and social transition regarding the roles and rules for marriage. These drastic changes in our relational patterns in the last century in the United States have seriously undermined successful families. These changes have had significant impact on our expectations of marriage and divorce.

American industrialization and wealth accumulation after the Depression and the growth of individualism and self-fulfillment after World War I began tremendous shifts in traditional marriages. The women's movement and women beginning to work during WW II continued the changes. Our societal changes were positive in many ways, especially for women. Nevertheless, they challenged former marriage values, and today they continue to contribute to the current instability. The 1960s saw a 50 percent decline in fertility from 3.7 children per family to 1.9 in 1989[5]. The total fertility rate fell to 2.1 percent in 2007 (http://en.wikipedia.org/ wiki/Total_ fertility_rate). A 2006 study found that the 95% rate of premarital sexual activity has really not changed much from the 1950's.[6] We certainly perceive that the rates of premarital sex have increased, but maybe it is just that the honesty of reporting it has increased. Birth control, abortions and out-of-wedlock births, increased cohabitation, and adultery are all related trends of our "sexual awakening" and have negatively impacted and redefined marriage. Divorce rates increased from 19 percent in 1960 to 54 percent by 1986, and have held firm at 50 percent in the twenty-five years since.

Some of our reluctance to discuss or address the decline in the two-parent family comes from fear of inferred criticism of the women's movement. The women's movement needed to occur for many reasons, but as is so often the case, the pendulum of change has been extreme, and now we need to observe and modulate its effects. The preliminary freedom of the "have it all" mantra for women has become the burden that we "do it all." This major burnout phenomenon for women has caused unending stress on ourselves and our marriages.

Both men and women need to adjust their demands for individual rights at the ongoing expense of the family. How do we do that? Not a simple question, not a simple answer, but it starts with admitting the problem and that the cost of the problem has become too much for us as individuals, families, and a society.

We need to integrate the values and commitment of the past with the freedom and equality of the present. We need to get off of the crazy-making drive for success and personal happiness as a mutually exclusive priority over marital success. We need to open our eyes and get educated about the problem and be willing to learn new ways of doing marriage.

Application Questions:

1. Are you tempted at times to think that getting a divorce will be a solution to your lack of satisfaction? If you were to divorce, how would that bring you closer to the life you want?

2. What could you do within your marriage to increase your life satisfaction?

LIVING STRONG

Kerri is a good example to examine the realities of a difficult marriage and potential divorce. After struggling with her husband's escalating control, verbal abuse, and unrepentant alcoholism for fourteen years, Kerri finally had enough. She secretly made financial arrangements, found an apartment and movers, and filed for divorce. Both she and her husband had come from alcoholic families. She was born again and went to individual counseling. She attended Adult Child of Alcoholic classes to learn about the effects of her family dysfunction. Her depressed and anxious husband had no interest in church or relational health. The day the movers came her husband uncharacteristically came home ill from work.

He was angry, and he broke down emotionally and tried to block the movers from taking her stuff. Her attitude was, "I worked on the relationship for fourteen years—now it is your turn."

Kerri established firm boundaries with her counselor before she separated. Due to her husband's controlling nature and paranoia, she did not give him information about where she was or her phone number. He got the message and backed off and began to do his own work. He sought help for his anxiety, attended a church-based twelve-step program for alcoholics, and stayed sober.

Through their sixteen-month separation they gradually crafted a new and healthier relationship. They both worked individually, and after some time began to have counseling sessions as a couple. Eventually they discussed the possibility of reconciliation. Kerri's primary work involved developing boundaries and sticking to them to prevent recurrence of past abuse. They went to church together, and Kerri was surprised at what kind of relationship was possible. Even though Kerri had some doubts, they did reconcile, as she felt sure that was what the Lord was asking her to do.

I spoke to Kerri again after being reconciled over two years. There have been difficulties; her husband continued to be anxious and depressed. He has experienced job layoffs and serious medical issues. Kerri is content with her choice most of the time. It is not a cakewalk, but for her it is still clearly what God would have her do.

Kerri worked to contribute to having a much different, albeit not perfect marriage. She:

- Stayed close to the Lord.
- Did her own work and healing.
- Took bold steps to say "no more."
- Learned to set and stick with healthy boundaries.
- Remained open to the Lord's leading for reconciliation.
- Stuck with her call to remain married, even though it was not easy.

Kerri certainly confronted in her heart and mind what divorce might mean in her life. People understandably consider divorce because of intense relational pain. Expectations of married life have not been met, our spouse is not who we thought, and the love and connection that drew us together have vanished. We see divorce as the solution to deadness, never-ending conflict, tension, and chaos of our lives. Marriage is much harder than most people imagine, and it is logical to think that our difficulties will be relieved by ending the marriage. Even though we realize that divorce causes children some struggles and adjustments, we generally think kids are resilient and that their upset over the divorce will be temporary. We believe that our children will be much happier if we are happier, and the reduced conflict will be better for us all. We tend to see divorce as a temporary crisis with a good overall outcome. We believe we will recover from a bit of financial and emotional strain and bounce back over time to a much better world. This is what we expect. Now let's look at some realities regarding divorce.

MYTH VS. TRUTH

Dr. Judith Wallerstein and colleagues have written an outstanding book on their twenty-five year landmark study called *The Unexpected Legacy of Divorce*. Many of their findings are given in the following section and were surprising even to them.

Myth: Divorce will bring us the happiness we are missing.

When we experience failed expectations and fall out of love, struggle with conflict, and have pain over relational issues, it is normal to believe that the marriage and spouse are the problem. This thinking leads us to conclude that dumping the marriage will bring happiness. The belief in this thinking comes from lack of knowledge, poor marriage skills, and societal support.

Truth: Divorce is unlikely to make you happy.

Some findings of Dr. Wallerstein's long-term study of divorced couples include:

- In two-thirds of divorced couples, one partner is unhappy, lonely, anxious, depressed, and financially precarious ten years after the divorce.
- Twenty-five percent of couples report both partners experience depression and loneliness after divorce.
- Only ten percent of divorces find both former partners with happier, fuller lives after ten years.[7]

The University of Chicago conducted a study of unhappy individuals who were considering divorce. The study found that on average, unhappily married adults who divorced were no happier than those who stayed married. Of those who were unhappy and did not divorce, *80 percent of them were found to be happy five years later.* Even more surprising, the most unhappy couples who did not divorce reported the most dramatic turnaround, being *very* happy five years later. They found three categories that explained the formerly unhappy couples' return to happiness:

- Couples showed the *marital endurance ethic* by outlasting problems, not solving them.
- Couples showed the *marital work ethic* by solving problems and learning skills to become happier.
- Individuals showed the *personal happiness ethic* by finding their own ways to happiness and building a good and happy life in spite of a mediocre marriage.[8]

One woman who was interviewed and happy after her divorce wished she had taken full responsibility for her happiness within her marriage prior to divorcing.

If you are not a happy person before you divorce, it is unlikely that divorce will make you happy. This study concluded that the benefits of divorce have been oversold. Half of divorced partners remain miserable, and the other half experience temporary relief.

Myth: Divorce will remove conflicts.

It makes sense to think that if we are not living with the person that we have conflict with, we won't have as much conflict. Unless we move away from each other and do not share custody of children, conflict does not end when we divorce. There are times when separation can be very helpful to grow emotionally and physically strong. Please be very careful when considering this option when your relationship is abusive, and see Appendix C for more information. The marriage researcher John Gottman found that couples who divorce and those who are happily married both have 69 percent of their conflicts irresolvable! What Dr. Gottman has found is that the key to the happily married couples was not that they did not have conflict, but that they had skills to manage conflict respectfully.[9] Elimination of conflict is not reasonable in any marriage. It is reasonable to manage it respectfully.

Truth: Divorce will not remove conflicts.

- Sixty-six percent of couples who divorce have a low to medium level of conflict.
- One-third of couples are still fighting at the same level ten years after their divorce.
- Life tends to become more chaotic and complicated after divorce. The mother typically needs to work more to make a living and is less available to the children. There are many more arrangements to get children back and forth to both parents. If either spouse begins to date and blended families occur, complexity and stress increase tremendously, evidenced in the 64 percent divorce rate for second marriages.
- If we have fights when we are married, they will most likely continue and even escalate when divorced. Divorce provides much more to fight about and the battles become uglier and more dramatic. We don't automatically learn the skills to manage differences respectfully when we are no longer together. This anger, hurt, and conflict also

commonly transfer to the next generation and the negative cycle continues.
- New sources of conflict with divorce include money concerns, splitting up the house, settlement, moving, housing, custody, raising of children, stepfamilies, family gatherings, visitation, holidays, and girlfriends and boyfriends—not to mention selfishness, greed, and payback.

Myth: Cohabitation improves marital success.

Cohabitation has increased tenfold over the last forty years, up to 5.5 million people in 2000. Cohabitation is the predominant way male-female unions are formed today, with approximately two-thirds of couples currently cohabiting. Fifty-five percent of people who cohabit think it is a good idea that helps them move closer to a permanent marriage. Couples think of cohabitation as a "trial marriage." The average cohabitation lasts 1.3 years and 40 percent of cohabitating couples never marry.

Truth: Cohabitation is really "trial divorce."

Professionals who know the facts have found that of the 60 percent of cohabiters who end up getting married, only 15 percent are still married at ten years. They feel that it is due to the carryover resistance to commit to marriage. Cohabitation contributes to a casual attitude that relationships are temporary and easily ended. The intimate intermingling of lives and property of cohabitation makes breaking up more complicated. Man and women often see cohabiting very differently. Men tend to see it as a convenience and money saving decision; women see it as a commitment and precursor to marriage. Many cohabiting couples end up sliding into marriage rather than making a commitment-based decision to marry. When we add the breakup of cohabiting families to our married divorce rate, we get a 75 percent total rate of family breakup.[10] Ouch! When a couple is either seriously committed or engaged when they live together, the statistics for success dramatically increase.

The pain of being torn apart by a very difficult marriage and considering how the breakup of the family might affect your children is a tortuous place to live. I experienced this heart-wrenching dilemma when my husband and I were separated in 1991. We had contemplated divorcing for many years, but the reality really hit when we separated and I saw a lawyer. This is what I remember: pain in my chest, crazy-making fears, tormented thoughts, gigantic guilt, indescribable anger, difficulty breathing, walking around like the living dead, being dumbfounded, confused, torn in half, ripped up, disjointed—that about covers it.

Our own pain and the sorrow we feel about hurting our children through divorce have to be some of life's most tormenting and conflicting experiences. I remember feeling like I was stuck. I couldn't see surviving within my marriage, but I also couldn't imagine living without it. I do not take the following information lightly, but it is important to examine the facts regarding children and divorce.

Myth: Children benefit from divorce.

- Children are better off when conflicting parents divorce.
- Children are resilient and able to recover from the initial pain of divorce.
- Children will get over the pain of divorce and have a happier life.
- Children are better off when parents are happy, even when divorced.
- Children will mirror adults in how they respond to divorce.

Truth: Divorce hurts children on many levels.

Judith Wallerstein's extensive longitudinal research of children of divorce is reported in her books, *Second Chances* and *The Unexpected Legacy of Divorce*. Dr. Wallerstein was very familiar with divorce and children, yet she was surprised at the severity and extensive nature of children's reactions to divorce as she followed them for five, ten, fifteen, and twenty-five years. She found children and adults perceive and process divorce in *very* different ways. Here are some of her findings:

- The adults have chosen to change their adult relationship, expecting to have a better life. Children are usually unaware of the suffering of the adults, but cannot comprehend how splitting the family will solve problems of the family.
- Children see divorce as the cause of the problem, not a solution.
- Children report that divorce results in loss of their childhood, a loss of choice, play, and trust.
- Children's pain and struggles are cumulative. They build in intensity and severity over time. Young adults feel hopeless, not knowing how to relate. They fear being able to pair up or being able to intimately bond to another.
- No matter how reassuring parents are, children think divorce is their fault and feel intensely rejected.
- Divorce does not lessen effects or change outcomes for children from chaotic families.
- Divorce permanently alters children's views of the world, which they judge as unreliable and dangerous.
- Children struggle with all types of attachment losses and fear of failure.
- Children of divorce take more time to grow up.
- Younger children's maturation is more affected, as they lose mothers to work, and even a good remarriage is less likely to be helpful.
- Parents who don't fight after divorce don't save their kids from pain; children still have much of the same relationship pain when they become adults.
- There is no "trickle down" effect of parent to child happiness.

> The effects of divorce on children are cumulative as they grow up.

- Children of unhappy parents who did not divorce learned how to stick together, and learned that marriage can be hard and takes work. They learned that if their parents could persevere, they could also.
- Initially girls seemed to do better emotionally, but their struggles increased as young adults, having difficulty with trust and fear of betrayal.
- In her long-term study, she found that half of the boys (then ages nineteen through twenty-three) were unhappy, lonely, and had few female relationships.[11]

MORE DIVORCE REALITIES

My parents had a moderately conflicted marriage and they divorced after thirty-two years. I had been married twelve years at the time and was in my early thirties. Even though I saw my reactions as irrational, I felt that the end of their marriage erased the fact that I ever had a family. I felt that all of my early life and experiences were discounted, were fake, meaningless, and lost. Gradually, over the thirty years since, I have been able to reclaim my upbringing as valid. Unfortunately, both of my parents died alone and still angry. The good which came out of it is that my own experience with my parents' divorce motivated me to do absolutely all that I could not to divorce and to encourage others to do the same.

- *Kids and fathers*: Fathers tend to be much less accessible to their children after divorce. Of the 60 families studied, 57 of the fathers remarried and stopped child support at age eighteen. This affected their children attending college, though fathers often paid for the education of stepchildren. The number of children who do not live with their fathers has increased from 7 million in 1960 to 24 million today.[12]
- *Adult "kids"*: Marriages of children of divorce have a much higher rate of divorce. They are frightened that their relationships will fail, wait for disaster, and are relationally

needy. They are not prepared for conflict, trust, love, and commitment. They experience more of these fears and uncertainty if their parents divorced with a seemingly no or low conflict marriage, because they don't understand why it happened and did not see it coming. Wallerstein discovered that adult children of divorce continued to struggle with anger toward aging parents who had caused them so much pain.[13]

- *Mothers and daughters* in divorced families have more conflict than intact families. Relationships are more unstable with much guilt and anger. Two-thirds of the adults in Wallerstein's twenty-five-year follow-up study chose not to have children because they feared what divorce would bring the kids.[14]

- *Subsequent relationships or marriages:* If you have not learned skills and/or resolved issues that contributed to the end of your first or subsequent marriage, it does not bode well for future relationships. The divorce rate for subsequent marriages increases significantly each time. The divorce rate for second marriage is reported to be 67 percent, and seventy four percent for third marriages.[15] Forty percent of women over thirty never remarry after a divorce. Second marriage failure rate with kids is an unbelievable 85 percent. In the twenty-five-year follow-up study, only five percent of children experienced a stable second family marriage with good step relationships.[16]

- *Financial costs of divorce:* The cost of divorce is not as simple as a fifty-fifty split. Lorie Fowlke, who wrote *Thinking Divorce*, knows firsthand about the expenses incurred in a divorce. She is a lawyer who has observed many families experience the financial pinch. A woman's income drops an average of 27 percent; a man's increases 10 percent through divorce. Those who divorce lose an average of three-fourths of their personal net worth. Expenses multiply when setting up a second household and paying lawyer fees. Court costs are particularly steep if there are custody issues. Fowlke also discusses how the pain and stress of divorce almost always affect our employment. Our production wanes with reduced concentration, more emotions, and time away for court, therapy, kids, and lawyers. Divorce costs U.S. taxpayers $150 billion per year.

- *Marriage as a private affair does not affect anyone else:* The effects of divorce definitely go beyond our families and have tremendous effects on society at large. On top of the huge economic cost, there is increased fatherlessness, poverty, stress, and struggle. All of this fallout continues to impact parents, children, and social systems for many years. Fowlke, the lawyer, talks about how conflict cycles to the future generations and the often-selfish decisions with divorce destroys our sense of community. Children have increased risk of troubled lives, and no one has the energy to give back to the communities when they expend all of their energy just surviving. Most of the books and articles I have read regarding divorce don't stop their discussions with individuals, but give significant attention to the traumatizing effects that divorce has on our society. David Popenoe says that successful and sound family life are the basis of any enduring civilization, and "as the family goes, so goes the society."[17]

IS A "GOOD DIVORCE" POSSIBLE?

Yes, it is possible, and here are some statistics. Fifteen percent of all divorces result in both individuals re-creating happy lives ten years after the divorce. Children of people who reported that they had a "good divorce" reportedly had the least successful marriages compared to couples who reported having a low conflict, but challenging, marriage. The worst effects of divorce in children do not often show up until they leave home and try to form intimate relationships and families of their own. Their difficulties with trust and insecurity in knowing what makes for a lasting marriage comes around to bite them. Half of all adult children of parents who reported having a "good divorce" state that as kids, they always felt like adults, compared with two-thirds of adults whose parents had a "bad divorce." Children of divorce are known to "fake happy" and keep secrets from their parents to avoid conflict because they know their parents are struggling and unhappy with divorcing. Dr. Wallerstein concludes her findings to say that children raised in divorced or remarried families are less well adjusted as adults.[18]

BECOMING STRONG AND COURAGEOUS

Mutual consent divorce (especially when children are involved) is a policy that some states are attempting to instate. Mike McManus believes that this one act has the potential of cutting the divorce rate in half because it will be harder for one person to end a marriage.

Even though your state may not have this policy, it is very possible for each of us to adopt this mindset. If your spouse wants a divorce, state your disagreement and refuse to go along with it. Do not listen to people who are skewed about divorce and downplay the effects on your future and children. Do not buy into the American way of believing that we deserve to be happy all the time, concluding that divorce will bring it. Four out of five divorces are cases where one spouse does not want to divorce. McManus says in his book, *How to Cut Divorce Rates in Half*, "Divorce laws are rigged to destroy families, not preserve them." He would like to see no-fault divorce replaced by mutual consent or "both fault divorce."[19]

Should I Stay or Go? by Lee Raffel is a unique and most helpful resource for those of us who struggle in marriage and just cannot see continuing in the same trap. Her controlled separation guidelines were developed from her thirty-year counseling career, having seen many couples at the cusp of staying or going. Raffel has rescued many from the precipice by giving guidelines for slowing down the process and giving some structure to lives and marriages on the edge. It has

"Divorce laws destroy families."

been called by some a time-out for troubled marriages. She starts by having couples sign a contract promising to not pursue divorce or other relationships when separated. She suggests that couples explore the "whys" of their difficulties, and develop ground rules for the separation involving such topics as where to live, care of children, and financial arrangements. The time apart is used to step back from hurtful chaos and the lost, almost panicky, feelings of a marriage in trouble. It gives both parties a chance to begin to heal, examine their needs and goals, and move forward with renewed hope and energy to make things work, or move on. The purpose here is not to allow separation to be the automatic prelude to divorce but to be the healthy break we so often need to make a rational decision rather than an emotional one. It is highly recommended that a controlled separation be facilitated by an experienced therapist or pastor who is pro-marriage.[20]

My introductory remark regarding planned obsolescence parallels our attitude about marriage. The initiation of "no-fault" divorce doubled the divorce rate. From a legal perspective, the debate which occurred discussed how a marriage could be terminated merely because it was no longer a "viable institution." To me this sounds eerily similar to the shortsighted and selfishly motivated manufacturing decisions regarding the "viability" of any given product.

The tragic outcome for no-fault divorce is that there is no real determination of the viability of the marriage. If you split up, it does not mean you didn't love each other; it means you weren't skillful at keeping love alive. We need to love smarter. Divorce seems like a solution because it is taking action, doing something. It is like cutting off your legs because your shoes are too tight.

Once again, I am not saying divorce should never happen if it is what God leads us to do. In one-third of difficult marriages where there is violence, abuse, addictions and unrelenting adultery, divorce is often the best option for all involved. I am saying this:

- Know the facts.
- Look at the effects.

- Get smarter and stronger about yourself and the system before you make this life altering decision.
- Make sure you have done every, every, everything to avoid divorce. Even if it means a time of long-suffering until you feel clearly led by God to do it.
- Do not be swayed by friends or family, not even spouse or pastor, but God.

I was actually quite mad at God when He did not seem to lead me to leave my husband. I was mad that He made me stay; I was mad that He made me grow up, I was mad that He thought I had more work to do from within the marriage. I was mad—until I did the work, stayed the time, grew up and out of some (not all!) of my dysfunctions.

And now, I am so glad I did. I sent my younger son a copy of my testimony a few years ago. And I guess he didn't know how close or how long we had lingered around divorcing. I get chills when I think of his response today. He was twenty at the time, and he said, "Mom, I am so glad you and Dad didn't divorce. I was really struggling with the death of a good friend, and I was really depressed. I don't know what would have happened to me if you guys had called it quits." In my case, that was another confirmation that, for me, staying and fighting for my family was the right thing to do. Please, friends, don't automatically buy into the social, distorted, misleading, and very devastating assumptions regarding the viability of your family.

Will you join me in fighting for your family?

NOTES

1. Diane Sollee, http://www.smartmarriages.com/marriage.quotes. html, accessed June 25, 2008.

2. Robert Anderson, http://www.smartmarriages.com/marriage. quotes.html, accessed June 20, 2008.

3. Diane Sollee, http://www.smartmarriages.com/marriage.quotes. html, accessed January 22, 2007

4. Elizabeth Marquardt, *Between Two Worlds* (New York: Crown, 2005), 3-4.

5. David Popenoe, *War Over the Family* (USA: Transaction, 2005), 4.

6. http://www.truthdig.com/eartotheground/item/20061219_95_of_ americans_have_had_premarital_sex/#, accessed June 10, 2009.

7. Judith Wallerstein, *The Unexpected Legacy of Divorce* (New York: Hyperion, 2000).

8. Linda Waite, University of Chicago study, cited at www. americanvalues.org, accessed July 5, 2009.

9. John Gottman, *Seven Principles for Making Marriage Work* (New York: Three Rivers Press, 1999), 130.

10. David Popenoe, http://www.smartmarriages.com/cohabit.html, accessed June 29, 2009.

11. Wallerstein, *The Unexpected Legacy of Divorce*, 169.

12. Marriage Savers.org, Resources, Articles: "Twenty-Five Tough Questions," 6/15/2009.

13. Wallerstein, *The Unexpected Legacy of Divorce*, 203.

14. Wallerstein, *The Unexpected Legacy of Divorce*, 202.

15. http://www.divorcerate.org/, accessed June 15, 2009.

16. Wallerstein, *The Unexpected Legacy of Divorce*. 29.

17. Popenoe, *War Over the Family*, 10.

18. Wallerstein, *The Unexpected Legacy of Divorce*. 297.

19. Mike McManus, *How to Cut the Divorce Rate in Half* (Potomac, MD: Marriage Savers, 2008).

20. Lee Raffel, *Should I Stay or Go?* (Chicago: Contemporary Books, 1999).

CHAPTER 6

WORK SMARTER, NOT HARDER

Whatever you do, work at it with all your heart,
as working for the Lord, not for men.
—Colossians 3:23

I T MADE PERFECT *sense to me. I have always wanted to communicate better with my husband. I have wanted it since I was
fifteen, when we were dating—and I wanted it last week, having been
married nearly forty years. So, doesn't it seem sensible to you that if
you want to talk more to someone, then what you should do is talk
to them? Yeah, me too. So I talked to him. Phil was not on the same
wavelength as me (never has been, never will be), so he didn't really
communicate the way I expected.*

*So what did I do? Of course, I talked more! Then I talked more
firmly, then I talked faster, then I talked with tears, then I talked louder,
then faster, then with bigger words, then with shaking fists, then all
of the above at the same time (I used to be a gymnast!). None of these
tactics to get my husband to talk have worked in the way I expected.
They were perfectly logical and sensible to me, yet they were totally
wrong! They didn't give me the outcome I expected.*

*It's common to get locked into thinking a particular approach will
solve a given problem. Often our thinking is very logical and sensible.
But "logical and sensible" to us does not mean it will be logical and
sensible to our situation or our hubbies. In fact, with my vast experience
at failure to communicate, I can pretty much guarantee that my logical
and sensible solution will be totally off of his radar! What we have to
ask ourselves about any issue that we want to improve in our marriage
and the focus of this chapter is:*

"Is what I am doing giving me what I want?

If the answer to this question is "no," you may want to consider
making some changes. If what you are doing is not working, chances
are it makes absolutely no difference how logical your efforts are,
or what worked for your mom, or your girlfriend. Unfortunately,
this is a very common problem in marriages.

The good news is that you are not alone and there is a solution.
Oftentimes we are so sure we are right that we don't step back long
enough to realize that what we are doing is not giving us what we
want. Oh yeah, and that's another common dilemma: we often do
not even identify for ourselves, or our spouses, what we really want!
As they say, "When you aim for nothing, you are guaranteed to

get it, every time!" Having been a practitioner of these unhealthy but common marital practices, it's no wonder that I entertained thoughts of bodily harm regarding my "failure to communicate."

SOLUTION-FOCUSED APPROACH

A *solution-focused* approach to marriage emphasizes finding answers to issues instead of focusing only on a deeper understanding of problems. Ineffective patterns of relating seriously contribute to the understandable hopelessness and pessimism in marriages today.

Having lived in this painful place for many years, I understand the desire to just be done with the round-and-round patterns of mutual hurting. I certainly understand the presumption of many in this position that divorce is the least painful option. Too often and too late, we often learn that it is not the partner who is the problem, but *our* patterns of relating. It makes logical sense for us to identify and change *our* ineffective relational patterns before we dump our partner! When we are stuck in hurt and dysfunction, especially in the blame game, we do not see other viable options and assume that leaving our partner is the only choice. Yet people who divorce without growing out of their destructive patterns often end up repeating them in their next relationship, and the one after that, and the one after that. The divorce rates of 67 percent in second marriages and 74 percent in third marriages speak volumes to this. The premise of the solution-focused approach is that traditional problem-focused and insight-oriented models and explanations of issues don't solve problems—solutions solve problems. Interestingly, traditional marital therapy is reported to be successful only 20 percent of the time. I hope these statistics motivate you to get out of the box of your logical but limited and ill-informed thinking about what works for successful marital problem management.

> It is often our patterns of relating that cause our problems, not our partner!

Michele Weiner Davis has developed and practiced the solution-focused approach in her counseling practice for many years. Many years ago, she made a major shift in how she practices marriage therapy. She noticed that many individuals she had counseled in her first decade as a therapist returned to her—remarried and unhappy, or still single and unhappy—five years after she had "helped" them divorce. She was convicted by this sad statistic and concluded that the traditional way she had been doing therapy was not "marriage friendly." She had been assisting couples to be "happy" and "fulfilled" as individuals, and for far too many, that translated into divorce. Because she had suffered through the divorce of her parents at sixteen, she was personally motivated to learn about what it took to save marriages and families from the surprisingly long-term pain of unnecessary divorce. Thus, she began her search for concrete solution-focused methods for saving families, helping them work smarter, not harder. She realized, as many marriage educators of today know, that marriage is a skill-based endeavor. She observed that the traditional insight-oriented approach, although sometimes helpful, mostly gives deeper insight into issues without giving couples the skills they need to be healthy. Through intensive study of what works for hurting couples, she discovered how to identify problems and negative patterns and then experimented with solutions, as relayed in her books, *Divorce Busting* and *Divorce Remedy*.[1]

NEGATIVE PATTERNS

Blame is the most pervasive negative pattern in marriage. For some reason, neither of us wants to be wrong about anything, so we blame our spouse. It is very evident that this fallen pattern began with Adam, Eve, and a serpent, where finger-pointing was rampant. Occasionally, we get into extreme mental gymnastics to convince ourselves that our spouses are to blame, but most times, it's sinfully natural to blame them.

My husband and I both participated in the blame game for many years, primarily so that we didn't have to look at ourselves and take responsibility for our own destructive habits. This is a game with no winner because when we are stuck in it, we have convinced ourselves that we're right! A primary consequence when we blame our spouse is that we lock ourselves out of figuring out a solution to the problem. After all, how can I, or why would I, attempt to figure out a solution for a problem when *I'm sure* it is his fault? He may very well not be innocent, but I am still responsible for *my* reaction and/or contribution to the issue.

Cloud and Townsend give a great example in their boundaries book about a woman, Ann, who blamed her husband for delaying the family dinner by coming home late from work. Nothing she had done had been effective in ending the problem. It was not until she took responsibility for her unhappiness and her negative reaction to his lateness that she was able to change the dynamics of the situation. As long as she saw the problem as his alone, she locked herself out of a solution.

She began by asking herself, "Is what I'm doing working to give me what I want?" Usually, we both play a role in the round-and-round pattern of blaming, much like the "What came first—the chicken or egg?" scenario. After a while, we don't even know what the issue is, much less where it began. Ann became the one courageous person to break their dead-end cycle of mutual blame. She took responsibility for her role and initiated a successful resolution.[2]

Blame is also part of the larger negative pattern of pride. We are all more interested in being right than accommodating our spouse's views. We want our spouse to change, we think our way is best, and we think we are right. It is not easy to die to our own views, opinions, and desires in our marriages, but our difficulties multiply proportionately as one or both of us allow our pride to rule. My husband and I are both very stubborn and strong-willed, which I'm sure was a major component of being locked into the "unwinnable" blame game for so many painful years.

A common mantra of the struggling marriage is, "Why do I have to be the first one, or the only one working or making changes in our relationship?" First, that question demands fairness, which in case you didn't notice, does not exist in this fallen world. We laughed when a woman in a group once said that her mother always told her, "The only thing that is fair is the State Fair!" Jesus tells us in Matthew 5:23-24 that finding fault in situations is irrelevant. We are to seek reconciliation with our brothers, no matter what their attitude is. *Ouch!*

It's also true that we're not blameless in the situation, either in an active or passive way. We are accountable to God for our behavior and our motives. When we are trying to "help" God by focusing on another's faults, we block God from working in both of our lives. It's common for women to be more relationally motivated and to desire deeper and more intimate relationships than men. If we are the ones who are dissatisfied, we need to take responsibility for our own happiness and learn to make things different. As believers, the more we focus on our personal accountability to God and His plans and purpose for our lives, the less hung up we will become on who takes the first step to change.[3] As I have coached many women (including myself), the one to change first in the marriage should be the more mature one.

Charles Darwin said, "It is not the strongest of the species that survive, nor the most intelligent, but the ones most responsive to change." May we each be strong and courageous in being the first to change!

We often lock ourselves out of being proactive with solutions due to *narrow views about the ability of one person to change* a relationship for the better. It's very easy to accept that we could turn any interaction in our marriage into a negative nightmare. It is therefore a little odd that we struggle with accepting that we could also have a positive influence on our relationship. We can change our negative interactions, moods, and conflicts to be less hurtful—and even positive—if we learn the appropriate skills. When a spouse infuses a tense scenario with appropriate humor, for example, the other party has much more difficulty escalating the situation to anger. It's also common to think that small changes won't impact our interactions. This approach can lock us out of the very changes we desire. The inertia of moving ahead positively is powerful, and even small changes can lead to the big change we desire if we are patient and persistent to wait for incremental changes to affect outcomes. Once again, it is helpful to adopt the bigger picture that we are changing our modes of interaction to honor the Lord with our lives. This motivation gives us a much greater ability to persevere and persist in change just because it is the right thing to do.

Viewing our changes as an experiment with both positive and negative outcomes is also helpful. We sometimes get locked into negative thinking, making *sweeping generalizations* regarding potential for change, such as saying, "He never...," "We will always....," "I can't," or "This is never going to work." These self-fulfilling prophecies lock us out of any chances of change, as our behaviors both directly and indirectly reflect our negative views. We are unlikely to try to find solutions in light of the perceived overwhelmingly negative odds. We are commonly deceived when we think, "The way my marriage is now is the way it always will be."

Not true! Marriages go through developmental stages over the years and vary depending on circumstances such as children, jobs, financial and family circumstances, and menopause!

We equally lock ourselves out of solutions by *presuming the intention* of another person in any given scenario. Take the case of the spouse who watches a lot of TV, spends time on the computer, or is a golfing aficionado. It is not uncommon for a wife to assume her spouse doesn't love her because he spends a lot of time on these endeavors rather than spending time with her. It's helpful for couples to discuss how they spend their time, but attributing meaning to another's behavior is a deadly habit that causes a vicious downward spiral. We need to check out our assumptions. I like what change expert Bill O'Hanlon says: "Don't believe everything you think."[4] I spent many years misinterpreting my husband's every move, mostly because of my own insecurity.

> Presuming intention of another is a deadly relational habit.

For thirty years Dr. John Gottman has been studying what makes marriages fail and succeed.[5] A habit that Dr. Gottman observed in women that predicts divorce is what he calls the *harsh startup*. A harsh startup is when we begin an interaction in a harsh, critical, demanding, or sarcastic way, even just with negative body language or tone of voice (you know what I mean!). The *only* reaction that is possible from our spouses in response is defensiveness. Beginning an interaction this way sets us up for guaranteed failure.

I was shocked and remorseful when I first heard this because I have (ashamedly) been the queen of the harsh startup. With my harsh startups I had unknowingly contributed to the defensiveness in my husband, which I had also loudly protested. Let it be known that he also carried responsibility for his defensiveness, but I did encourage it when I started an interaction in a harsh way.

Please, friends, let's honor the Lord by learning to address our spouses in a softer way. I am not saying "let's be doormats." Let's follow the command in Ephesians 4:15 and reduce our speaking out of hurt, anger, and immaturity and learn to speak the truth in love, to grow up in Christ.

Dr. Gottman also identified a pattern he calls *negative sentiment override*.[6] In this common pattern of couples, one of us interprets all spousal activities in a negative way. For example, if I am in a negative sentiment override frame of mind and my spouse brings me roses, I might reply, "Oh, sure, you just brought me flowers to butter me up, so you could get what you want."

It's a sad and difficult place to live, but it is possible to turn even this negativity around. We begin the process by acknowledging it exists, followed by accepting that we may be contributing to the system that hurts us. Then, we can decide to learn to replace our negativity with positives.

Application Questions:

1. Is what you are doing now in your relationship giving you what you want? Explain.

2. Do you have any negative views about change or are you currently practicing any habits that may be blocking you from making the changes you desire in your life? (Blame, depression, negative sentiment, and harsh startup)

3. What are some specific problems that you want to find solutions for? (Don't pick the largest or most emotionally charged issues to start with.)

SEARCHING FOR SOLUTIONS

The solution-focused approach helps us to replace ineffective patterns of relating with positive solutions. We have all typically experienced times when things ran more smoothly, with fewer difficulties in our relationships. Over time, we often get away from what works. This model assumes that there have been exceptions when we were more successful with any given problem. We need to observe, identify, and then be consistent in doing what works.

Sometimes we struggle with creating solutions to our problems because we do not step back to identify specific problems or think about the specific goals we want. We just know we are unhappy with how it is. The problem with this common scenario is manifold. Our spouse has no clue about what we want when we just complain about what we don't have. It becomes even more of a dilemma when I haven't even figured out what I want! Oftentimes, as women, we spend our time helping family members to be happy and fulfilled. Then when the essence of who we are gradually slips away over the years, it is very easy to blame our family or spouse. But truthfully, if we don't even know what we want, how is our husband supposed to know?

In his book, *How Can I Get Through To You?*, Terry Real discusses intimacy differences between men and women. He concludes that we need to clarify what we need and be empowered to speak up in a way that can be heard.[7] This change can be the beginning of figuring out successful solutions. As you read Molly's story, you will see how using these methods played out in her marriage.

LIVING STRONG

Molly came to the group I facilitated in dire need of courage to change the destructive, religiously based, and distorted patterns of abusive interaction of her twenty-five-year marriage. She desperately feared divorce and was dumbfounded that her lifetime of motherly accommodating and taking care of everyone around her was not giving her the fairy-tale life she had imagined. She was absolutely exhausted. She suspected her husband might be having an affair. Her frantic and sponge-like approach to Christian counseling, group work, and scriptural studies led her to a realization that she had not been the innocent, submissive, and perfect wife that she had perceived. She realized that she had been enabling (encouraging) her husband's controlling and verbally abusive treatment of her by accommodating him and attempting to work hard to ensure his happiness.

No wonder she felt both fearful and hopeful as she began to make a plan to try something different! She feared making things worse, but realized she had nothing more to lose. She lived in hope of her plans working and anticipated that God wanted something better for her, and would bless her efforts. Molly was the queen of the solution-focused approach, and we both chuckle as we recall her carrying around her dog-eared copy of Michele Weiner Davis' book, *Divorce Busting*, in a brown paper bag! She devoured the book and took copious notes to learn how to change her patterns within her dying marriage. Fear and hope replaced her helpless exhaustion at the prospect.

I remember one of Molly's first attempts at "doing something different." It involved her family's habit of watching movies together on Friday nights. Their habit had been to go pick out a movie with her sons and then return to the cozy family room to watch. Before starting the film, Molly had the self-appointed job of going in to her husband's study to beg, plead, convince, and cajole him into joining them. This went on for some time, as he was reluctant and resistant. Finally, he would come and join the family, who of course was expected to be very grateful for his presence!

This was a pattern that Molly realized was unhealthy, and one of the first she wished to change. She asked herself, "What can I do that will be different?" She decided to go into his study and announce that the movie was starting at 8 p.m., and then walk out and allow him to decide if he would join them or not.

The first few times, it was very difficult for her, as she had taken responsibility for his happiness for so many years. He was usually crabby and liked to be "convinced," so he didn't join them for a few weeks. The first week he decided to join in, there was no seat for him, so he walked right out! After that, *he* made the choice to join the family for movie night. A few weeks later, he was eager to go with them to pick out the movies. Molly had changed *her* behavior and developed a solution that changed the pattern! She was elated with her successful experiments that motivated her to keep trying something different.

Remember, there is no guarantee that our partner will change their reactions, but like Molly, our purpose is to get healthy ourselves. Hopefully there will also be a carryover in the relationship. If her husband had not adapted to her change, she still would have accomplished her goal of not taking responsibility for her husband's happiness and would be more content with her life and family movie night.

Molly went on to be extremely successful at changing her accommodations to the whole world and in finding her own solutions to the unhealthy patterns of her past. Her husband never got involved in counseling and often did not like her changing their marital dance. But today she cannot believe how different her marriage is. She sees in hindsight how the long process of "doing something different" many times has made her a different person. Her husband experienced the differences and *could no longer* behave the same. As she stood her ground in her new behavior, he saw that she was no longer made of straw. He could huff and puff as much as he chose, but he was left wondering why his old methods were not working for him!

Today Molly is a happy, confident, strong, and empowered woman, glad that she took responsibility for changing negative patterns, and is incredulous about how it has affected her marriage. She got serious about studying God's Word to correct her former distorted views of God and marriage. She continues to keep healthy boundaries, but doesn't see herself returning to the fear and insecurity, false responsibility, or guilt-based submissiveness of the past. She cries when she talks of the peace and freedom she has experienced in having the courage to step out beyond her fears as she has experimented with solutions in her life.

Becoming Strong and Courageous with Positive Patterns

There is so much *we* can do to change patterns with effective solutions. For an endless plethora of options, I recommend that you check out Michele Weiner Davis's books, *Divorce Busting* and *Divorce Remedy*. Even though we can get very discouraged, we must:

- First, believe that change is possible. If we don't have any experience with these methods, we have no idea how it could work for us until we try. This step alone is a great motivator, and empowers us to move from hopelessness to having a specific method to apply.
- Begin to identify the negative patterns in our lives, taking responsibility to grow out of them. Negative patterns include thinking change is not possible, family patterns of negativity, blame, being right, nagging, criticism, controlling, presuming negative intentions, harsh startup, negative sentiment over ride, and other selfish, prideful motives. After we have identified our negative patterns, we can commit to changing them.
- Next, we need to establish some goals of what we would like to see happen in these areas. Our goals must be specific, measurable, and reasonable to attain.
- Identify what will be the first hint that the pendulum of negativity is swinging in the positive direction so that we can appreciate it when things begin to turn around.
- Have realistic expectations, and appreciate even small changes.
- Remember that addictions and abuse are unique and challenging situations. A woman in this situation can establish goals around getting help for herself, creating safety and boundaries, and not getting pulled into the dysfunctional dance.

After we have reduced our negativity, identified patterns to change, and made appropriate goals, we are on the road to the great experiment seeing what will work in our situation. A scientist is not discouraged when his experiment doesn't give his expected answer. He's gotten information about what doesn't work, which brings him closer to what does.

We would do well to adopt this non-emotional and pragmatic scientist-experimenter attitude for marital solution hunting! It can be helpful to think of a time when your problem was not so bad and did not cause conflict, in order to brainstorm about feasible solutions. It's also helpful to make a mental note about what methods have not helped our situation in the past. The timing of our efforts is particularly important to success.

Application Questions:

4. What specific problem areas in your marriage do you want to begin to find solutions for?

5. Can you think of a time when things were not as difficult in these areas? What were you doing differently then? (For example, you did not have as short a fuse, were not depressed, thought things could be better, had more going on in your life that was pleasurable, exercised more, and were not as stressed out)

"WALKING THE LINE"

Molly is a perfect example of how one person can change the patterns in a marriage. She took responsibility and changed her part of the marital dance. When one person has the courage and perseverance to change a dysfunctional marital dance, the whole marriage is thrown off-balance. When we change the unhealthy steps and throw off our partner's balance, we can be assured that it may not be received with love and appreciation. My husband tells me today that he was very unhappy with me changing our patterns in the past. My changing made his previous dysfunctional responses ineffective. Today, he says he is glad I changed things, and thanks me!

We don't know if our spouse will desire to learn a new healthy dance with us and do things differently in our marriages. That doesn't mean that we should not proceed or that it is wrong to change patterns. Spousal change is typically more resistant and complicated when we are dealing with abuse, addictions, or adultery. But no matter, we still need to be sure that our motives are pure and not manipulative. We cannot change our spouse, or fix him up, or even fix up the marriage. Our best hope is to be a positive influence on our relational patterns, taking responsibility for our own behaviors and happiness. We hope that our more positive and healthy behaviors will affect our spouse, but our purpose is not to fix or change him.

We need to walk the line. We need to address difficulties so that we don't become bitter and angry, and we need to do it respectfully. We can gently confront and challenge our spouses to be their best, while we extract ourselves from their dysfunction. We are speaking the truth to them while holding them accountable to be the best they can be. As we examine and change our own behaviors, we are strengthened, empowered, and freed from the fetters of whatever our spouses decide to be or do. This certainly contributes to our contentment and honors God, no matter what the outcome.

Will you join Molly in having the courage from God to lead the way to changing your dance? Start by asking yourself this question:

Is what I'm doing working?

NOTES

1. Michele Weiner Davis, *Divorce Busting* (New York: Fireside, 1992), and *Divorce Remedy* (New York: Simon & Schuster, 2001).
2. Henry Cloud and John Townsend, *Boundaries in Marriage* (Grand Rapids: Zondervan, 1999), 60.
3. Romans 14:12 and Jeremiah 29:11.
4. Bill O'Hanlon, *Change 101* (New York: W. W. Norton & Company, 2006), 114.
5. John Gottman, *Seven Principles for Making Marriage Work* (New York: Three Rivers Press, 1999), 26.
6. Gottman, *Seven Principles for Making Marriage Work,* 21.
7. Terrence Real, *How Can I Get Through to You?* (New York: Fireside, 2002), 206.

CHAPTER 7

STINKIN' THINKIN'

You were taught, with regard to your former way of life,
to put off your old self, which is being corrupted by its deceitful
desires; to be made new in the attitude of your minds;
and to put on the new self, created to be like
God in true righteousness and holiness.
—Ephesians 4:22-24

When my attitudes are right, there's no barrier too high, no valley
too deep, no dream too extreme, no challenge too great for me.[1]
—Charles Swindoll

I *F YOU KEEP on doin' whatcha' been doin', you'll keep on gettin'*
whatcha' been gettin'." This quote by one of my favorite Christian
motivational speakers sums up the dilemma of negative thinking that
many of us are stuck in and usually not aware of. Zig Ziglar came
to this conclusion through the "School of Hard Knocks." He grew up
poor in a little town in rural Alabama. His father died when he was
young, and his mother and he began the difficult task of getting by. Zig's
"light bulb moment" came when he was a forty-five-year-old, married
with children, not-so- successful door-to-door cookware salesman. He
was spinning his wheels and going nowhere fast, stuck in a pattern of
"stinkin' thinkin'." He began his phenomenal turnaround by giving his
life to God. Jesus and other mentors played a major role in encouraging
him to change his thinking around. He "met" some mentors in person
and some in books, but all of them had what he wanted. He wanted
to be positive, moral, and successful. Although our first steps might
vary, they often don't begin until we are finally hurt and tired enough
to really want to grow out of old thought patterns.

I remember when the counselor I had as a thirty-year-old gradu-
ate student revealed that my negative beliefs were a product of my
upbringing. This was not so hard to believe, but I was incredulous
when she said they might not really be true and I could decide if I
wanted to change them!

"Youuuuu gottttttaaaa be kidddddin meeeeeeee?!!!!" So began
my longer than desired road to changing my own stinkin' thinkin'.
Therapists call this negative self-talk *distorted thinking* or *cognitive
distortions.* Some of my deeply ingrained beliefs were:

- "You will never amount to anything."
- "You are not lovable."
- "You are not acceptable the way you are."

THE FORK IN THE ROAD

Many of us come to this fork in the road. We are tired of the
same old negativity and confused about why we keep sabotaging
our lives, sick of our dysfunctional behaviors. We are overwhelmed

by the feelings of going around in the hamster wheel of negativity, not even aware that we *can* make different choices. Our common "stuckness" is aptly expressed in Romans 7:19: "For what I do is not the good I want to do; no, the evil I do not want to do—this I keep on doing."

When you identify and challenge the thoughts you are stuck in and replace them with God's truths, you experience great freedom and peace, and the potential for change in your life has never been more precipitous. If you have yet to examine what you believe about yourself, you are in for a newfound joy as you embrace the *real* truth of who you are in Christ!

Strongly believed, yet deceptively hidden from awareness, our negative thinking patterns are slimy rulers of unhealthy feelings and behaviors. This negativity will continue to pervade and play havoc with our lives until we stop and examine them at their source. Once uncovered, we can reduce their prevalence in our subconscious as we replace the lies with God's perfect truth about us.

There are a variety of sources for our untrue thoughts and feelings. They arise from hereditary patterns, our personalities, our families, and our life and faith experiences. We may have heard some negatives, such as those in the list below, directly from our parents or caretakers:

- "You won't amount to much."
- "You are unattractive."
- "No one will ever love you."
- "You must work to earn God's love."

Other negative thoughts were not seated in our subconscious from actual spoken words, but rather what was *not* done or said. A little kid will make "little-kid" assumptions about being overlooked, ignored, or dismissed by adults. A rebuffed youngster makes sense of this treatment by assuming what it means. He might think, "I must not be worthy of being around others," or "I must not be very lovable," or "I have to work to be acceptable." We might also make those little-kid assumptions from dismissive comments such as, "Don't bother me," "Kids should be seen but not heard," "I will give you something to cry about," "You're not angry," or "If you can't do it right, don't do it at all."

Children develop their views of themselves as if their image were being mirrored back from what big people around them say and how they are treated. Children believe adults without question—because, after all, "they are the big people; they must really know the truth about me." *Not!* Many of us end up with a set of beliefs about ourselves that are eighty percent negative, and, tragically, believed without question.

COMMON LIES

Do any of the mantras below sound familiar? They represent some common lies many women have come to accept as truth.

- I must be perfect.
- I must have everyone's love and approval.
- I can have it all.
- Life should be fair.
- If it takes hard work, we must not be right for each other.
- My spouse should meet all my needs.
- God's love must be earned.
- A good Christian does not feel anxious, angry, or depressed.
- God can't use me unless I am spiritually strong.
- Things have to go my way for me to be happy.[2]

Application Questions:

1. Are you aware of any of these or other negative thoughts that you have about yourself?
2. Do you know where any of these negative thoughts may have come from?
3. What are some consequences of negative thoughts in your life and relationships?

CHALLENGING THE LIES

As adults, we are very capable of revisiting our negative self-talk, to update it to the real and healing truths about ourselves from our heavenly Father. This is *great* news! But how do we do it? We start by identifying the vicious cycle that ties together our thoughts, feelings, and behaviors. Let's say we have a negative feeling about ourselves such as, "I have to earn God's love."

When we have that negative thought, it leads to negative feelings such as discouragement, hopelessness, anger, depression, or anxiety. These feelings then lead to varied negative behaviors such as withdrawing from friends, perfectionism, burnout levels of serving, "acting out" with addictions to medicate the pain, yelling, crying, and avoiding responsibilities, to name a few possibilities. You can see in this example how our negativity in thoughts, behaviors, and feelings all intermingle and feed one another. These patterns allow us to break in and change the cycle in a variety of ways.

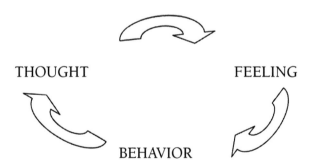

THOUGHT   FEELING

BEHAVIOR

First, we can identify any negative thoughts we are aware of from our current thinking or childhood experiences. Remember, this can be both what was directly said about us or indirectly inferred. If you are not aware of any negative thinking patterns, the second method is to identify any persistent negative feelings that you have. For example, are you often angry, depressed, anxious, or insecure? The third way to identify this cycle is to observe any persistent negative behaviors you struggle with. They might be things like acting out, drinking, yelling, retreating, addictions, people pleasing, avoiding intimacy, crying, to name just a few. The cycle of negative thoughts, feelings, and behaviors goes round and round unless we are proactive about breaking through. So, once we identify our cyclical patterns, we change them with the following steps:

> We can change our negative patterns of self talk by replacing them with God's truths.

- First, we identify our persistent negative beliefs (or lies) about ourselves.
- Second, we identify the real truth from God's Word.
- Third, we continue to replace the lies with the truth over and over until we believe it!

When we begin to convince ourselves of this truth, it will carry over to changing our feelings and behaviors. (There are more details about this process in Chris Thurman's book, *The Lies We Believe.*)

LIVING STRONG

It's no wonder Sharon has had difficulty getting over the lies she believes. Her dad was emotionally unavailable to her family and his father had been a verbally abusive alcoholic. Sharon still experiences pain thirty years later when she tells about the rejection she felt as a vulnerable fourteen-year-old. She recalled how she excitedly scooted to the middle of the front seat for a family car trip. She really did it to be close to her dad, even though it appeared she was making room for others. She still tears up today as she recounts his response, "What do you think you're doing? Get away from me." The words cut her to the core and the contempt twisted the blade. When asked today about how she internalized these types of direct and indirect negative messages, she said she believed she was not lovable, worthy, or loved. She remembers thinking, "What's wrong with me?"

It's no surprise that Sharon married an emotionally unavailable man who was disapproved of by her family. She was merely repeating what she knew. The marriage was difficult for the seven years that it lasted. The last straw was a volatile fight where he pushed her against the kitchen counter when she had their six-month-old son in her arms. He blamed Sharon for his affair that he refused to discontinue. Sharon took her toddler son and left, and filed for divorce.

The unconditional support that she received from her mom and dad at this time was the beginning of her belief that she might be lovable after all. She quickly entered another relationship, marrying a man who she erroneously thought would make her happy and meet all of her needs. Unfortunately, it was a perfect match of dysfunction. Sharon reported that no sooner had they said "I do" than her husband did a 180-degree turn in his expressions of caring. He refused to help around the house, assist with the baby, or be intimate with her emotionally or physically.

Never one to mince words, Sharon freely expressed her anger and disbelief with this dramatic change. It was almost like a replay of the event in the car with her dad. "I'm not lovable! What's wrong with me?" she repeated to herself. Blame and shame accompanied the rejection.

When Sharon came to the women's group that I facilitated, she had a big chip of anger and hurt on her shoulder. Yet she was willing to begin to look at herself more deeply. She identified more clearly the false messages from her childhood and identified how to replace them with God's truth about her.

See her negative messages below; the second column identifies God's truth.

LIES	TRUTH
Thought: I am unworthy of being loved	**Thought:** God loves me unconditionally
Feeling: Depressed, sad, angry, hurt	**Feeling:** Content, secure, loved, at peace, disappointed in lack of human love
Behavior: Verbally defensive, short fuse, chip on shoulder	**Behavior:** Relaxed, more controlled verbally, slower to express anger

You can see by the above chart that Sharon is on her way to changing the old lies with God's truth about her lovability. I wish I could tell you that this is a one-time-fixes-all event. The truth is that it takes time, work, and perseverance to change these deep and enduring messages that are seared into our little-girl brains. Sharon now knows and fully believes that God is the only one who can meet her love needs. Little by little she is getting better at replacing her lies with God's truth. She continues to focus on her own growth and become stronger in herself. She is less affected by her husband's choices and more comfortable in her own skin.

Even though Sharon and her husband are both believers, they have had a painstaking seventeen-year marriage with slow healing of their mutual childhood wounds. Hurt people *hurt* people. They are committed to their marriage and periodically see a theologian-counselor who assists them in growing out of their negative beliefs about themselves and each other.

Becoming Strong and Courageous

Friends, God knows it all. He knows our thoughts, our feelings, and our behaviors. He wants us to live in truth. He wants us to reason like adults and give up our childlike, often distorted beliefs about ourselves. He tells us in His Word to put off our old selves and put on the new truths from Him. It is unfortunate we are often unaware of how pervasive, painful, and destructive our negative patterns are. It can be very disheartening when we first discover the depth of these negative cycles in our life.

Becoming tired of the pain and chaos in our lives is the first step we take. We can then turn the corner to hope as we recognize that it is *our choice* to reduce their death grip on our lives. It is daunting, yet freeing to put those little-kid lies behind us with their unhealthy feelings and behaviors. We rejoice as we believe and become more fully who God made us to be, what He has known all along!

I believe the single most significant decision I can make on a day-to-day basis is my choice of attitude. It is more important than my past, my education, my bankroll, my successes or failures, fame or pain, what other people think of me or say about me, my circumstances, or my position. Attitude is that "single string" that keeps me going or cripples my progress. It alone fuels my fire or assaults my hope. When my attitudes are right, there's no barrier too high, no valley too deep, no dream too extreme, no challenge too great for me.[3]
—Charles Swindoll

It's true; it is our *choice* what we believe about ourselves: the little-kid lies of our youth, or the everlasting truths of our Creator!

What will you choose to believe today?

NOTES

1. http://www.quotesdaddy.com/author/Charles+R.+Swindoll
2. Chris Thurman, *The Lies We Believe* (Nashville: Thomas Nelson, 1989).
3. http://www.quotesdaddy.com/author/Charles+R.+Swindoll

CHAPTER 8

"¿CÓMO ESTÁS TU?"—
"WHAT DID YOU SAY?"

*Everyone should be quick to listen, slow to speak and slow to
become angry, for man's anger does not bring about
the righteous life that God desires.*
—James 1:19-20

*I*T WAS A great spring day at the start of recess on the grade school playground. Children were flying around gleefully with jackets open. When the initial squeals diminished to occasional shouts, the rhythm of a normal recess settled in. Over in the far corner near the chain-link fence a group of boys was setting up for a game of baseball. Teams were picked without fanfare. The boys proceeded to follow the clipped orders of their self-appointed leader. They began the first inning with their normal banter, teasing, and arguing about who was first at bat. I could hear them taunting the first batter, with a great thirst for winning, each team hungry for a win.

Just to the side of the building, a small group of girls began their game of hopscotch. Pairs of friends waited their turn, holding hands while sharing the intimacies of the morning in school. There was a brief hesitation as they chatted about who should go first. "Let's count off," one girl said. "Let's have the shortest person go first," laughed another. Somehow, one girl stepped up to the square and their time of sharing recess began.

Did you notice that these two grade school groups play differently? The girls are openly cooperative, communicative, and inclusive, and the boys are competitive, status-seeking, and independent. Both the boys and the girls want to get their own ways, but they go about it in totally different ways. These early patterns follow us for life. They lay the groundwork for gender-based communication and greatly affect how we get along with each other. What we say, what we want, and how we interpret our partners' words and actions are all colored by these early boy or girl lessons.

As we get older we no sooner want to be paired up last with boyfriends or husbands than we want to be picked last for those playground games. We greatly desire intimate closeness with another person. Someone we can count on, someone who will be there for us when we need them. So, you ask, if we crave this closeness so much, why is it so difficult to attain?

Sue Johnson has extensively researched adult attachment needs for the last twenty years. She has found that an adult's need to bond or attach is a survival imperative. When bonding fails to happen, we experience what she calls *primal panic*. This is the place where our deep need to connect meets with our fear of not connecting. It is at this juncture of great need and fear that our differing verbal and nonverbal communication patterns and skills greatly impact our relationship. Johnson relates our panic to being distracted by our own agendas, not knowing how to speak in attachment terms, not giving clear messages and being tentative about what we need.[1] Our poorly communicated needs set off our two-person tug-of-war for emotional survival.

Have you ever tried to have a deep and meaningful conversation with your spouse and felt like you were not being heard? Then you begin to realize he does not understand you at all. You make a few attempts at clarification, and still no connection. You sense a growing distance with each risky attempt to connect. At this point, you get frustrated and hurt about not being heard and understood. This situation leads to the primal panic Dr. Johnson identifies. Our great desire to connect is paired with the realization that it isn't happening. Ever been there? It hurts. It's scary. It's "crazy-making."

Our ability to have needs met and fears relieved depends on communication skills that allow us to understand each other on a deep level. A major block to our connection happens when we interpret others' messages according to our system of understanding. For example, when my husband is just silent in the middle of a conversation, I tend to think he isn't listening to me and doesn't care. Typically, he is just processing what I have said and contemplating his response. My interpretations in these cases are not reflective of what he actually feels, and commonly lead to my misunderstanding his reaction.

Metamessages are another means of misunderstanding. A metamessage is the underlying or implied message behind the words. For example, if I am constantly picking up after my husband, saying, "I'll do this," or "Let me get that," he may get the message that I don't think he does things well. His metamessage may see my gestures as criticism. If he reminds me that I have to take the car in tomorrow, my underlying metamessage may be "He thinks I'm too stupid to remember." Our metamessages reflect the relationship or attitude between the individual and our histories.[2] These failures to accurately translate each others' messages cause much relational misunderstanding and pain. I hope this chapter can help us clarify our communication problems and move past gender differences toward more fulfilling connections.

Connecting on the deep and vulnerable level that God intended is risky business! We have to risk moving beyond just the words to a deeper level of knowing what others mean and feel. We greatly improve our effectiveness if we have skills and rules for safety in communications. Here is where it gets dicey when we are discussing men and women. We are sooooooo different! We are designed, raised, and socialized differently. We commonly view others' speech and actions through the lens of our own system of understanding. Deborah Tannen in *You Just Don't Understand*, says, "Girls' rules don't fit boys, and boys' rules don't fit girls."[3] Dr. Tannen and I agree that it is very helpful to envision patterns of interaction between men and women as cross-cultural.

When we enter a different culture around the world, we do not expect to understand or see things exactly the same as our counterparts from a foreign land. In these cases we accept that we have vastly differing meanings, cues, language, and intentions behind our words and actions. We give the benefit of the doubt in assuming good intentions. We attribute most of the words and actions of people in those countries as not intentionally offensive. We attribute them to the differing culture. We extend an extra measure of grace to be able to connect and seek clarification of intent when necessary.

In a similar way, it is helpful to see men and women as having different cultures. This view allows us to depersonalize differences and connect more deeply heart-to-heart. Then when we do perceive negativity or have misunderstandings, we do not automatically get defensive but are able to clarify what is intended.

Gary Smalley defines connecting heart-to-heart as going beyond hearing the words to understanding the feelings underlying the words. He informs us that this level of listening does not imply agreement, but is a dynamic, changing process requiring skills and rules for safety. In his *DNA of Relationships* book, he even goes so far as to claim that this deeper level of listening and understanding is a primary key to saving marriages.[4]

"CROSS-CULTURAL" DIFFERENCES

Even though God made both men and women in His image (Genesis 1:27), we are still different. We have been brought up with differing roles and rules. As a result of the fall, we struggle to have a healthy balance of desire and control in our relationships (Genesis 3:16-18). This eternal battleground is often fought out and expressed through communication styles. Acceptance of gender-based differences is controversial. Some well-meaning people think that gender stereotypes influence what we notice, and that they end up shaping the very behaviors they describe as a self-fulfilling prophecy. There is an ongoing argument whether these differences are due to heredity or to environment.

I could care less where gender-based differences come from, but from my perspective from fifty-nine years as a girl, I have noticed that differences do exist. Over the last decade or so, I have observed some consistencies in the differences and have realized that significant relational problems commonly result.

This is what I care about. I want us to be smart and observant and proactive as women. I don't want us to get sidetracked by debating the real, imagined, self-fulfilling, or hereditary source of our differences. I want us to learn about them and observe if our differing ways of communicating, interpreting, or viewing the world cause us marital problems. I want us to move ahead proactively to learn to translate accurately each other's communications in order to promote deeper connection.

> Understanding gender differences greatly improves communication.

There are many gender characteristics that can greatly influence our ability to communicate with our spouse. Deborah Tannen is a sociolinguist who has spent her career analyzing how our everyday conversations impact relationships. She did not set out to focus on gender differences, but they stood out, and she found them so intriguing that they became the focus of her work. Her fascinating book, *You Just Don't Understand: Men and Women in Conversation*, discusses her findings. I've listed some of them below. Although they are stereotypical to some degree, they are based on her stringent research findings. My purpose in listing them is to help us identify differences in our relationships in order to reduce our habits of jumping to conclusions. If we increase our understanding and acceptance of these differences, our intimate connections will almost certainly improve.[5]

CHARACTERISTIC	MEN	WOMEN
Talking style	Focus on reporting things	Focus on rapport with others
One up	Often lecture when engaged with women, trying to be "one up" from another person	Listen for mutual knowing, seek equality
Focus	Focus on themselves, seek to control and have their needs met	Focus on connecting, getting consensus and giving to others
Listening	Are competitive, facts oriented; need time to process information	Are cooperative, feelings oriented; process thoughts and feelings immediately
Decision-making	Decide by force, persuasion, or majority rule	Decide by consensus
Speaking	Speak up more in public	Speak up more in private
Problems	Want to solve	Want to understand
Relating	Relate as rivals	Relate as equals
Speech centers in brain	Have two	Have seven; girls speak at an earlier age

CHARACTERISTIC	MEN	WOMEN
Words per day	Use 12,000	Use 25,000
Motivation	Motivated for independence	Motivated for intimacy
Problem-solving	Cope by being silent	Talk to solve problems
Asking	See asking as inferior	See it as chance to connect
Talking	See excessive talking as wasteful	See lack of talking as not caring
Home	See it as a place where they don't have to talk	See it as a place to be free to talk

Application Question:

1. Which differences listed above do you observe between you and your spouse and what difficulties do they present?

The differences that men and women experience in play, thought, behavior, and conversation have huge implications for our ability for intimate connection. We have different views of intimacy, different intimacy needs, and different interpretations of our communications. These differences result in much confusion, hurt, and anger in our marriages.

Terry Real is a male therapist and researcher who has examined and confronted many of our differences around intimacy. Terry has observed that women today still carry some traits of our passive and overly accommodating mothers. Yet we also desperately want to become modern women, able to identify clearly and ask that our relational intimacy needs to be met. We have been raised to know more and expect more from our marriages. Yet our desires for closeness commonly exceed our skills and those of our partner. In his book about male-female intimacy differences, *How Can I Get Through to You?*, Dr. Real observes that men have typically not been socialized to understand or desire intimacy the same as women. He goes so far to say that the very historical definition of masculinity is synonymous with disconnection! Men have been taught to vie for power and to seek being one up. Their drive for independence and competition run contrary to intimacy. Women can become dissatisfied and resentful about being left with unbalanced responsibility for marital intimacy. Men may like things to be different as well, but are uncertain about how to go about it. Our dilemma as women then becomes learning to bring together our desire for equal relational responsibility while we develop our skills and voice to identify and express our needs for change. Our underlying fear of abandonment contributes heavily to our demanding and overly accommodating styles. These issues can turn to bitterness, anger, criticism, or nagging, leading to further emotional disconnection.

Dr. Real has recommendations for this current intimacy gap that we are experiencing. He recommends that women be empowered to find their voice and speak up about intimacy needs in reasonable, direct, and non-offensive ways. We are not responsible for men opening up, but our attitude helps them. If I am critical, demanding, or angry, I know from experience that my husband is not drawn to me (not that surprising), and I know those behaviors do not honor God.

> Intimacy improves by learning to express our needs more effectively.

I remember a "light bulb moment" I had about this. My husband and I were having a loud disagreement and I screamed, red-faced, crying, pleading, "Why can't you just love me?" In the way that only God can do, He lovingly convicted me, making me realize, "Kathy, you aren't exactly very lovable right now." That memorable experience helped me learn about the ugliness and consequences of negativity born out of hurt.

In a perfect world, a man would adjust and compliment our growth by addressing the unhelpful communication code they learned early in their lives: "Don't cry, don't be vulnerable, and don't show you care." In his relational intimacy book, Real states that men need to step down from their often dominating and disconnected position to risk and connect emotionally with their wives.[6] Our new approach regarding intimacy differences has the potential to help us to develop the pattern of healthy interdependence that God desires.

NEGATIVE PATTERNS THAT DESTROY ONENESS

Remember the saying "Sticks and stones will break my bones, but words will never hurt me"? We all know that words *do* hurt. Most of us have been hurt by another's words, yet we have also been a source of hurtful statements toward others. Our poor role models regarding marital communication resulted in my husband and I not knowing what good communication looked like. Our childhood hurts fueled our fear-based negative communication and kept us apart for many years. This resulted in the common pattern—hurt people *hurt* people. Our great desire to connect was thwarted big time, not only by lack of skills and past hurts, but our great fears of abandonment and unworthiness. These deeper fears were not identified or addressed for many years, but rather acted out in the form of protective negative communication—"I'll hurt you before you hurt me." Each of us was like the usually gentle dog that bares his teeth and bites when he is injured. Negative patterns destroy relationships.

In his book, *A Lasting Promise*, Scott Stanley identifies and discusses four key negative patterns that put marriages at risk.[7] They destroy the oneness that God intended us to have. It makes sense that when we reduce the negative interactions listed below, there is more hope for healing.

- *Escalation*: Arguing back and forth with increasing hostility. Partners try to "one up" the hurting of each other and say things they don't mean and can't take back.

- *Invalidation:* Subtle or not-so-subtle character assassination with words, sarcasm, contempt, and criticism. Found to be a serious contributor to marriage problems and divorce.
- *Negative interpretations:* Occur when we believe the worst about a partner's motives and behaviors. It fuels hopelessness. We then tend to collect evidence that the negative views are true, which locks us into this system. When a person is stuck in negative interpretation, little can be done to change the interaction, because it won't be believed.
- *Withdrawal and avoidance:* Refusing to get in to or address difficulties. Partner can leave physically or emotionally or both. Damage worsens if allowed to continue.

John Gottman, a prolific marriage researcher from Seattle, has examined what makes marriages fail or succeed.[8] He identified what women do and what men do to contribute to divorce. As mentioned previously, a woman's primary destructive act is what he calls the *harsh startup.* This is when we begin an interaction in a blaming, attacking, sarcastic, or otherwise harsh way. The harsh startup can also be nonverbal—a look, tone, stance, or body language. Starting this way *guarantees* that our partner will respond defensively. I embarrassingly admit that I have been the queen of the harsh startup, and I am probably more lucky than not that I am not divorced because of it.

Dr. Gottman coined the phrase "Four Horsemen of the Apocalypse" to describe the damaging traits of criticism, contempt, defensiveness, and stonewalling, which also contribute to marital breakdown. Other miscellaneous poor communication tactics include using too many words, "being right," nagging, and communicating through hints. Dr. Gottman found that a man's major block to relational success is his unwillingness to be influenced by his spouse.

There are many biblical mandates regarding negative communication patterns:

- James 3:8 refers to the tongue as a restless evil, unable to be tamed.
- James 1:26 warns us to keep a tight rein on our tongue if we consider ourselves religious.

- Galatians 5:15 warns us that we will destroy each other if we keep on biting and devouring each other.
- James 1:19 tells us to be quick to listen and slow to speak.
- Proverbs 19:13 speaks of a contentious woman being like a constant dripping, and restraining her is like trying to restrain the wind. Not very likely, huh?
- Romans 14:12 informs us that we will be accountable to God for ourselves, whether our spouse desires to grow in communication skills or not.

I wish memorizing these verses and praying were guaranteed to bring about change in our marital communications for *both* spouses. Unfortunately, willingness to change often requires that we dig out and heal from our childhood hurts and work hard and long to replace negative patterns with healthy skills. Still, these biblical mandates remain personal challenges for our own growth, no matter what choices our spouse makes.

A very common male female pattern of interaction described by many marriage experts is what is called the *pursual-withdrawal pattern*. (Dr. Stanley actually calls this the "gender dance."⁹) My husband and I have lived this out to a T. In our marriage, I have been the pursuer who desires connection and brings up issues for discussion. My husband, the classic withdrawer, is either not interested, is self-protective, or does not feel safe in the disagreement. The pursuer tends to see the withdrawer as not caring, and the withdrawer tends to see the pursuer as attacking. We experienced firsthand and for too many years how this pattern of interaction with negative interpretations can escalate out of control.

Fortunately, but not without much damage, we have been able to improve our interactions by identifying the pattern, then applying skills and boundaries to reduce the harm done. We still maintain our basic styles, but each of us is less quick to make negative interpretations. Because we know the pattern, even when we slip into old habits, the negativity does not usually escalate as in the past, and forgiveness comes more quickly. I grieve today about the hurtful, cutting words I have spewed out of my hurting self at my husband. I don't even remember many of them, but he does, and I can't take them back. It just didn't have to go on and on that way. Please believe me, it is hard, hard, hard (and sometimes impossible) to overcome the hurts that come from harsh words. I not only hurt my husband, but my speech and selfish pushiness has dishonored the Lord.

P.S.: I still pursue, but more softly and with respect most of the time.

SAFETY IN COMMUNICATION

An imperative step toward relational health is to develop boundaries or ground rules for safety in communication. Many of the problems that we can have are a result of wildly out-of-control random attempts to be heard. (Remember the injured dog?) Through my poor communication role models, I learned that couples either yelled or ran away from each other in tears. My husband learned that anger and conflict is wrong. What preparation we had! A perfect setup for a pursuer and withdrawer.

One of the reasons for poor communication is that we do not feel safe enough to be vulnerable. It is imperative that we develop some ground rules for safer communication that will also be discussed in the chapter about boundaries. If you suspect that the communication in your marriage is abusive (or verges on abusive), please read the details of this pattern in Appendix C. Although you can still grow and apply techniques of healthy relating alone, there may be cases where your changes may threaten your safety and you need to be wise and have support to proceed.

Some general principles before outlining how to make a safe structure for discussions:

- Listening and understanding another person's position and saying "I understand" is not the same as agreeing with them.
- If either of you is stuck in an "I'm right-You're wrong" mode, no skills will help you. I like the saying "You can either be right or you can be married." Not both!
- Having problems and differences is normal, what make them damaging is our negative reactions to them.

- Issues such as addictions, mental illness, affairs, and abuse will complicate communication and safety.

Dr. Stanley and Dr. Smalley both outline a few basic guidelines for safety in communication:[10, 11]

- Couples should schedule weekly meetings at mutually agreeable times.
- A person can decline, but must reschedule discussion time.
- One person speaks at a time, speaker first, no more than three minutes.
- Separate "problem discussions" from "solution discussions".
- Take a time out if discussion escalates or gets off track.
- Accept differences, suspend judgment.

Application Questions:

2. What are some negative patterns that you could reduce?

3. Which safety guidelines would help you feel safer in your communications with your spouse?

BECOMING STRONG AND COURAGEOUS WITH POSITIVE SKILLS

After we have identified our differences and negative patterns and have set up healthy communication boundaries, it is time to apply positive communication skills. Even reducing a few of our negative patterns allows room for positive patterns to develop. Here are some suggestions for developing positive patterns:

- Do your own healing so you can operate from a position of strength.
- Commit to truthful talking, even when it's hard.
- Ask your spouse just to listen if you want to process something in a rambling way.
- Make sure to schedule talks at a good time for both parties.

- Identify your wants and needs and learn to express them directly and positively.
- Learn to speak assertively with "I" messages.
- Learn to listen with intent to understand and empathize with the other person.
- Learn about your spouse's special patterns and learn to work with them.
- Don't expect your man to be able to relate to you like a woman.
- Learn to say, "I was wrong."
- Learn to say, "It is not your fault."
- Learn to say, "I hear what you are saying. I don't see it the same way, but that's OK."
- Learn to say, "Will you forgive me?"
- Give positive reinforcement and affirmations.
- Develop your friendship, go on dates, have fun times without "problem" discussions.

LIVING STRONG

- As I have tried my best to put these skills into practice within my marriage, I continue to keep a few key principles in mind:
- I am different from my spouse.
- Learning and accepting and adjusting to differences is important.
- I need to translate communications into the language of the speaker.
- When I am stronger, our negative patterns and differences do not hurt as much.
- Increasing positive and reducing negative communications is imperative.
- One person focused on honoring the Lord in attitude, speech, acceptance, and love can change the destructive dance of marriage.

Will you commit to changing your dance steps with more effective communication?

NOTES

1. Sue Johnson, *Hold Me Tight* (New York: Little, Brown and Company, 2008), 30.
2. Deborah Tannen, *You Just Don't Understand* (New York: Ballantine Books, 1990), 32.
3. Tannen, *You Just Don't Understand Me*, 43.
4. Gary Smalley, *The DNA of Relationship* (Wheaton, IL: Tyndale House, 2004), 132.
5. Tannen, *You Just Don't Understand Me*, 49-148.
6. Terrence Real, *How Can I Get Through to You?* (New York: Fireside, 2002), 134.
7. Scott Stanley, *A Lasting Promise* (San Francisco: Jossey-Bass, 2002), 26.
8. John Gottman, *Seven Principles for Making Marriage Work* (New York: Three Rivers Press, 1999), 26.
9. Stanley, *A Lasting Promise*, 42.
10. Stanley, *A Lasting Promise*, 94.
11. Smalley, *The DNA of Relationship*, 89.

CHAPTER 9

STAND UP, STAND DOWN

*If it is possible, as far as it depends on you
live at peace with everyone.*
—Romans 12:18

Speak the truth in love.
—Ephesians 4:15

MR PASSIVE AND MS. AGGRESSIVE—A TWO-ACT PLAY

Act 1: The Fight

Scene 1

Ms. Aggressive: Well, I can't believe you've done it again!

Mr. Passive: *What?*

Ms. Aggressive: You promised to follow through with a serious talk with Bill about his prom plans and the prom is tomorrow night and you haven't talked to him yet.

Mr. Passive: I was just going to do it.

Ms. Aggressive: I can't count on you for anything.

(Mr. Passive is silent.)

Ms. Aggressive: I really thought you cared enough about his safety to follow through on this.

(Mr. Passive is silent.)

Ms. Aggressive: Who do you think should talk to him about his plans for the night and drinking and sex and safety? Do I have to do that, too? I can't stand it! I am so tired of being the only parent in this family. Are you ever going to grow up?

(Mr. Passive is silent.)

Ms. Aggressive: I don't think you drop the ball at work like this, or you wouldn't have a job. But, of course, you *care* about your job. I wonder how Bill will feel if his mom has to be the one who talks to him about sex. Why do I always have to be the responsible one?

(Mr. Passive is silent and walks away.)

Act 2: The Subconscious

Scene 1

Ms. Aggressive *(expressing subconscious thoughts to herself)*: I will start off on the attack, so the focus isn't on me. Then I'll blame him so I feel more confident about my sorry self. Next comes the ever-popular guilt trip. It will make him feel responsible for the wrong in our family so I can continue to avoid looking at myself. Then no one will see how hurt and insecure I really am. I wish I could really believe in his badness and my goodness. Then I would be "successful" and I wouldn't have to play these games. Now I will keep my superior position with a little "you don't care" talk, and "you only care about work" jabs. I think I'm convincing him, because he's not talking. I get tired of being overly responsible, but I sure wish it gave me a sense of accomplishment instead of hollow emptiness. One last personal dig about his character, and this job of self-protection is done. I just wish it felt a little more satisfying, and it doesn't seem to be making me feel as superior and in control as it used to… I guess I have won for now…

Scene 2

Mr. Passive (*expressing subconscious thoughts to himself*): Uh-oh, this doesn't look good. I didn't remember that prom was tomorrow. Here we go. I wish she would get off her high horse. I hope this doesn't go on very long; I have a show I want to watch at 7:00. I'll just not say much. Oh, she's on the old "I'm responsible-you're not" kick. If she only knew, I like it that way. That's how I keep under the radar. If I don't do much, I can't be wrong as much. I'm enough of a loser; I don't need any more opportunities to be wrong. I'll just do my usual silence thing, and it will be over soon. This method has worked for me for a long time. Although you'd think if it was working so well, I'd begin to feel a little better about myself. I know I'm a lousy person and parent, but I sure get tired of hearing it constantly. Who does she think she is? I think I'll count the ceiling tiles again. One, two, three… Boy, she's really going on and on tonight. I wonder what's for dinner. I hope Billy has a good time at the prom. I really like to see her escalate a little; it makes me feel powerful and superior, even though I'm not. Yea, I'm tired of you being my parent also; but go for it! I know I'm not going to step into that role as long as you are willing to do it all. I know I'd never do anything right, anyway. I don't think I will grow up—it's overrated and scary—and I gave up on me a long time ago, too… I wonder what's for dinner…

I remember similar interactions back in the day. I felt like I was screaming at the top of my lungs (sometimes I was), yet my voice wasn't heard. The reality was, and is, we can't be heard until we learn to overrule our unhealthy subconscious voice and learn the language of mutually respectful assertive communication. In order to be heard, we need to learn skills of speaking the truth in love.[1] I have needed to learn to *stand down* from being aggressive and bullying and protective and my passive husband has needed to learn to *stand up* for truth and honesty. We needed to learn to be neither dominating nor disengaged, to learn to speak truth in love through respectful, assertive communication.

My aggression and my husband's passivity have both caused damage to our marriage. At first glance, the passive person may seem healthier, but passivity is a killer. John Gottman and other marriage researchers have determined that avoiding conflict is a major contributor to divorce.[2] We all experience conflict, but avoiding it causes the buildup of anger and bitterness, eventually leading to disconnected and parallel lives.

This is certainly not the pattern that God intends for marriage. When passive individuals do not speak up for themselves, they often end up being overpowered and taken advantage of. Through passive acceptance, they teach their partners and others to treat them disrespectfully. They live to keep the peace at any price; for women, often to please others. At first, peace-at-any-price people may appear to be super spiritual martyrs in a difficult situation. The cost to them is the loss of themselves, and often the loss of relationships. Changing our harmful communication patterns is difficult, but very possible.

Both my husband and I needed to become more assertive. I have to admit, when my husband began to be more assertive, it was not easy for me to receive, but it was right. Learning these skills has been a scary and uncomfortable process, but very, very healthy and rewarding as we both learned to speak the truth in love and as we have grown to be more respectful of ourselves and each other.

The irony with the couple who represent opposite ends of the passive-aggressive continuum is that subconsciously they are very similar. Commonly, they both come from positions of insecurity and poor communication skills, yet are acting them out in opposite ways. The passive person runs and hides, trying to keep peace. The aggressive person's tactic (of which I am all too familiar) is to be loud and verbose, hiding insecurity behind dominating methods. Each person is

> Both passive and aggressive persons are often operating out of insecurity.

being disrespectful, insecure, and dysfunctional when they play out their natural passive or aggressive dance.

Jesus can be the real "leveler" here, as he gives the passive person the courage to *stand up* for himself and speak the truth. Jesus can give the aggressive person the humility and courage to *stand down* from their high horse of protection to make room for the other person's voice. The courage and humility from the Lord can help both individuals to either step up or step down to the healthy assertive communication style.

I was shocked as I examined definitions of assertiveness over the years. My 1969 *Webster's Dictionary* says assertiveness means "disposed to bold or confident assertion, stating confidently; synonym: aggressive."[3] The 1989 *World Book Dictionary* said assertiveness means: "too confident, to insist on." Assertiveness training was defined as "a method of training submissive individuals to behave with confidence, usually by adapting an aggressive attitude." [4]In 2003 *Webster's* says assertive means "to declare, affirm, to insist on one's rights."[5] The 2010 Web-based dictionary definition says assertive is "self-assured; positive; aggressive."[6]

These serial definitions of assertiveness over the last forty years reflect the ongoing confusion between being assertive and aggressive. I was particularly surprised to see the word *aggressive* interchanged once again with assertiveness in the 2010 definition. We are *still* confused! Historically, especially in the church, being assertive has gotten a bad rap, particularly for women. Assertiveness is often characterized as a method for being abusive, aggressive, and disrespectful to others in order to get our own way. It seems that many individuals continue to think that there are only two choices in communication styles—either aggressive (often seen as the same as assertive) or passive.

The following quote from Robert Alberti's 2008 edition of *Your Perfect Right* (updated from 1970) compares the forty-year historical pendulum swing.[7]

> It seems that we have—as a society—reached a point of much greater openness and freedom of expression. That may not be all to the good....Some folks have used "assertiveness" as a pretext for all sorts of uncivil behavior—misinterpreting the concept as if it gave them license for rudeness, road rage, and boorishness. Fortunately that's not the rule, but I sometimes think we may have created a monster, despite our best efforts to teach a self-expressive style that is respectful of others.

COMMUNICATION STYLES

- *Assertive:* A way of communicating feelings, opinions, and views in an open and truthful way that is respectful to both parties. It is a way for others to know us for who we truly are as we also know and respect them.
- *Passive:* Passive people avoid conflict at any cost and communicate indirectly. They do not express their own needs and feelings and have difficulty saying no without guilt. Passive people do not require others to respect them.
- *Aggressive:* Asserting one's rights at the expense of the other party. An aggressive person demands, disrupts peace, and often insists on winning at any cost. The aggressive person uses anger, put-downs, verbal abuse, threats, and manipulation to get his or her way, and disrespects and alienates others.
- *Passive-aggressive:* These individuals use trickery, manipulation, and seduction to get their way. They dominate and disrespect others, while outwardly playing the nice guy. They will agree with others and then go behind their back to get their own way. They control others through

withdrawal of affection, tattling, and not cooperating. They will make promises, then procrastinate and "forget." This communication style is challenging to figure out because "what you see is not what you get."

Some have observed an increase in passive-aggressive men that has run parallel to the women's movement. They suppose that the changing balance of power may have caused a shift which challenges the old pattern of the macho man and submissive woman. Some men may have moved to an indirect passive-aggressive mode rather than learning healthy and mutually respectful methods of communication.

Below is a line representing a continuum of communication styles from passive on the left, to aggressive on the right, with the balanced style of mutual respect, assertiveness, in the middle.

"You only"	"Us"	"Me only"
Care for others at my own expense	Balanced asking and giving	Care only for self

$$\longleftarrow \qquad\qquad\qquad\qquad\qquad\qquad \longrightarrow$$

PASSIVE	ASSERTIVE	AGGRESSIVE

Application Questions:

1. Where do you see yourself on this assertiveness continuum?

2. Are there certain people that you have more difficulty being assertive with? For example, authority figures, parents, spouse, friends, co-workers?

3. What situations cause you most difficulty in being assertive?

IMPORTANCE OF ASSERTIVENESS

Assertiveness is not a personality trait but a skill to be learned. The communication styles that got us what we needed as children are not necessarily effective in our adult lives. It's helpful to stop and examine our automatic patterns as adults. When honest feelings are not expressed in healthy ways, they get acted out through destructive habits and traits. Unexpressed emotions do not go away and can even lead to life-threatening physical ailments. Learning to communicate with others honestly is important for our mental and physical health, our confidence, and the well-being of our relationships.

Passive or peace-at-any-price individuals tend to feel unappreciated and taken for granted. They spend a lot of energy and years walking on eggshells, giving in, and swallowing their feelings. They are frustrated and unacknowledged for their efforts, disappointed with the lack of peace. They often learned communication from an angry and unpredictable parent. They were motivated by fear and learned it was better to give in to the tyrant in their life. This method was logical and got them through childhood, but breaks down in adult interactions. Passivity reinforces the hurtful behaviors of tyrants and does not bring change or peace. The passive style can lead to many emotional and physical ailments such as anxiety, depression, bitterness, headaches, and heart and intestinal problems. Passive individuals often see themselves as being nice and keeping the peace, when in reality they perpetuate dysfunction by fearing honest expression of their real selves.

Aggressive individuals assert themselves, their rights, and opinions at the expense of others. They are disrespectful and imply by their actions that they are right or superior. Some tools of these individuals include being demanding, attacking, blaming, humiliating, and using sarcasm and put-downs. It is a shock to most passive individuals that the bullies in their lives often feel inferior and are hiding behind the mask of their loud bravado to appear strong and in control. When aggressive individuals hurt and offend others, they are often protecting themselves from being hurt or connecting closely to others. They often hide to avoid feeling emotions and create the illusion of control and power to avoid revealing their vulnerable self. Inside, they feel angry, sad, fearful, hopeless, and guilty. Their background might include a bully who drove them within, only to become a fearful bully themselves.

A passive-aggressive communication style was first coined as an "immaturity reaction." A person who uses this method usually has poor self-worth, lacking power and resources to challenge authority directly. These inadequacies and a perceived helplessness all result in their indirect and covert communications. These individuals can be confusing and challenging because outwardly they appear cooperative, but they are also resistant. The increasing prevalence of passive-aggressive men may be partially due to the women's movement. When the power base in relationships was challenged to become more equal, men responded by becoming passive-aggressive. It is hoped that they can also learn to become healthfully assertive and share relational power.

LIVING STRONG

Gina is a good example of a woman who has worked at and overcome the long-standing trait of being a peace-at-any-price person. For the first twenty years of her marriage she knew something was wrong, but she thought she was being a good submissive Christian wife as she attempted to soothe and tolerate her husband's tantrums, which included severe verbal abuse. Through spiritual and secular counseling she found out that she had been enabling his sinful treatment of her. Armed with a clearer view of submission and the unhealthy patterns of enabling that hadn't kept the peace anyway, she finally said "*No more!*" She was tired of being mistreated and manipulated to be what he needed her to be. She learned to be strong and assertive and developed boundaries to protect herself from the former abuse. She describes her deep yearning to stand up tall and fill her lungs with air. She felt free and liberated. For the first time in her marriage she was able to more fully become the woman God made her to be.

The marriage is not healed today, but she is. She lives in wholeness and peace and freedom, with no fear. She is still disappointed about the marriage, but has learned to value truth-telling above peacekeeping. She continues to grow in the process of becoming more assertive. She has blossomed as she has a strong network of

Christian friends who help her live a full life. The Lord has not released her from her marriage; she believes He would lead her out of it if He wanted that. She is amazed at what is possible with Him. He is all we need, a husband in every way. She has encouraged many younger women to follow the Lord.

BECOMING STRONG AND COURAGEOUS

There is great confusion with women being assertive in the church. We somehow think that being biblically submissive and assertive are opposite and mutually exclusive traits. The attitude that assertive behavior is only appropriate for adult white males is a deep and die-hard concept in our culture, coming out of the Victorian age, when women were to be seen but not heard. This philosophy began to change with the suffragettes and was further challenged with the women's movement of the 1960s and '70s. Women have experienced a lot of resistance to their efforts in speaking up for themselves, but have made strides in asserting their rights. We are breaking through stereotypes and have more equal representation in society. We have more freedom to speak and voice our own opinions, feelings, and self-expressions. Church teachings on submission, self-denial, sacrifice, and humility lead some to believe that being assertive is incompatible with Christian principles. The Bible does not use the word *assertiveness* but calls us to behaviors that are components of assertive communication. We are able to live out the following verses more effectively when we learn assertive and respectful communication skills.

> Being assertive and submissive are not mutually exclusive.

- We are both created equally in God's image. (Genesis 1:27)
- We are to love our neighbors as ourselves. (Matthew 19:19, 22:39)

- We are to speak the truth. (Proverbs 12:22; Ephesians 4:15; Col. 3:9)
- We are to respect others. (1 Peter 2:17, 3:7; Ephesians 5:33)
- We are to live in peace. (Romans 12:18; Hebrews 12:14; 1 Peter 3:11)

Communicating clearly, directly, and truthfully in an assertive style is the best method for keeping peace. The results of being untruthful, passive, aggressive, or indirect in communication are anger, bitterness, and strife, along with a plethora of psychological and physical ailments. In his popular book, *Love and Respect*, Dr. Emerson Eggerich elaborates on the outcome of what he calls the "crazy cycle." This is where we go round and round in the dysfunctional dance of indirect, hurtful, and disrespectful communication.

However, as Dr. Eggerich says, it is a chicken-and-egg scenario and it only takes one to turn around the destructiveness of the crazy cycle.[8] It is up to each of us, to the best of our ability and the Spirit's help, to live out these biblical mandates. We need to balance personal acceptance and love with honest communication of differences. Assuming we are praying, learning to speak up respectfully and assertively is the next best way to honor God in our relationships. This is not an easy task, but once again, it is the right thing to do, and we have a great big God to guide us and give us the courage to move ahead in spite of our fear.

We both need to access the great leveler, Jesus, in these two extremes of relational communication. He can help the aggressive person *stand down*, acknowledging his or her childhood hurt and false bravado style of bullying. Aggressive people need to be empowered by Jesus to become humble and grow in mutual respect, acceptance and equality. The passive person needs to accept their equality as a child of God, to learn to love themselves and courageously speak the truth. Standing up for themselves will allow the passive person to experience a peace never experienced before. The Lord helps both of us communicate more successfully, whether male or female, whether passive or aggressive.

Honest mutual communication of our thoughts, feelings, and needs are necessary components for knowing and loving each other. Sometimes our mistaken assumptions confound being assertive. Chris Thurman details some of the major assumptions in his book, *The Lies We Believe*.[9] Learning to be assertive is a process to be learned like many other skills in this book. Assertiveness starts having a clear definition of what it is and what it isn't. When you are assured that the mutual respect definition does not contradict your religious beliefs, you can move forward to become assertive. You need to identify the people and circumstances that you have the most difficulty being assertive with.

It is then helpful to rank order these people and circumstances from least to most difficult and begin practicing assertive "I" messages with the least difficult circumstances. One thing you can be assured of is that as you begin to assert yourself, not everyone will automatically be a cheerleader for your new skills—especially those who are particularly fond of your manipulability (a new word!) and former doormat role. But that is OK. This is where it is particularly helpful to be sure your motive is to be assertive, not aggressive or manipulative, as well as a time to be sure of your "I" messages. When others bristle or balk as you ask to be respected, you will be confident and more able to let it be *their* problem!

When we do not learn how to communicate in a respectful way, the marriage suffers. Being either passive and thus losing ourselves, or aggressive and constantly attacking others to defend ourselves, either communication style prevents us both from having peace. We often are not able to discover who God made us to be, much less to identify and use our gifts. One brave and committed person in a marriage can step up to the plate and dramatically improve disrespectful communications.

Will you join me in learning to step up or step down to respectful communication?

NOTES

1. Ephesians 4:15.
2. John Gottman, *Seven Principles for Making Marriage Work* (New York: Three Rivers Press, 1999), 15.
3. *Webster's Seventh New Collegiate Dictionary*, (G.& C. Merriam Company Publishing,1969),
4. Robert O. Zelemy. Editor,*World Book Dictionary*, (Chicago, World Book, Inc.,1989).
5. Michael Agnes, Editor, *Webster's New World Dictionary*, (N.Y., Pocket Books,2003).
6. http://dictionary.reference.com/browse/assertive.
7. Robert Alberti and Michael Emmons, *Your Perfect Right* (Atascadero, CA: Impact, 2008), 23.
8. Emerson Eggerichs, *Love & Respect: The Love She Most Desires; The Respect He Desperately Needs* (Nashville: Integrity, 2004), 16.
9. Chris Thurman, *The Lies We Believe* (Nashville: Thomas Nelson, 1989), 28.

CHAPTER 10

WHO REIGNS?

Emotions make good slaves and terrible masters.
—Dallas Willard

A fool gives vent to his anger.
—Proverbs 29:11

*T*HE OLD-TIME WESTERN *movie* Oklahoma *has a runaway covered wagon scene. The cooking wagon is ambling along a flat stretch of desolated rolling desert. The two drivers move in unison with the slight creak, creak of the slow moving wagon. It looks like that late afternoon, "I could take a nap" type of time. A young calf playfully breaks loose from the herd. The alert cowboy jerks his horse around and takes off like there is a fire. The older, sedate wagon horsies lift their heads and jangle their harnesses, prancing around a bit. This wakes up the drivers, but too late. The trusty steeds are spooked and now the whole herd is restless. The wagon begins to rumble along with increasing speed and the drivers are saying all sorts of cowboy things to calm them. It is ineffective, as they are now approaching a downward hill and picking up speed. They gallop faster and the wagon shifts precariously back and forth. They hit a few rocks and the hill gets steeper. One of the drivers bails just as the cooking supplies begin to fly out the back of the wagon. The moviegoers hold their breath as the wagon breaks apart. All of the movement and speed and hill and rocks and yelling and breaking apart escalate until the wagon is merely a platform and three wheels. The driver throws up the reins and jumps off as the remaining horse goes left and the wheels go right.*

Wow, what a ride! How out of control was that? It had started out to be such a peaceful afternoon. I have a question: Who was holding the reins? This Wild West scene reminds me of myself and my emotions. Things are quiet at times, then all of a sudden, my thoughts, body, and feelings begin going down an uncertain path. The intensity escalates, and the driver leaves. The wildly out-of-control person hardly knew what happened. My question to you is this:

" Who reigns" in controlling your emotions?

Our emotions are given to us by God to enrich our lives and motivate us to action. As a woman who was not taught at all about emotions, in my earlier life it seemed that they were given to drive me and others close to me crazy! I wore my emotions on my sleeve and was out of control. My thirty-something PMS years were especially painful. The only emotions shown in the family I grew up in (although of course they were never talked about) were anger from my dad and sadness and anxiety from my mom. My dysfunctional family mantra was "Don't talk, don't trust, and don't feel." I was clueless in identifying, expressing, and controlling emotions, and experienced much personal and family pain and confusion as a result. I hope this chapter can assist us all to continue to move toward a more healthy, balanced emotional life.

Our emotions are a mixed blessing, a reflex of our thoughts and automatic bodily reactions. The best definition I have ever heard is emotions are like our own "personal weather." This "weather" varies wildly, is always there, and is neither right or wrong, good or bad. Our emotions can be denied, expressed unreservedly, or controlled and used for good. They can be our friend or our foe. The choices we make with our emotions can lead to our enrichment or personal and relational struggles.

BASIC EMOTIONS

Six basic human emotions have been universally identified from the facial expressions of cultures all around the world. These biological and God-given emotions are innately hardwired into our brains to give us information about our internal and external worlds. Emotions are cues that lead us to scan our bodies and environment to mobilize us for action. It is thought that the information that we receive can be processed along two paths in our brain. One path causes us to respond to events automatically and quickly for our survival. The second pathway allows us time to thoughtfully contemplate a response. Opinions differ regarding whether our emotions and physiological reactions occur simultaneously, or if our physical reactions trigger our thoughts and emotional reactions. Listed below are the six basic emotions with actions they signal us to take.[1]

We may first become aware of sadness from tightness in our chest, a tear, or awareness of an imaginary black cloud around us. This is our bodies' signal to slow down, to possibly adjust to a loss, or seek support. When afraid, we may notice shallow breathing, a racing heart, or darting eyes. This alerts us to scan our environment for danger, to run, fight, or cope with a threat. With surprise, we may notice a catch in our breath, or slight tension in our muscles that alerts us to stop and take in the scene. There are many similarities in human emotional responses, we are responsible to observe and learn how our own bodies respond to any given emotion.

FEELING	ACTION
Anger	Danger, prepare to defend self
Fear	Warning, protect self, run, fight, or cope
Sadness	Slow down, adjust to loss, seek support
Disgust/shame	Hide, avoid
Surprise	Stop, be alert, explore
Joy	Continue, engage

Application Questions:

1. Are you able to identify and express the six basic emotions? Which ones do you have more difficulty with?

2. What forms of emotional expression did you observe in your upbringing?

It is important in growing emotionally that we examine our past for sources of emotional pain. God can certainly heal anyone spontaneously, yet we commonly need to acknowledge and excavate past hurts for good emotional health. Our relief will only be temporary if we blame our current difficulties without examining our past. Like with many things, ignoring emotions does not make them go away! Negative emotions can be windows to past wounds. When they are ignored, they come out in other ways such as perfectionism, emotional deadness, acting out, or bitterness. Additional expressions can include anger disproportionate to the offense, hostility, feeling misunderstood, relational problems, stress related physical illness, depression, and anxiety.

There are powerful physiological components related to emotions. Don Colbert's recent book, *Deadly Emotions, Understanding the Mind-Body-Spirit Connection that Can Heal or Destroy You*, tells it all. Emotionally traumatic experiences are deeply buried in our survival brain as a result of physical, emotional, and sexual abuse, or exposure to violence and other traumas. Traumatic events increase the likelihood that buried emotions will trigger negative thoughts, feelings and behaviors, and dysfunction. Over time, our unresolved toxic emotions can fuel deadly and painful diseases.

Colbert reports the estimation from the American Institute of Stress that 75 to 90 percent of visits to our primary physicians in the United States today are for physical disorders caused by emotional factors.[2] Individuals who do not learn to manage their emotional stress have a 40 percent increased risk of death over those who do. The stress hormone cortisol has significant negative effects on our body and its functioning. It affects our immune system, our bones, our use of glucose, our muscle mass and percentage of body fat, our memory, and our ability to learn, to name a few.

There is a strong mind and body connection to many physical diseases such as cardiovascular disease, infection and immune disease, and cancer. Mental difficulties such as depression, anxiety, panic attacks, and fear, are also a result or at least greatly exacerbated by stress and emotional difficulties. Dr. Colbert also reports that trapped emotions seek expression.[3] Luckily, we get to choose if we will grow in awareness and skill in identifying and letting go of unexpressed emotions and past traumas, or wait for the likelihood that they show up as physical or emotional illness.

Living Strong

Karen was not aware of her many buried emotions until she looked below the surface of her struggles with her husband of sixteen years. She felt insecure, fearful, and threatened when her husband raised his voice, even a little. She began to have confusing flashbacks of childhood abuse, which led to her shutting down and fearing intimacy.

Her father was alcoholic and verbally abusive. He would yell and scream, "Let's be one big happy family!" She got the messages that anger is wrong and bad. Conflict is bad, and pretending is better. She saw that anger could hurt people and she vowed never to get angry. Her mother retreated from the anger and was emotionally unavailable to her seven children. Karen became her mother's helper by doing a lot of housework.

Karen escaped by babysitting at the neighbors' home when she was ten and eleven. Unfortunately, this experience also groomed her for future abuse. The playful punching and "accidental" touching by the children's father felt wrong to Karen, but she also liked the male attention. The neighbor's wife provided Karen with the companionship and fun that she did not have at home. It turned ugly when Karen was sexually abused as she slept on the neighbors' couch as the wife was in the hospital giving birth. Karen kicked and screamed to fight off the husband, to no avail. Later that night she tried to overdose with a half of a bottle of aspirin. This event triggered difficult teenage years for Karen, as her mother did not believe her, and she feared telling her angry father.

The sexual abuse continued even when she left for a year to stay at the home of a relative. She returned home at fourteen, questioning her parents in her heart, "Why didn't you pursue me?" She apologized to her parents and was told she needed to shape up and not shame her parents or make waves. Her relatives called her a home wrecker and a slut and threatened to kill her if she reported the abuse.

Karen buried the pain and emotions through her later adolescence, but they were expressed as insecurity, fear of conflict, and fear of intimacy. Her suppressed emotions did not remain buried and finally came to the surface uninvited, as flashbacks during times of marital intimacy. The safety she felt with her husband supported her in opening up as she became more cognizant of the complexity of her childhood abuses. Karen has had counseling, attended my class, and has rethought her childhood issues regarding abuse, emotions, and boundaries. She has been able to be angry about the abuse and now sees anger as helpful and a good motivator. She can face conflicts and have discussions, even agreeing to disagree. She is coming alive to her longings and feelings and is able to love much more freely without fear. She has great compassion for abused women, and desires that God would use her pain for His glory.

In the four years since Karen was part of the women's group, she has done tremendous work. She has continued in counseling for her own awareness. She has excavated much childhood abuse and prayed her heart out to be able to let it go and forgive. Of course, this also involved expressing the hurt and anger and injustice of it all. Karen was able to reconcile deeply with her mother before her death two years ago. She found out that an uncle had also sexually abused her mother. She has experienced being part of Grace Groups through Open Hearts Ministry, a group for women in the church who have been sexually abused.[4] She has gone on to be trained to facilitate a group in her own church.

She hasn't stopped there. She has gone back to confront and prosecute her abuser. This has led her to channel her righteous indignation through going to court for her own abuse and testifying for the larger population of sexual abuse victims at the state level. As Karen has submitted her past to the Lord and cried out for healing, I think you would agree that He has been more than faithful in transforming her pain to bring Him glory. She is living strong. God is good.

Learning How to Express Anger

Women's emotional struggles often involve difficulty with anger, depression, and anxiety. Some say that depression is anger turned inward. Traditionally, women have not been encouraged to either have or express their anger (especially in the church). Any women who do are called names I can't repeat here! Not only do we not have skills for expressing our anger, but often we fear it because it is so unfamiliar and culturally forbidden. Our fear of being accepted and valued may also affect healthy anger expression.

Anger is unique as a secondary emotion. It reflects our deeper feelings of hurt, frustration, or fear. Anger motivates us for self-protection or drives us to accomplish our goals. Denial of anger prevents us from discovering the source and results in ineffective expression or emotional and physical problems. Our response to having an emotion which has not traditionally been "allowed" is that we bury it and find alternative ways of expressing it, such as one or more of the following ways:

- Passive-aggressive expression (sarcasm, stubbornness, procrastination, forgetting)
- Perfectionism, controlling attitude
- Performance-based living
- Silent submission, emotional distancing
- Fighting or blaming

These understandable but highly ineffective methods of expressing anger have delayed our development toward healthy anger management.

The Dance of Anger by Harriet Goldhor Lerner helps provide understanding of the sociological and personal history of women and anger. It helped me validate and understand my struggle with anger. I can see how my failure to acknowledge and voice my anger kept me an emotional cripple. Even though anger is a normal emotion, I accepted my family and societal views that women (especially Christians) should not have anger. So I did what we do when we are raised to keep the peace and please others—I denied my feelings. My anger came out anyway, becoming my generic emotional expression for anything and everything, including my husband's feelings. It is not uncommon at all for the emotionally expressive partner in a marriage to take on the "job "of expressing all of the emotions for family members. This allows others to not be engaged, as it also inhibits the development of their own personal emotional expressiveness.

I was also totally clueless of the many legitimate reasons women have for their anger. These include childhood hurts, low self-esteem, fear, injustice (social and personal), inequality and sexism, double standards, unequal workload, stress, unrewarding work, and more.

Anger is necessary and appropriate to protect us from abuse. Dr. Oliver defines abuse as "any behavior designed to control and/or subjugate another person through fear, humiliation, and verbal or physical assaults." He follows by saying, "Fists and feet are the weapons of physical abuse and words and looks are the weapons of emotional abuse."[5] The low self-esteem of the women involved in abusive situation allows them to believe their partners' lies and accept blame for being abused. When the abused woman develops a more accurate self-perception, she can begin to operate from a position of strength to put a stop to the abuse. Her normal righteous anger is the motivator to change abuse dynamics.

With abuse of any kind, I recommend getting support from professionals for the necessary safety, wisdom, and strength to be able to move away from a specific situation. When abuse is involved, it is not safe or wise to do this alone. (See Appendix C)

Our growth in acknowledging and appropriately expressing anger starts by accepting that it is a valid God-given emotion. We know that Jesus felt and expressed his anger, and did it without sinning.[6] It is helpful to explore messages we received regarding anger expression in our families. This role modeling, especially from our female ancestors, helps us understand from whence we have come. In doing my family tree (*genogram*), I was shocked yet also validated to observe that many women in my family were angry and depressed! No wonder I had "issues."

The more you read about anger and the more you identify, validate, and express your feelings underneath, the less angry you will become. There are several ways to make this process a little easier. A trained professional is helpful to walk this path with us because of our blindness to our own patterns. Journaling is a habit that has greatly helped many people, including me, to defuse anger. Anyone with anger issues would also benefit from therapy, classes, or reading that helps them learn communication, assertiveness, and boundary skills.

In the 1980s and '90s there was a big movement to express and vent fully any and every angry feeling a person had, thinking that was the way to get rid of it. It was a time of hitting pillows with fists, hitting things with Styrofoam bats, and shooting darts at objects of our anger. This was a failed experiment. It was discovered that this type of unbridled self-expression escalated and perpetuated anger rather than relieved us of it. Current thought is that the best method for dealing with anger is to identify it, be honest and admit it, and process and express it in appropriate ways, such as discussing and venting it with a counselor or friend, journaling it, and praying to God about it. It is helpful to ask ourselves questions such as, "What am I feeling, what am I angry about, who am I angry with, what is the appropriate way to respond?" It is also typically helpful to let some time pass when we are angry, so that our initial "hot" feelings do not result in an inappropriate or regrettable reactions.

LEARNING TO RECOGNIZE AND DEAL WITH DEPRESSION

Depression is called "the common cold of mental illness."[7] Almost 19 million (almost 10 percent) adults in America suffer depression. Women report depression twice as much as men, and it is the leading cause of disability. Depression can be biological or related to situational issues such as loss, abuse, life change, stress, or other external factors. Psychological factors contributing to depression include faulty thinking, repressed anger, and personality traits such as pessimism, dependency, and passivity. Factors contributing to women's higher rate of depression include low self-esteem, societal treatment and injustices, hormonal changes, low economic status, trying to "do it all," and lack of support.

Depression is more than the occasional sadness due to loss or being temporarily unhappy due to circumstances. Depression involves a distorted perspective that colors every area of our life. According to Oliver and Wright in *Good Women Get Angry*, "depression is a negative emotion due to self-defeating perceptions and appraisals."[8] Levels and causes of depression vary widely from mild to very severe. We all experience brief times of sadness. More severe depression affects daily functions such as eating, sleeping, maintaining energy level, concentrating, having the ability to work, and relating to others.

Some depressions can be either caused by or result in a chemical imbalance in our brain that will only improve with medication. I have seen women who struggle intensely with either anxiety or depression be shamed into refusing a medical approach and advised to take a prayer, Bible study, or "suffering for Jesus" type of approach instead. I am not saying any of these methods are wrong, but each individual situation needs to be evaluated by skilled professionals for the most effective approach. I recommend that each woman who struggles with depression find a well-balanced advocate for herself and learn to ignore any judgmental and untrained audiences.

Treatment modalities for depression vary widely and need to be customized to each person. It is helpful to see a physician first to rule out any medical and hormonal causes, then to follow up with a trained counselor or psychologist for a specialized treatment plan. David Burns wrote a classic book, *Feeling Good, New Mood Therapy,* for successfully overcoming depression with a cognitive behavioral approach that I described in Chapter 7, regarding attitude. Along with exercise, it has been an integral piece for me to stay out of the pit of depression. Other common recommendations include ongoing counseling, medication that might include hormonal and herbal remedies, exercise, prayer, and spiritual support.

It is always best to also be in counseling when on medication. If medication is recommended, it often takes time to find the right medication for you and the dosage needed to relieve your symptoms.

If a person is so depressed and hopeless that he or she considers ending their life, they need to tell someone so they can be helped. Often a person sees ending their life as the only way out of their pain. In fact, there are many options for reducing the emotional pain that can be difficult to see from inside the fog of depression. If you are at this place, tell someone.

LEARNING TO CONQUER ANXIETY

Anxiety disorders are the most common mental health disorders in the United States. Anxiety is an unpleasant sense of nervousness and apprehension that takes many forms. Normal anxiety occurs when we hear the proverbial "bump in the night" and our heart pounds, our breathing changes, and our eyes bulge. This fight-or-flight response is the alarm system our Creator built into us to kick in our adrenaline and prepare us to respond and protect ourselves from possible danger. If our body does not return to normal after the threat has passed, or if we have an anxiety response with no apparent trigger, we are moving into having an anxiety disorder.

The *Generalized anxiety disorder* (GAD) is a chronic, mild to moderate anxiety. It is the most common of anxiety disorders, and a person who has it is often called "a worrier." I liked the description I once heard for anxiety: it is in our bodies like a car with the accelerator stuck. Our body is revved up due to stress, and is unable to, or doesn't bother to, come back to neutral. Over time our body gets worn out from staying revved up due to this low-level drip of internal stress hormones.

Post-traumatic stress disorder (PTSD) is severe anxiety caused by a traumatic experience that does not go away after the threat is gone. This disorder was first identified in soldiers returning from war who experienced jumpiness, flashbacks, nervousness, and nightmares. PTSD can occur from any fearful or stressful experience, including sexual and physical assault, divorce, death, and violence. The consequences of the trauma can go on for many years. This disorder often benefits from treatment.

A *panic disorder* occurs when a person has extreme feelings of terror and anxiety without warning. A panic attack can come on in any circumstance and commonly includes a sense of impending doom, including fear of death. After a person has had one panic attack, the fear of subsequent attacks can contribute to reoccurrence.

Obsessive-compulsive disorder (OCD) is anxiety brought on by fears that drive a person to perform repetitive functions. Fear of germs resulting in repetitive hand washing is a common form of OCD.

Phobias are fears of specific things that are out of proportion to the situation and beyond voluntary control. People can have fears of objects, such as snakes or large crowds, or they can have fears of situations, such as flying, heights, and crowds.

Our culture is prone to the quick fix of medicating for anxiety disorders. Medication is sometimes necessary for some severe disorders, but often only reduces the symptoms without eliminating the underlying cause. Physical factors can contribute to anxiety, so it is best to begin seeking treatment with a complete physical examination. Other factors that can play a role in anxiety include family background, early experiences and trauma, personality, and our thought patterns. Starting with a professional evaluation, there are many ways we can work to regain equilibrium in our lives. Nutrition, exercise, hormone balance, counseling, prayer, medication, stress management, sleep management, and emotional healing can all play significant roles in our healing.

PMS-RELATED DEPRESSION, MOOD SWINGS, AND HOPELESSNESS

I have to add a special word for any woman who struggles with PMS-related emotional difficulties. I struggled for many years with PMS-related depression, mood swings, and hopelessness. It is very hard. I did a lot of damage to myself and my marriage during those years. Our society and many medical professionals don't always accurately diagnose or support women with PMS. I hope the support is better these days. I often felt labeled as crazy or at least mentally unstable as I tried to describe my situation to my husband or helping professionals. I finally found a local clinic where I was evaluated and received a treatment plan. I was most successful with a combination of strategies, regular exercise, balanced eating with lower salt and sugar intake, good self-care, and at times anti-depressant medication. The hopeless thoughts and feelings of my PMS state prevented me from being totally faithful and successful to my own treatment. I found myself believing and acting as if I was a hopeless loser for one week, then spent the next three weeks mopping up the damage I had done. Over the years naturopathic and hormone therapy, along with maturity and psychological healing, allowed me to experience further symptom reduction.

If you think PMS may be a part of your emotional struggle, do not discount it. Read all you can on PMS and find a local advocate. You might have to go outside your regular medical community for proactive care. Do not give up—you are not crazy! You deserve to be the best that you can be. If PMS is a part of your life, it is most likely greatly affecting your primary relationships. I regret not being more proactive about seeking help in this area earlier in my life. I am still mopping up damage done during my untreated PMS years, and I want so much more for you!

EMOTIONS IN RELATIONSHIPS

John Gottman talks about how our emotional heritage impacts our adult emotional connections. Our heritage reflects how we were treated as children. We observe how people close to us acted when they were angry, sad, happy or afraid. We learn to trust in these relationships, and we learn about feelings and love. We learn about our worth. We learned about emotions and ourselves by what they said or did not say to us when they tried to express their own emotions. Dr. Gottman describes differing emotional heritages below:

- If our emotions were *dismissed,* we heard things like "You'll get over it" or "Cheer up." This causes us to be uncertain and insecure about how to connect with others and we learn to *turn away from others.*
- If our emotions were *disapproved* of, we heard "You shouldn't feel that way" or "You'd better change your attitude, Missy." This response leads us to be insecure and fearful of disapproval so we *turn against* connections with others.
- If we heard "I understand how you feel," we may be *more able to connect* with others, but not have much guidance for coping with difficulties.

- If we heard "I understand how you feel. *Let me help you,*" we are much more *secure* in how to connect as adults.[9]

When our childhood experiences are less than healthy, we are insecure and untrusting, and we struggle with emotions and have trouble connecting with others as adults. It can be disheartening to acknowledge the past experiences that have shaped us when the past cannot be changed. It is never too late to address old patterns to become the best that God made us to be.

Sue Johnson has revolutionized adult attachment theory by confirming that adults continue to have deep survival needs for one another. It is not something we outgrow. Unfortunately, depending on our emotional heritage, we commonly struggle with how to do that. In marriage we respond to unmet childhood needs by either becoming overly dependent or overly independent. This is complicated by our tendency to match up with a partner who is equally dysfunctional as ourselves (sorry about that). We have also overdone the independence thing in our society of rugged individualism and mis-labeled our need of each other as *dysfunctional*. What we really need, according to Johnson and other current marriage experts, is to learn to accept that we *do* need each other and learn how to develop a healthy mutual interdependence. We need to adopt a different attitude about our struggles and we need new language and skills to support it. Since God has made us for each other and for mutual love and acceptance, I believe this fits God's perfect plan for marriage.

> We do not outgrow our deep, interdependent need for each other.

The dysfunctional dance that we do is based on our emotional heritage paired with the complexities of our great desire for, and fear of not, connecting with our spouse. When we desire connection but do not have the background or skills to make it happen, we feel fear, anger, and rejection. These feelings lead us to behave in destructive ways. Fear and anger feed each other and perpetuate a vicious cycle of hurt and conflict. Many marriage experts describe the same cyclical dance in differing terms:

- Pursuer/withdrawer pattern: Scott Stanley[10]
- Fear dance: Gary Smalley[11]
- Angry women/passive men: James Dobson[12]
- Blamer/distancer: Sue Johnson[13]
- Crazy cycle: Emerson Eggerich[14]
- Allergy Loop: Lori Gordon[15]

Within these well-studied and destructive patterns, our great desire to connect is thwarted by a triggering event from our partner or our perceptions. When our fear of not connecting is triggered, it is followed closely by self-protective behaviors that block connecting. We may attack or fly off the handle. We may withdraw or shut down. Either extreme of protective response will typically trigger our partner's fear. When our partner is also triggered, we are off to our repetitive cyclical and destructive marital dance that Sue Johnson aptly calls the "demon dialogues."

We usually are unaware of what sets off this deadly dance, and the solution seems even more elusive in the midst of it. Both parties have been emotionally triggered. We are functioning in our out-of-control survival brain with no brakes in sight. (Remember the covered wagon?) Typically, these awful patterns escalate quickly, cause much damage and hurt, and repeat in similar veins for each couple. It is important to remember that this cycle usually is not purposeful and it is a chicken-and-egg scenario. It is automatic and subconscious out of our great need and fear.

BECOMING STRONG AND COURAGEOUS

The good news is that one person can greatly reduce our destructive marital dance. So what do we do? The first place to start is to understand that we are both most likely hurt little kids inside, reacting out of the conflict of our great need for each other paired with our great fear of not connecting. It would be preferable that both parties come to this awareness, but it is not necessary for change to begin. We need to see the destructive dance pattern as the enemy, not our partner. When we choose to see the pattern as the enemy, we can be united with our partner against the pattern and have much greater power to change the dance.[16] We can:

- Allow God to become our one and only, 100 percent trustworthy Soul Mate.
- Take full responsibility for our own emotional life.
- Work to understand and overcome our own emotional heritage.
- Learn to recognize and listen to our emotions.
- Learn not to sin in healthy emotional expression.
- Learn from healthy friends, be vulnerable and get support for growth.
- Learn about our part in any unhealthy relational dance we are involved in.
- Identify the pattern of the dance and your part in it.
- Align with our partner against the pattern.

Will you join me in allowing the Lord to reign supreme in your emotional life?

NOTES

1. John Gottman, *The Relationship Cure* (New York: Crown, 2001), 174.

2. Don Colbert, *Deadly Emotions* (Nashville: Thomas Nelson, 2003), 6.

3. Colbert, *Deadly Emotions*, 58.

4. http://www.ohmin.org/gracegroups/about

5. Gary Oliver, *Good Women Get Angry* (New York: Harper & Row, 1985), 184.

6. Mark 11:12-17.

7. Colbert, *Deadly Emotions*, 63.

8. Oliver, *Good Women Get Angry*, 164

9. Gottman, *The Relationship Cure*, 136.

10. Scott Stanley, *A Lasting Promise* (San Francisco: Josey-Bass, 2002),42.

11. Gary Smalley, *The DNA of Relationship* (Wheaton, IL: Tyndale House, 2004), 43.

12. James Dobson, *Love Must Be Tough* (Dallas: Word, 1996), 193.

13. Sue Johnson, *Hold Me Tight* (New York: Little, Brown and Company, 2008), 67, 80.

14. Emerson Eggerich, *Love & Respect: The Love She Most Desires; The Respect He Desperately Needs* (Nashville: Integrity, 2004), 5.

15. Lori Gordon, *Passage to Intimacy* (n.p. 1993, 2000), 238.

16. Johnson, *Hold Me Tight*, 42, 124.

CHAPTER 11

GROWING LOVE

We love each other because He loved us first.
—1 John 4:19

Love is not the culprit, not loving in God's model is.[1]
—Tim Clinton

*S*PRING FLOWERS ARE *amazing as they pop up in unbelievably harsh surroundings in Wisconsin. They peek out in bright, lime green clusters from turf that looks like old concrete. Covered with snow at times, but still growing. Ice storms, still growing. They bring hope out of the long, harsh winter and defy all odds of survival. They show me that what appears impossible isn't always so. They give me hope for love.*

The tulip is a good depiction of the growth of healthy love in our lives. The bulb and roots are their sources of life, representing our source of love from God. His unconditional agape love is the love that we were made for and the only one that fulfills us. It needs to be the source of all other love in our lives. The soil around the bulb represents our family, early experiences, and expectations of love. The quality of some soil is poor, lacking necessary nutrients for healthy plants. Good gardeners know that poor soil can be amended any time to reinvigorate and grow a healthy plant. So it is with our inadequate upbringings and early experiences of love. The stem and leaves represent our self-love, which is imperative for survival of the species. If we "over-feed" the newly growing greenery, it gets leggy and weak and will not stand up or support a flower. So our self-love has to be tempered and balanced. We need to respect, accept, and love ourselves as God loves us, so that we can flourish into the fully functioning healthy person He made us to be. When we have appropriately cultivated our bulb from healthy soil, have strong leaves and stem, we at last have a chance to see the successful culmination in a beautiful flower. The flower represents our healthy human love relationships as God intended. The health of this love is dependent on the rest of the plant. It is a beautiful outgrowth of God, family, and healthy self-love. It takes work and tending, but that amazing blossom is worth working and waiting for.

Ah, if only we all had green thumbs to grow healthy love! The route to God's intended pattern for love is often indirect, takes much more time than we think it should, and involves much struggle and pain. I have certainly taken a circuitous path to a healthier pattern of love. I wouldn't recommend this to others, but it is common in our fallen world. There is often an *emptiness to love* when it is not rooted in God's love or healthy family love. There are many expectations and cultural patterns which make us *blind about love*. These issues which contribute to marital difficulties can commonly result in what I call *"crazy love."*

I invite you to examine these hurtful patterns of love with me, so that you can be challenged to surrender to the soul-filling, fear-relieving, power-giving, satisfying, *real love* of God.

It sounds so unromantic to discuss technical details about love. But our physical, emotional, spiritual, and sociological perspectives on love can derail our marriages faster than the blink of an eye. It is therefore imperative that we get smarter about love.

EMPTY LOVE

If we are not rooted and established securely in God's love and did not receive healthy love from our families, we have reduced ability to give or receive love as adults. The love we did or did not receive from our earthly fathers also greatly affects our ability to receive love from our heavenly Father. In our early years we collect information about our worth, our ability to receive love, and whether others are trustworthy and responsive to our needs. We get the "answers" to these questions by how our needs are met by our caretakers, according to Tim Clinton in his book, *Attachments*.[2] Our interactions of giving and receiving love with our spouse will reflect these early messages until we make a conscious effort of loving differently.

Traditional attachment literature focused on how our childhood attachment experiences affected our ability to connect in adult love relationships. It has been stated directly and implied indirectly that to "recover" from poor attachment in our upbringings we must grow out of our needs for deep connections. Adults who were too needy had labels such as codependent, enmeshed, fused, and merged. It was thought that spouses who depended on each other too much wrecked their marriages. Healthy people were characterized by independence and self-sufficiency, not neediness of others.[3]

This never sat well with me. I *did* need deeply attached relationships with others. I thought maybe I was just a needy parasite of a person. It seemed to contradict my knowing that God *did* make us for relationship. He *did* make Eve so Adam would not be alone. My dysfunctional past also confused my understanding of attachment. Thankfully, I came across the radical but well-respected work on adult attachment by Sue Johnson in her book, *Hold Me Tight*.[4]

Sue has gone beyond early attachment theory, which limited the effects of poor attachment to children. She has acknowledged adult attachment needs by saying that these needs *do not* diminish as we age, but continue to be *critical* for our survival. This well-researched position certainly aligns with the biblical position that God made us to bond and be united in intimate marriage relationships. Dr. Johnson has found that our inherent human need for love, our longings to feel special, and know that loved ones will be there for us, are hard-wired in our brains from "the cradle to the grave."[5] She claims that conflicts about kids, sex, or money are not what make or break a relationship, but the security of our bond does. When we know that our partners are there for us and we can count on them to respond to us, only then can we relax and feel loved. Problems also arise when we do not know how to send clear signals about emotional needs to our partners.

I was excited to discover this outlook that affirmed our God-given adult needs for adult bonding. This was a missing piece for me, allowing me to be validated in my desire for closeness with my husband, rather than being dysfunctional. Unfortunately, just because we know we need it doesn't mean we know how to get it. Thank the Lord, these skills for connecting with our spouse can be learned.

Some more truths about love relationships from Sue Johnson's research:

- We are born to need each other.
- Emotional hurt in love relationships comes from fear, but also anger and sadness.
- We can survive being very different from our partners.

- There is not a perfect lover.
- When we can't connect in love, we either build walls or break them down through anger.
- Loving relationships are the best recipe for a long and happy life.
- Lasting passion is possible.
- Key moments in love occur when we open up and ask for what we need.[6]

Our strong emptiness in love around marital conflict makes it imperative that we learn more about the real truths regarding conflict. It is normal to have disagreements that aren't readily resolved. All couples will have ten to twelve issues that they will *never* resolve in their married lives. The marriage researcher, John Gottman, found that whether couples divorced or thrived in marriage, 69 percent all couples' conflicts are irresolvable. The difference in the groups was that the couples who remained contentedly married managed their conflicts respectfully.[7]

We need to accept that we *will* have differences, we *will* disagree, we *will* even be angry and hurt and distant at times. These feelings and experiences in our love relationships are *normal*. They do not need to threaten our security or unity if we are able to accept them and to learn the skills to deal with them in nondestructive ways. It has been determined that the healthiest couples learn to live with a certain amount of discomfort in their relationship.

My husband and I both grew up in homes with alcoholic fathers, where love was assumed but not shown. Our scary and critical environments taught us that love is unreliable and it hurts. My husband and I reacted in opposite ways to our similar "emptiness in love" and insecure attachments. I attempted to earn love through performance and getting attention through myriad good and bad methods. As a kid my husband, Phil, tended toward building walls of self-protection and being disobedient for protection from being hurt. These are our primary "tools" for dealing with fear of attachment. This is one of many ways we match up in our "perfect imperfect" ways. Since neither of us knew how to receive the love we needed, we were forced to cry out to God in our pain and frustrated efforts at loving.

We thank God that we *did* come to Him out of our marital pain. We regret that it took fifteen years due to our dysfunctions and mutual stubbornness. I think this was what was so enormously sad and frustrating, especially for me in our earlier years. We were both really hurt and damaged little kids. We were hungry for love. Yet we had no clue or ability about how to love each other.

The truth is that none of us can give the deep love that we long for to each other. That ever present and totally dependable love can only come from God. This is our starting place to heal from any less than ideal childhood love experience. After we surrender our hearts and are rooted and growing in God's love, He can help us heal from our empty love and we are on our way to living strong. (See Appendix A.)

Blind Love

Social influences, expectations, infatuation, and other distortions often contribute to our being blind about love. Our American infatuation and romantic love is sure fun, especially as it is bathed in hormones called the "the Love Cocktail" by Pat Love.[8] This potion contains amphetamine-like neurotransmitters, dopamine, and norepinephrine. I happily recall the unending energy, lack of need for sleep, and euphoric feelings of new love. I have less recollection of the equal presence of reduced concentration, reduced fear, and lowered ability to make complex decisions. This brain-fog stage of a love relationship allows us to overlook and explain away annoyances, giving us a false notion that our love will never involve serious struggle or discord. This "Love Cocktail" really does deaden our brain! This potent natural hormone serves its purpose to draw us to another person and rudely diminishes after eighteen months to three years. The problem is, matching up with physiological attraction to a person, has nothing to do with whether we will be relationally compatible. Oftentimes others observe our mis-matches, but we are blind.

These early infatuation distortions often set us up to misinterpret difficulties when they come later on. We say things like "He must not really be right for me" or "We just fell out of love" or "He just can't communicate," and so on and so on. When the hotness of new love diminishes, it really means that we can now get down to the real work of loving. We can build our friendship, learn skills to manage conflicts, learn more effective communication, and much more. Part of the problem is that it is much more fun to fall in love than to do the work to stay in love. Did you know that societies which are infatuation-based have the highest divorce rates?

> It is much more fun to fall in love than do the hard work of staying in love!

Another blindness when it comes to love is the concept of soul mate. You know, the Tom Cruise, "you complete me" type of love. Plato first coined the term *soul mate*, believing that prior to birth a perfect soul was split into male and female. It was believed that to be complete, they must find each other and reunite their souls, encouraging the idea that there is only one person in the whole world we could be happily married to. This notion is certainly disproved in societies that have arranged marriages, which are more successful than our soul mate matches! God made us to have a deep and intimate connection with our mate. This type of connection takes a lot of hard work, commitment, perseverance, and prayer and does not happen automatically with anyone. God designed real and lasting love to be something you do, not something you mystically have. Tim Gardner says, "A soul mate isn't something you find; it is someone you intentionally and prayerfully become."[9]

I was a normal, young, infatuated American who chose to pay more attention to information I *wanted* to be true about marriage than to learn real truths. I thought happy couples never argued or got angry, were not dependent on each other, wanted sex equally, had their needs met, shared responsibility, thought alike, never got lonely, knew what each other wanted and resolved their problems. This doesn't seem like much to ask, does it? According to Pat Love in *The Truth About Love*, all of these statements are false.[10]

Whoa, boy, I am in trouble now! Blindness strikes again. "Unmet expectations" is listed on many "Why People Divorce" lists for good reason. We develop our expectations regarding marriage from family, friends, society, Hollywood movies, and novels, as well as just in our own little fairy-tale brains.

Most of us don't take the time to identify and challenge these expectations, so we believe them as truth. If that isn't bad enough, subconsciously we tend to match up with an equally dysfunctional love partner. We usually do not discuss expectations with them, and if we do it in the infatuation stage, we are either not honest or we are blind to the consequences as we giggle at our cute differences. So we enter marriage with many conscious and unconscious expectations about love, roles, chores, goals, finances, kids, and future plans. Blindness.

I fell hook, line, and sinker into blind love on many levels. I may have been told by my family that I was young and immature to be marrying at twenty, but I didn't hear it. I could not fathom that there could be any possibility that this love of mine would ever cause any significant pain or disappointment in my life. I believed that my love would carry us through. I was sooooo blind. After all, my future spouse and I had dated on and off since we were fifteen and seventeen. We were very complimentary opposites who completed each other in magical ways. We had the common experience of having alcoholic fathers. We both felt ignored in our families, so we were sure we would never ignore each other or repeat any of the hurtful patterns of our families. Blind, blind, blind.

CRAZY LOVE

The grave disappointment which occurs when infatuation fades and power struggles prevail results in what I call "crazy love." The tension and subconscious awareness of unmet love needs cause both people to scramble to maintain power. In our subconscious selves, we clung to an impossible hope that our childhood hurts would be met and totally healed by each other. Crazy, isn't it? It was equally crazy that two hurting little kids could fulfill the love

160

needs in each other even though they had not been loved. We were, as I say a "perfect imperfect" match. His retreating matched my chasing, his fear of failure matched my critical spirit, his emotional unavailability matched my fear of abandonment. We acted out what Sue Johnson calls "demon dialogues" as we scrambled to have our attachment needs met with no awareness or skills.[11] This resulted in the round-and-round craziness of the power struggle of marriage. This is a time when, according to Harville Hendrix, we either wake up, heal and learn the skills, or we continue to struggle.[12]

Fear plays a significant role in our struggles with love. We greatly desire the connection which we also fear. David Benner talks about the irony of our efforts to avoid fear, which keeps us from seeing and getting past our fears. He talks about us needing to surrender fully to God, who will then fill us with His love. When we are filled with His love, we are able to be obedient to Him and be transformed in our pain and able to love others. The huge paradox which is so powerful is that we fear love, but only God's love can release us from our fears so that we are able to love.[13] His perfect love casts out our fears.[14]

Ray and Nancy Kane continue the discussion on fear and love in their book, *From Fear to Love*. Through their experience in counseling couples, they identify fear as the most destructive relationship emotion. They see couples having fears of failure, pain, abandonment, rejection, and death. They observed that fearful individuals responded with the following patterns of controlling behaviors:

- *Power controllers:* These individuals strive to dominate and manipulate their partners.
- *Pride controllers:* These people are described as two year olds in adult bodies. They are self-centered and need to be the center of attention.
- *Passive controllers:* These people are not engaged with others—"Ignore it and it will go away" is their approach.
- *Protective controllers:* These folks hover over others to show love.

It was so helpful (and validating) to see how when we fear love, we control others to have our needs met. The Kanes go on to say that when our needs are then not met, we get angry, and then fear and controlling increase.[15] This certainly describes the fear- and control-based round-and-round cycle of marital craziness that we can get stuck in.

Another common characteristic when we are stuck in the negativity of the power struggle stage is called *confirmation bias*.[16] It is a scientific term that describes what we do when we hold a negative view with few facts to back it up. What we do is look for and file away any and all information that confirms our belief. If I believe that my husband doesn't love me because he goes to bed early, I will look for and interpret anything and everything he does in that light. He comes home late; therefore he doesn't love me. He cooked dinner; therefore he doesn't love me or my cooking. He stayed up with me; therefore he doesn't love me because he doesn't want me to have time on my own. He...get the point? We can sabotage many things with confirmation bias thinking. Especially when we invite family and friends to join the game.

Application Questions:

1. Can you identify with any sources or consequences of unmet love needs in yourself?

2. Can you identify which fear-based control position you tend toward in your marriage?

BECOMING STRONG AND COURAGEOUS, ROOTED IN REAL LOVE

We can peek out from the "stuckness" of this crazy love when we realize a few things:

- Surrendering and being rooted in God's love is the source of all love.[17]
- Our hurt, fear, and confusion often begin in childhood love and attachment experiences.

- Men and women have individual and gender-based differences in their desire for closeness, which can cause much hurt and conflict about love.
- Marriage is a constantly changing process that goes through developmental stages and life stages related to schooling, careers, finances, and children.
- Marital conflict is not as much resolved as managed.
- Marital power struggles are normal.
- We can learn how to turn our own lives around to a healthier path.
- We cannot predict what effect our actions could have in our marriages until we implement them.

Getting the Love You Want by Harville Hendrix is a resource that will guide you in identifying the patterns of love in your families and understand the effects on your marital love. Dr. Hendrix surmises that we match up with individuals who cannot give us the love that we need. This primarily forces us to connect with God. The power struggles that nearly drive us crazy can then lead us to heal from our childhood hurts. For example, if I had married a man who was proactive in loving me, instead of one who kept his distance, I would not have had to heal from my sensitivity to abandonment or rejection. If we let them, the things that bring us pain often can become the vehicles for our healing.

I remember how I struggled to accept this concept, the first fifty times I read it. I just did not want to accept that I could have been contributing to my marital struggles by not doing my own healing. Especially when I had spent so many years gathering the data to prove that my husband was to blame!

This is a very challenging concept to grasp and believe, but I have seen it be true over and over again in all sorts of scenarios. Miracles can happen as we turn the finger of blame back at ourselves to examine and heal our dysfunctional selves. It is difficult to view our struggling marriages this way. One reason may be that we hope against hope that the tragedy of our pain will somehow, someday, some way receive the magic wand of healing and we won't have to struggle or work our way out of it. I am sorry to say that is called wishful thinking. The good news is that when we *are* able to make a shift from wishful thinking and embrace the concept that our pain can become the source of our healing, we are possibly facing the truth of our marriage for the first time. We can then have more hope and purpose for healing than we have had in a long time. People are hurt in relationship and they are healed in relationship.

Living Strong

Kristi's story of love began as one of six children in a loving but functionally unavailable home. Why I describe her home with those words is because even though she felt loved, hers was the first generation in her family to live without alcohol and active abuse from the adults. Even though her parents eliminated the active physical abuse and the alcohol, the unfortunate fallout from previous generations of abuse carried over through instances of sexual abuse and addictions in the kids. Kristi was emotionally tormented by older brothers who suffocated her under a bean bag chair and put her in a garbage bag that they hung from the swing set. She was also verbally abused, threatened, and sexually abused by a brother. Kristi went to church regularly with her parents and knew about Jesus from a young age. In grade school she was quiet and shy and hid behind her straggly hair and poor hygiene. This failed to prepare her to deal with becoming popular in junior high when she got contacts and cleaned herself up. She grew to feel good about herself through her popularity, good looks, and easy promiscuity.

As a young adult, Kristi continued this free and easy lifestyle, working as a model and marrying a professional sports celebrity. She had the world by the tail! They quieted down and were contented until their second child, Brandon, died ten hours after his birth. This sent Kristi into a crisis of faith as she searched for answers. She saw this loss as her wake-up call, and she gave her life to the Lord two years later. She had incredible peace and joy in her first few years as a believer, soaking up God's incredible love. God repeatedly turned the pain of her loss into magnificent blessings.

Over the years, she and her husband had drifted apart. Because they had experienced the loss of a child, they knew and feared the heartbreak that their sexual intimacy could create. She sought all the Christian resources she could, but none could break her husband's, hardness and refusal to address the issues that separated them. In her pain and frustration, Kristi prayed and searched for answers. In her Bible study, prayer, and talking to others she observed one message over and over again: "Stay in the truth." She compares her life at this time to Job's, being tested by Satan and needing to cling to God in spite of her circumstances or feelings. She and her husband separated, during which time she learned on the deepest level that God is enough. She did not believe that any pain could compare to the loss of a child, but she was heartsick and devastated by the possibility of a divorce.

She recalls a specific time of despair as she stood hopeless at the kitchen sink. God met her in this dark hour and encouraged her that He would get her through, no matter what the outcome. His peace and assurance followed. God guided her in staying in His truth through journaling, Bible studies, praying, and study of His word. She continued to identify with Job's testing, personally learning that no matter what happens in our lives, God is enough and can bring blessings from sorrow. Kristi was amazed when God used her eleven year-old daughter to affirm His message of hope to her as she gave her mom a verse on a card. The verse which she considers her life verse is Joshua 1:9 which says "Have I not commanded you? Be strong and courageous. Do not be terrified, do not be discouraged, for the Lord your God will be with you wherever you go."

Today Kristi praises God for her reunion with her spouse and the Lord's continued strengthening. She admits she would not recommend separation for all struggling couples, and that her life and marriage aren't perfect, but she continues to run the race that God has set before her and praises Him that she is His child!

Kristi was brought to her knees and into the healing arms of the Lord through the painful loss of her infant son. She has developed and been involved in a support group whose mission is to help parents whose children have died. The Lord has showered her with amazing grace and blessing as she has been privileged to help others that are hurting. She fell head over heels in love with the lover of her soul, who guided her in healing from the dysfunction of her childhood abuse. She was broken again as she experienced the pain of marital separation, and God proved himself faithful once again. She has since been blessed with a reconciled marriage, three more children, and redemption of the pain from the loss of her son, as she comforts others with the comfort she has received from God.[18]

God does not promise that we will all have such blessed outcomes, but He does promise never to leave us, to love us with everlasting love, and to give us the strength and courage to face the struggles in our lives. Will you join Kristi in trusting God in love and in life?

Kristi and I have both struggled with love. Hurt as kids, acting out to be loved as young people, our pain finally led us to fall on our knees to the Lord. He rescued us, but the pain did not end quickly. Growing in love is hard work. God continues to do his work in us today as we more deeply receive His unfailing love. He has blessed us with renewed love for our husbands. Kristi and I have both experienced the tender transformation expressed by Thomas Hardy:

> New love is the brightest, long love is the greatest,
> but revived love is the tenderest thing known on earth.
> —Thomas Hardy

Our prayer for you is this:

> *I pray that out of his glorious riches he may strengthen you*
> *with power through his Spirit in our inner being,*
> *so that Christ*
> *may dwell in your hearts through faith.*
> *And I pray that you,*

being rooted and established in love,
may have power, together with all the saints,
to grasp how wide and long and high
and deep is the love of Christ and to know
this love that surpasses
knowledge—that you may be filled to the measure
of all the fullness of God.
Now to Him who is able to do immeasurably more
than all we ask or imagine,
according to his power that is at work within us,
to him be glory
in the church and in Christ Jesus throughout
all generations, for ever and ever! Amen
—Ephesians 3:16-21

Will you join Kristi and me in
being filled with real love?

NOTES

1. Tim Clinton, *Before a Bad Goodbye: How to Turn Your Marriage Around* (Nashville: W Publishing Group, 1999), 143.
2. Tim Clinton, *Attachments* (Brentwood, TN: Integrity, 2002), 12.
3. Sue Johnson, *Hold Me Tight* (New York: Little, Brown and Company, 2008), 7.
4. Johnson, *Hold Me Tight*, 21.
5. Johnson, *Hold Me Tight*, 21.
6. Johnson, *Hold Me Tight*, 258.
7. John Gottman, *Seven Principles for Making Marriage Work* (New York: Three Rivers Press, 1999), 130.
8. Pat Love, *The Truth About Love* (New York: Simon & Schuster, 2001), 29.
9. Tim Gardner, *Sacred Sex* (Colorado Springs: WaterBrook, 2002).
10. Love, *The Truth About Love*, 29, 21.
11. Johnson, *Hold Me Tight*, 65.
12. Harville Hendrix, *Getting the Love You Want* (New York: Henry Holt, 1988), 80.
13. David G. Benner, *Surrender to Love* (Downers Grove, IL: IVP Books, 2003), 11.
14. 1 John 4:18.
15. Raymond Kane and Nancy Kane, *From Fear to Love* (Chicago: Moody, 2002), 134.
16. Love, *The Truth About Love*, 18.
17. 1 John 4:7-12.

CHAPTER 12

THE RULE BOOK

Above all else, guard your heart, for it is the wellspring of life.
—Proverbs 4:23

P *AM WAS BORN into my family a year and a half after me. We grew up in the same environment and are as much alike as we are different. We share memories of picnics and hide n' go seek in the picket-fenced Ohio yard. We sat together with our older sister at the top of the stairs in our homemade pj's. We clung together in fear and uncertainty as our parents argued below. We remember summer trips to Lake Cormorant. Those were carefree days in Minnesota, hunting frogs and boys and jumping the wake on water skis. Pam was a boy-crazy cheerleader. I was a tomboy and athlete.*

One memory that I still chuckle about is when we shared that basement room as young teens. Dad made some minor adjustments to the large paneled room and we moved in with our twin beds with the lime green striped bedspreads. It must have been in the early 'sixties. Although Pam and I got along for the most part, tensions must have built up for some long-forgotten reason. My logical response was to put masking tape down the exact middle of our respective territory. Then I said, "Don't get your cooties on myyyyy side. Keep your stinky clothes over there, too! I don't care if you have to go to the bathroom—I don't want you over here ever again...or else!" A pretty immature but firm expression of personal boundaries, don't you think?

As it turns out, that was one of the more clear boundaries of my early years. I remember in my late teens and early twenties, feeling that someone had forgotten to give me the "rule book" for life. It seemed like everyone else had clear directions on how to live, love, and relate. They must have gotten that secret book and I didn't.

- I didn't know how to be fully me and allow you to be fully you.
- I didn't know how to develop trust.
- I didn't know how to share tough emotions or differences of opinion.
- I had no clue how to manage conflict.

I needed these rules, or boundaries, to know who I was and how to relate. The main boundaries that I learned in my alcoholic family of origin were "don't talk, don't trust, and don't feel." These harmful rules instilled a great fear in me about asking anyone about the real rules. I feared that the reason I didn't "get it" was that I really was as stupid as my dad said. Everyone else seemed to know how to "be" and I didn't, they had gotten the "rule book" after all. Boundaries would have helped me know and accept myself so that I wouldn't have had to stumble around shamefully for that book. Since many of us have experienced a similar confusing and painful path of a boundary-less upbringing and marriage, it is very worthy of our attention.

THE RULE BOOK

We have been made in God's image, and He expects us to take responsibility for our own life and tasks. We are accountable to Him for our lives.[1] We need to know what is our job and what isn't. Confusion of responsibilities is a boundary issue. As noted in the classic boundary book by Cloud and Townsend, each spouse should take responsibility for their own feelings, attitudes, choices, behaviors, limits, desires, thoughts, values, talents, and love.[2] Boundaries are relational property lines telling everyone where I begin and end. Clearly defining who we are honors God and gives us the freedom to become fully who He made us to be. They give us a healthy sense of ourselves paired with the freedom and security to be individuals. Boundaries allow us to connect with God, ourselves, and others without losing ourselves.

Our connection with other humans is important to our emotional and physical health. Infants and children exhibit clear needs to be nurtured, loved, and secure. In extreme cases of neglect infants can even die (called *failure to thrive*) when their basic needs are not met. Although we haven't experienced such a critical lack of love, we may experience challenging consequences of lack of adequate nurturing. The love, safety, and dependability of our caretakers affect our adult relationships. Successful bonding or attachment results from the consistent meeting of our needs for food, changing, and comforting. When these basic needs are met from an early age, we develop the ability to trust and relate successfully with others. We develop a clear and strong sense of our self-worth. Tim Clinton states it succinctly by saying a healthy family has respect with a good balance of closeness and structure. There is a closeness without either over-involvement or too much distance. There is just enough structure that is neither too rigid or too chaotic.[3] Boundaries or rules for interactions are what provide these healthy balances.

Growing up without consistent boundaries contributes to our insecurity. When we are insecure we either over- or under-protect ourselves. Overprotection causes us to be controlling to prevent others from hurting us, while under-protection opens us up to being abused. Both options are based in fear and mistrust. Remember, we have a God-given need to connect, which causes many problems when paired with our fear and inability to know how to do it. Our childhood attachment wounds profoundly affect our adult love relationships.[4] We struggle with issues such as our lovability, others' trustworthiness, fear of abandonment, and insecurity. According to Tim Clinton, we all ask these questions of our caretakers. When they have not been dependably answered, we continue to ask them of our adult relationships. Do you ask yourself any of these questions?

- Am I worthy of being loved?
- Am I competent to get the love I need"
- Are others reliable and trustworthy?
- Are others available and willing to respond to my needs?[5]

The mantra of "don't talk, don't feel, and don't trust" is the common boundary rule for dysfunctional families. These rules are developed to protect us from further hurt and to prevent closeness. In my case, for example, because emotions were not identified or acceptable, I learned that it was not OK to have feelings. In my family, it was not OK to talk about anything deep or meaningful. We never knew when Mom would respond with tears, or Dad would put us down, so we learned not to talk.

This unpredictable atmosphere, Mom's emotional unavailability with Dad being controlling or drunk, taught me to distrust others. Their responses were not safe or dependable. Other adult outcomes from unhealthy family rules include living to please others, shutting down completely, faking happiness, depression, abuse, addictions, and not being able to say no or yes to relationships. "Don't talk, don't trust, and don't feel" rules protected me from deeper harm as a child, but they left me without successful relationship tools as an adult.

Commonly, measures which were necessary for survival as children are no longer effective for adults. No matter what form our childhood coping took, we need to give ourselves the grace to accept that as kids we had to do what we had to do. But as adults, praise God, we can re-examine our childhood defensive coping skills and adjust them for improved effectiveness in our relationships.

OPEN VS. CLOSED SYSTEMS: HEALTHY VS. UNHEALTHY BOUNDARIES

In her classic book on families as systems, *Peoplemaking*, Virginia Satir spends some time describing the two options of family outcomes as either *open* or *closed*. She concludes that humans cannot flourish within the closed system. You can see, as she compares the two below, that the open family system has clear and fair rules with flexibility, allowing for individual differences. The closed system is just that—fuzzy, uncertain, and unsupportive of individual development, closed to relationship.

FEATURE	OPEN SYSTEM (interdependent)	CLOSED SYSTEM (dependent)
Communication	Direct, clear, specific	Indirect, unclear, unspecific
Rules	Freedom to comment	Restricted comments
	Open to change as needed	Closed, fixed, unchangeable
Outcome	Reality based, constructive, appropriate	Chaotic, destructive
Self-worth	Confident in self	Doubtful, dependent on others[6]

173

The open or healthy family is secure, clearly communicating rules or boundaries, and individuals in this system learn to be interdependent. Within the closed system, individuals live with unclear rules, and learn one of two flawed approaches in relationships:

- Overly dependent, unprotected, or enmeshed with others, or
- Overly independent, protected, and controlling

Both of the responses to this closed system are dysfunctional and interfere with both individual development and intimate relating as well. As Tim Clinton said, the open or healthy family has a good balance of closeness and structure. The closed family is either over- or under- involved, with either too many or too few rules.

Open System

In our relationship, being as stubbornly versatile that we are, we have attempted functioning within all of the above methods. Thankfully in more recent years, having experienced the pain and ineffectiveness of our closed system, we have been able to develop a more healthy and interdependent relationship. We have more clear boundaries of where we both begin and end and we have more clear rules for relating. We are more secure as individuals and much more accepting of each other. We are growing in healthy intimacy. Boundaries have helped us to grow out of our old dysfunctional family mantras. We are learning to accept our differences and see them as more complimentary, instead of contentious.

About thirteen years ago we felt led by the Lord to start our own business together. This challenging endeavor was crucial to acceptance of our differences and growth of mutual respect and boundaries. The Lord must have known that is what we needed, and thankfully we were able to respond by growing together instead of apart. Truthfully, though, there were times that we were tempted to give up because it did not come easily. Fortunately, our mutual stubbornness has both created challenges and fueled our refusal to give up.

In *How Can I Get Through to You?*, Terry Real talks about the need for healthy interdependence in our relationships. I really like that word. It expresses that we *do* have a need for each other, a dependency of sorts. But we also have to care for ourselves and others in a balanced way. We need to not be either overly dependent or independent. Women commonly need to learn to care for themselves and learn to ask for and allow others to care for them. Men tend to need to learn to listen and connect relationally to reduce their tendencies for independence. Terry also says that we both need to learn to be protected and connected with effective boundaries.[7]

CLOSED SYSTEM

When we are dependent or enmeshed with another person, we have either inappropriately rigid or few boundaries. We are dependent on our partners for how we feel about ourselves, but are also closed and fear letting them into our inner lives. We desperately desire connection yet protect ourselves from it. This scenario makes it impossible to connect on a deep level.

This enmeshed pattern is sometimes called *codependent*. The term *codependent* came out of the alcohol recovery movement. A codependent is a person who can be either overly controlling or dependent. Both scenarios look to others to get a sense of themselves. Their fear-based neediness distracts them from looking honestly at themselves, as it allows others to influence their identity and emotional state. Codependents do not know how to meet unmet emotional needs, so they just give themselves up to others.

Boundaries help us move from "other control" to self-control. Codependent terminology is not used as much today, but is well-elucidated in the book *Love is a Choice* by the Minirth Meier psychologists. As a recovering codependent, I thought the way to be connected with another in love was to become the same as him. It did not take long to experience the fallibility of this approach. My husband and I almost destroyed each other emotionally with this method. We were lost in how to love or accept each other. At least good came out of it, as our time of struggle led us both to the Lord.

Since being enmeshed codependents was not effective, we moved on to another equally unhelpful approach for connection. Our subconscious thinking was that since trying to be clones of each other did not work, we must have to be totally separate to get along. During this period of our lives we were very protected, closed down, and angry. We had constant power struggles, needed to be right, blamed each other, and—surprise, surprise—remained insecure and disconnected.

Cloud and Townsend have helpful descriptions of four patterns we might adopt if we have not had good rules or boundaries for relationships. The first two examples represent the unprotected individual and the last two are the overprotected people.

- A *compliant* person cannot say no to others, but feels guilty and controlled by them.
- The *avoidant* says no to the good, and can't ask for help or let others into their lives. This prevents them from receiving care from others.
- The *controllers* cannot hear 'no' from others, and they violate others' boundaries by being aggressive or manipulative.
- The *nonresponsive* person cannot say yes to relationships and therefore sets boundaries against taking responsibility in love.[8]

These patterns all reflect a closed family system and comprise combinations of overly dependent and overly independent individuals. It is interesting that although the patterns operate very differently, they all indicate poor boundaries. Each pattern is put into place subconsciously to cope with insecurity from not having early needs met. They are all fear based and protect us from further hurt as adults. Unfortunately, they also perpetuate dysfunction and disconnection in our lives.

I would say that early on in our relationship I was a compliant-avoidant and my husband was an avoidant-controller in our relationship. In our second stage of dysfunction, when we attempted to be totally independent, I became an avoidant-controller, and my husband was more nonresponsive. Like anyone, we can still slip into these patterns especially under stress, but it is more and more rare that we have a full-blown mutual dysfunctional breakdown, where one of us is unable to stop the slide down the slippery slope. There is hope!

Application Questions:

1. Which of Cloud's four boundary patterns describe you? Your spouse?

2. What consequences do you experience due to your patterns as a couple?

LIVING STRONG

Lynn was raised to be a caretaker by her depressed mother and controlling father. She had a rather uneventful childhood but was attracted to "wild boys" as a rebellion against her strict family. She was not allowed to date until she was eighteen, but dated some wild boys at sixteen and married her husband at nineteen. She became a believer within the first very difficult year of marriage. She struggled with the marriage all along as her husband continued to live as a single person, going out with friends, and they lived separate lives.

Four children and thirteen years into the marriage, Lynn found out about his first affair, which he'd had after five years of marriage. Her faith became deeply important to her and she thought she was being a submissive Christian wife by tolerating his verbal abuse and critical and demeaning treatment. What she was actually doing was perpetuating the father-controlling, mother-depressed system that she came from.

Lynn attended counseling on her own. When her husband refused to stop the verbal abuse, she left with the children for a few days, hoping to make a statement. She began to struggle with depression. After much prayer and counsel, she moved out with her four children and began a period of applying principles of tough love.[9] She remained separated for six months, got stronger, and she and her husband attended counseling as a couple. Lynn felt led to move back. Although her husband ended his physical relationships with women, in hindsight she realized that he did not have the heart change that he professed. She can see now how their values and beliefs were very different. The verbal abuse was reduced, affairs were over, but the distance and lack of connection persisted.

Years later, Lynn discovered her husband had a sexual addiction, including use of pornography. He went to a ministry treatment weekend for sexual addictions at her insistence. He came back very excited about his transformation, but the effects fizzled quickly.

Lynn got more education regarding sexual addictions. When her husband continued to go out with male friends, spoke in a degrading way about women, saw a prostitute, asked a woman on a date, and brought home an STD, Lynn filed for divorce. Her husband never liked boundaries, and Lynn had been weak at standing firm with boundaries. She had become a fearful, enmeshed, dependent personality, having not learned boundaries from her controlling father.

Throughout all the years of applying and sticking with boundaries, for the first time in her life she had peace from the Lord. She found herself asking the Lord over and over, "Now what? Now what?" She felt Him encouraging her to stand firm, something she had not been very good at. She awaited His timing to move ahead, and she continued to do her own growth work in spite of how her husband behaved.

When she finally felt led to divorce him, she was prepared and had done a lot of grieving already. She was in a position of strength herself and followed the Lord through the valley. She continues to encourage young wives in their relationships. All four of their children come to her to discuss openly their lives and struggles. She senses that God's hand was in her divorce and she still prays and asks Him, "Now what?" She continues to be encouraged by His "saying" to her, *"Whether you turn to the left or the right, follow me."*

What I appreciate about Lynn's testimony is that she did all the things recommended for a person who has a "boundary resistant spouse."[10] She:

- Got stronger herself, no matter how her husband chose to live.
- Solved her own problems, acting righteously with her spouse.
- Learned about boundaries and how to stick with them.
- Used others to intervene, including pastors, programs, counselors.
- Accepted reality and grieved expectations.
- Repeatedly forgave her husband and did not stay angry or bitter.
- Gave change a chance after she quit enabling or contributing to their problems.
- Initiated separation for possible motivation for change.
- Waited and waited in longsuffering until she felt led to divorce.

BOUNDARY PROBLEMS

We can experience many indicators of a lack of personal boundaries. They all reflect the fear and desire that we all have regarding our need to connect but not having the rules or boundaries to know how to do it. Ineffective boundaries can contribute to many individual problems, including:

- Fear and uncertainty
- Controlling behaviors
- Seeking fulfillment in all the wrong places such as success, acquiring material goods, performance-based living, hiding behind spirituality
- Denying of our need for love and connection

- Medicating pain with drugs, alcohol, or other addictive behaviors
- Depression and anxiety
- Psychosomatic physical illnesses
- Sarcasm, name calling, blaming, shaming others, lying and manipulation

Lack of sufficient boundaries shows up symptomatically in our relationships. We may experience a general lack of trust or inability to talk intimately. We may be at opposite ends of the disconnection continuum and feel either dead or out of control in relationships. We may experience a lack of closeness, or intimacy problems in our relationships. We may struggle with communication and knowing how to face and manage conflict.

When we learn about boundaries, we are taking ownership of our lives. We learn to focus on our own well-being and issues more than our spouse's. We learn the fine balance of loving and supporting, accepting and giving, but not at our own expense. We learn to be healthily interdependent. We know that we are accountable to God for our own lives and will not fully fulfill His plan for us if we do not insist on discovering and defending who we are with appropriate boundaries. There is a real freedom in being more concerned in who God wants us to be rather than being enslaved to others. As we learn to set boundaries and eliminate destructive cycles, we can fully grow and love in the way God intended.

> Setting boundaries gives us ownership of our lives.

Be Strong and Courageous in Developing Boundaries

God has clearly allowed us to have free will, knowing that we are accountable to Him as individuals.[11] We can only become who He fully made us to be when we take responsibility for our own lives. Even if we have not learned to have healthy relationships in the past, it is never too late. In *Boundaries*, Cloud and Townsend explain God's design for boundaries in an excellent way.

Galatians 6:2 says we are to carry each other's burdens. At first glimpse, this might look like we are to take care of and help others at all times. When paired with Galatians 6:5, which says "for each one should carry his own load," we get a different overall message. Remember the Scripture interpretation guideline: that we always use Scripture to further explain Scripture. This means that we cannot take one verse and draw conclusions for that verse alone, but we need to look at other Scriptures to get the most accurate and complete meaning of any given verse. Galatians 6:5 says that each one should carry his own load, which at first glance seems to contradict Galatians 6:2, to carry each other's burdens.

The key to these seemingly confusing verses is in the definitions of *burden* versus *load*. A *burden* is an unusual and excessive task. *Loads* are the everyday tasks that each of us has to carry on our own. We are to help each other when our challenges are above and beyond the everyday. We are to each take responsibility for our everyday responsibilities. I cannot carry the load of my husband's past or his method of coping. I am not responsible for that. But if he has a health crisis, I should expect to help him carry that burden for a reasonable time. Cloud and Townsend conclude, "We are responsible *to* others and *for* ourselves."[12]

BOUNDARY MYTHS

Christians sometimes think that setting boundaries is in opposition to loving and accepting each other, but Cloud and Townsend address many common myths:

- If I set boundaries, I am selfish.
- Boundaries are a sign of disobedience.
- If I set boundaries, I will be hurt by others.
- If I set boundaries, I will hurt others.
- Boundaries mean I am angry.
- When others set boundaries, it injures me.
- Boundaries cause feelings of guilt.
- Boundaries are permanent, and I fear burning my bridges.

I will refer you to Cloud and Townsend's *Boundaries* for specific details regarding these boundary myths.[13] Briefly, the answers are very similar to the above comparison of burdens and loads. We need to use the whole of Scripture to determine appropriate behavior and not depend on unspoken religious or cultural expectations.

It is imperative that, before we go down this road of setting boundaries in our marriages, we approach the process with the right motives. We need to be non-emotional, not angry or vindictive. We need to have prayed and hopefully spoken to wise advisors regarding setting boundaries. When we have not had experience with boundaries in our lives, it is very hard to have an accurate gauge of what is right, wrong, and realistic, which makes professional advice very helpful. If your relationship has been abusive in any way, outside help is imperative for your safety. (See Appendix C)

We can do significant work on developing boundaries by first looking only at ourselves and learning and growing out of any overly dependent or independent and controlling ways. As we learn to speak up for ourselves and develop a healthier self-image, we will be more prepared to approach our marriages from a position of strength. Terry Real calls this form of personal boundary having a "strong psychic boundary."[14] Having a strong boundary allows us to assess what is said in our relationships as true or not, and stand up for the truth and reject what is false. This boundary will assist us in growing into a healthy interdependent partner.

Speaking of which: our partner may have no interest in better boundaries or change. When we go about changing the dance of our marriage, by establishing different boundaries we are changing the rules that our partner has helped to develop and has been complicit with over the years. It would be similar to starting a board game with one set of rules, and midway through the game our opponent decides the rules should be different. When we discuss it in this way, it is understandable that our partner might not like the changes.

It is important to keep in mind that he is not necessarily personally resistant to you, but he is resistant to opening himself up to hurt, fear of abandonment, fear of past hurts and fear of change. The dysfunctional place of your marriage has become safe and comfortable, and moving out of that space will probably be met with resistance. That does not mean you shouldn't change the dance, but it's all the more reason that we make sure our motives come from a pure heart. I want to encourage you to experience the joyful freedom, which will result as you learn about that rule book of life.

Will you join me in breaking down the prison walls of a boundary-less life?

Walls

Once my life seemed a prison—
Walls I thought I needed to hold me up, held me in.
Afraid to risk, fearful of change, my cell was small, confining, safe.
One day you stood at the door, Lord, and called my name.
You asked to come in, gently leading me to risk.
To follow, to change.
Surrounded by your love and filled with your grace,
I found myself free—to love with the Spirit's love.
To grow in becoming who you want me to be.
To praise you always for removing the walls
and for the revelation of your risky, grace-filled freedom.
—Roberta Porter

Notes

1. Hebrews 4:13.
2. Henry Cloud and John Townsend, *Boundaries in Marriage* (Grand Rapids: Zondervan, 1999), 21.
3. Tim Clinton, *Attachments* (Brentwood, TN: Integrity, 2002), 45.
4. Clinton, *Attachments*, 41.
5. Clinton, *Attachments*, 12
6. Virginia Satir, *Peoplemaking* (Palo Alto, CA: Science and Behavior Books, 1972), 112.
7. Terrence Real, *How Can I Get Through to You?* (New York: Fireside, 2002), 204.
8. Cloud and Townsend, *Boundaries in Marriage*, 52.
9. James Dobson, *Love Must Be Tough* (Dallas: Word, 1996).
10. Cloud and Townsend, *Boundaries in Marriage*, 200.
11. Hebrews 4:13.
12. Cloud and Townsend, *Boundaries in Marriage*, 30.
13. Cloud and Townsend, *Boundaries in Marriage*, 103.
14. Terry Real, *How Can I Get Through to You?* Smart Marriages Conference Talk, July 10, 2004, Dallas TX.

CHAPTER 13

FIRST, DO NO HARM

*Do not repay anyone evil for evil. If it is possible, as far as it
depends on you, live at peace with everyone.*
—Romans 12:17a, 18

*Reckless words pierce like a sword, but the tongue of
the wise brings healing.*
—Proverbs 12:18

P RIMUM NON NOCERE," or "First, do no harm," is to some people an outdated oath of healthcare. Others revere it as the cornerstone of the Hippocratic Oath of medical doctors. Written 2,500 years ago, most would agree it is one of the most famous oaths of medicine. It has been recited by graduating doctors throughout the ages, a promise to first and foremost "do no harm" in caring for their future patients. I like this simple adage, which for me speaks very strongly about the attitude we need to have regarding conflict in marriage.

Dr. John Gottman, who specializes in researching what makes marriages fail and succeed, says that the way that we deal with conflict is a major determinant of the success of our marriages. He can predict with 91 percent accuracy in as little as five minutes of observation whether a marriage will fail or succeed. What he is looking for is the couple's negativity during conflict. By following more than seven hundred couples in seven studies, he discovered that emotionally intelligent couples were able to keep their negative thoughts and feelings from overwhelming their positive ones.[1]

We wrongly assume that good marriages have limited conflict and that resolving conflicts is a cure all for troubled marriages. The truth is, a major key to contentment is accepting that we all have conflicts and we will *always* have conflicts. Effective conflict resolution is not the key to successful marriages. We need to learn to manage conflict respectfully and reduce negative and increase positive interactions. Dr. Gottman calls this skill "successful repair attempts."[2]

Here are some more facts to become more emotionally intelligent about conflict:

- Conflict is a necessary aspect of every marriage.
- Avoidance of conflict greatly increases risk of divorce.
- Sixty-nine percent of conflicts in successful and divorcing marriages are irresolvable.
- All couples have ten to twelve issues that will not be resolved in their lifetimes.

- Happily married couples do not have less conflict, but deal with differences more respectfully.
- Respectfully managed conflict improves marital closeness.
- Skills for effective conflict management and respect for differences can be learned.

DEALING WITH MARITAL CONFLICT

The unhealthy responses of avoiding or attacking and defending in conflict result in mutual hurt and greatly increased risk of divorce. Both negative extremes foster an unsafe and unloving atmosphere. These fear-based and protective responses are an outcome of what we learned or did not learn about conflict in our earlier years. Observe how this conflict continuum closely replicates the assertiveness continuum in Chapter 9. Passive individuals often withdraw and aggressive people attack or defend in response to conflict. Once again, it is interesting that even with these opposing behavioral responses, each individual reaction often comes from the same basis of fear, insecurity, and self-protection. As with the assertiveness continuum, both extreme and unhealthy reactors need to come to the middle to connect and manage conflict in the most healthy way. Successful couples are able to apply skills and stay more emotionally connected and respectful, even when they disagree.[3]

Let's look at these three responses to conflict: avoid/withdraw, attack/defend, and connect/manage.

Avoid/Withdraw

At first glance it seems that withdrawing or avoiding conflict would be a good choice for our marriages. But the opposite is true. Avoidance of conflict is the number one predictor of divorce. Diane Sollee, of Smartmarriages.com, explains our logical but ineffective reasoning. We avoid conflict when we are first married because we believe that staying in love is about agreeing and we fear that fighting will hurt our marriages. Later, we avoid conflict because when we face our disagreements we end up having hurtful and destructive fights. After we have had a few damaging conflicts, we are more determined to avoid them.[4] Even though this line of thinking is very logical regarding conflict, it is totally wrong. Successful couples know how to discuss differences in a respectful way that actually strengthens their relationship. Diane goes on in her article to talk about the erroneous reason for divorcing due to "irreconcilable differences." Many marriage researchers agree with Diane when she says that irreconcilable differences isn't a reason to divorce, but is a normal part of any marriage.[5]

> Avoiding conflict is a strong predictor of divorce.

If my husband, Phil, and I have thirty areas of differences, we will have those differences until we die. I will always be Kathy, he will always be Phil. He will always be a morning person and I will be a non-morning person. I will always be more strict with the kids and he will play more. He will always like quiet and remote vacations and I will always like a mix of activity and quiet. I will be social and he will not. I will be more relaxed around finances. We will always be different. If I decided to divorce Phil because of the problems these differences cause, my next husband and I wouldn't have the exact same differences. But husband number two and I would for sure be different, and our differences would cause us problems. The answer to our differences is not to dump the spouse, but to learn to manage our differences and unsolvable problems more respectfully. Once again, our problems in marriage are frequently due to the patterns we have, not the specific partners.

We withdraw or avoid conflict because of fear. Maybe we fear connection, or fear not having connections. Maybe we have grown up with either no conflict or a lot of conflict. It is common that we have not learned the skills for handling conflict in a healthy way. We might have unresolved past hurts that now influence our withdrawal or fear of conflict. We may be insecure and have fears of abandonment or rejection that now contribute to conflict avoidance. Our personalities and life experiences affect how we manage conflict. No matter what the reason for not addressing conflicts in marriage, avoidance is the very worst thing we can do. The next worst response is when we attack and are negative in our response to conflicts.

Attack/Defend

There are many ways to negatively attack and defend ourselves when we disagree with our spouse. These negative methods damage the individuals and their marriage, making it emotionally unsafe. As mentioned above, Dr. Gottman found that 69 percent of disagreements both in healthy marriages and in those that are divorcing are irresolvable. His research of these two groups found that couples who were content in their marriages had much less negativity and much more respect than those near divorce.[6] Power struggles are normal. When a couple does not have sufficient skills, the struggles turn nasty and result in unfair fighting, growing apart, living parallel lives, and possibly divorce.

Dr. Gottman has identified some gender tendencies that occur related to conflict. As you recall, he found that women are often guilty of what he calls the *harsh startup*, which guarantees a defensive response from our spouse.[7] Women also create conflict when they indirectly hint for what they want or assume their spouse will automatically know what they want, as a test of their love. If we don't get what we hinted at, we might turn to criticizing, complaining, or nagging. All of these ineffective strategies guarantee defensiveness or withdrawal of our partners caught in this "no-win" situation.

Men's negative tendencies exacerbate conflict when they are unwilling to be influenced by their partner and when they withdraw from conflict. Dr. Gottman found that many men have difficulty being influenced by their wives. Accepting influence does not mean giving up their manhood and letting their wife run the show. Being influenced means that he listens to his wife, considering her views as valid and worthwhile in marital decisions. An emotionally intelligent man accepts influence from his wife.[8] Those who do not accept influence are four times more likely to be divorced. When men withdraw from conflict, they contribute to putting the nail in the coffin regarding the life of the marriage. Although we are not responsible for our spouse's withdrawal, our approach, skills, safety, and understanding of conflict greatly influence them. Knowing these tendencies helps us learn to be smarter in managing interactions most effectively and depersonalize their resistance.

Dr. Gottman's "Four Horsemen of the Apocalypse" are worthy of repetition, as they are damaging communication traits in a relationship. *Criticism* goes a step beyond complaining by attacking the person, not just the behaviors. *Contempt* is criticism gone viral. With contempt we convey our disgust of our spouse through sarcasm, name-calling, eye rolling, mocking, and belligerence. *Defensiveness* occurs to protect and end conflict, but because it is really a form of blaming our spouse, it only causes escalation. *Stonewalling* is the ultimate defensive protection, which involves shutting down and disconnecting from the conflict and the spouse. Dr. Gottman puts it well to say that stonewalling is meant to avoid the fight, but it results in avoiding the marriage. When our spouse stonewalls and acts like he could care less about what is going on, it increases our difficulties and distance apart. Men stonewall 85 percent more than women, at least partially because marital conflict is more uncomfortable for most men and they flood more frequently.[9]

Flooding occurs when the negativity of our spouse during conflict makes us shut down emotionally. We cannot do any problem-solving when we are flooded. A flooded person needs a time-out, a minimum of twenty minutes of relaxation, before they return to discuss an issue effectively. Flooding is an automatic self-protective mechanism that cannot be willfully avoided, and is a mini fight-or-flight response. In Dr. Gottman's love lab, where he studies couples' interactions, a staff member told a couple having a heated discussion that they needed to take a break because the video equipment had malfunctioned. When the couple returned to their discussion twenty minutes later, they were both calmed down and able to resume more effective problem-solving.[10] All of these negative patterns contribute to growing distance in marriage, and can lead to being "walking dead" and divorced.

Many marriage researchers have their own names for the round-and-round escalating cycle of negative patterns that occur repeatedly over the years of a marriage (also mentioned in chapter 10). They are called many things: power struggles, the cycle of disaffection, the allergy loop, the pursual-withdrawal pattern, the fear dance, and the demon dialogue, to name a few. These patterns are similarly automatic, repetitive, negative, mutually hurtful, out of control, and they escalate in intensity. They are born out of past hurts, life, and marriage experiences. We all have particular sensitivities, which when triggered cause negative defensive reactions in us. When triggered by circumstances or our spouse, our reaction tends to trigger the sensitivity in our spouse as well. For example, when I am feeling abandoned, I tend to lash out in anger (which is really hurt) and criticism of my spouse. His reaction to my negativity is to feel unworthy, which he responds to by withdrawing. When he withdraws I lash out more, which triggers him to withdraw more, and off we go into our own unique cycle of negativity. At any given time when our negative loop is going on, we may be arguing about any or every topic under the sun besides abandonment or unworthiness. Our negative loop is based in our deep need to connect, and fear that it won't happen. Our protective and defensive responses do a lot of damage.

Sue Johnson observes that these "demon dialogues" occur in all love relationships, but when they become habitual and toxic, they can destroy a relationship.[11] Typical fears that underlie our dangerous dances include:

- Fear of abandonment or rejection
- Fear of not being loved or valued
- Fear of being inadequate or unworthy

When these deep-seated fears get triggered, our automatic response is to either fight or withdraw as if our life depended on it. These triggered responses are an unconscious reaction based in our survival brain. Our response is automatic and defensive. It would be like the reaction we would have if we just missed having a car accident. This does not mean we cannot change these patterns, but it takes consistent awareness and lots of practice. And, yes, it is possible for one person to change this defeating dance.

The marital therapist Terry Real has studied intimacy differences between men and women. He has identified five more losing agendas of couples:[12]

- Being right
- Controlling spouse
- Retaliation
- Withdrawal
- Unbridled self-expression

Additional unfair fighting styles are bad timing, blaming, bringing in many issues, covering deeper feelings with anger, making unrealistic demands, and threatening with ultimatums. These and other unfair fighting techniques usually stem from wrong assumptions that conflict is awful, that my needs are more important than yours, and that only one person can win a disagreement. Poor techniques stemming from inaccurate assumptions are deadly for marital contentment, according to McKay and Davis in their helpful book, *Messages*.[13]

We often assume that the most damaging styles of unfair fighting are the loud and obvious ones. The PAIRS program for marriages teaches couples to recognize and avoid a more subtle style of fighting, called "velvet glove." This technique outwardly appears to be less damaging than louder methods such as yelling, blaming, putting down, demanding, criticizing, and lying. The passive velvet glove control includes whining, denying, a "poor me" and martyr attitude, making excuses, changing topics, and keeping score. Velvet glove techniques are even more damaging because of their subtlety, their exploitation of weakness, and their underhanded methods, which anger and confuse the partner, making it difficult to respond to.[14]

Application Questions:

1. Which of the above negative patterns do you sometimes get stuck in?

2. Which of the fears listed do you think might be fueling your defensive reactions?

3. What type of statement or situation triggers your negative response?

Conflict is defined in *Webster's New World Dictionary* as "antagonistic and sharp disagreement of interests or ideas."[15]That definition makes it a given that spouses will have conflict; we will disagree. In fact, in John 16:22 Jesus declares, "In this world you will have trouble." First Corinthians 7:28 tells us that those who marry will face *many* troubles. Conflict and troubles are expected in life and marriage. We presume also that we will have anger, but Ephesians 4:26 tells us to not sin in our anger or let the sun go down while we are angry. Proverbs 29:11 says only a fool will give full vent to his anger. In his book *The Pillars of Marriage*, Norman Wright gives a helpful distinction between conflict and quarreling. He defines a quarrel as verbal strife involving angry emotions and attack of another person instead of the issue.[16]

What causes quarreling? The Bible has a lot to say about it:

Pride only breeds quarrels, but wisdom is found in those who take advice.

—Proverbs 13:10

What causes fights and quarrels among you? They come from your desires that battle within you. You want something but don't get it. You kill and covet, but you cannot have what you want. You quarrel and fight. You do not have, because you do not ask God.

—James 4:12

What are some outcomes of quarreling?

Starting a quarrel is like breaching a dam; so drop the matter before a dispute breaks out.

—Proverbs 17:14

Better to live on a corner of the roof than share a house with a quarrelsome wife.

—Proverbs 21:9

Better to live in a desert than with a quarrelsome and ill-tempered wife.

—Proverbs 21:19

What are we to do with quarreling?

And the Lord's servant must not quarrel.

—2 Timothy 2:24

A hot-tempered man stirs up dissension, but a patient man calms a quarrel.

—Proverbs 15:18

It is to a man's honor to avoid strife, but every fool is quick to quarrel.

—Proverbs 20:3

We have spent a lot of time on negativity in this chapter. There is agreement from the Bible, experienced marriage researchers, and from our own experience that negativity in conflict kills a relationship. This makes it imperative that we neither avoid nor attack in response to conflicts. If we do not spend time and energy reducing our negativity in conflict, we will always struggle with finding positives in our marriages. It is commonly said that it takes five positive actions to make up for each negative one. Dr. Scott Stanley claims that it takes from five to a whopping twenty positives to cancel out each negative action in marriage.[17] We know it's not true that "sticks and stones can hurt my bones, but words will never hurt me." Words do hurt. We have all heard

> Reduce negatives and develop respectful skills for more effective conflict management.

from our moms that "If you don't have anything nice to say, don't say anything at all."

Words hurt, and they can't be taken back. This is why I have emphasized the primary importance of reducing negative behaviors and to "First, do no harm" as a major tenant of conflict management. It means everything for the survival of marriage. I know from personal experience it is hard, often impossible, to make up for hurtful words said in anger. These negative patterns break trust in a relationship and push others away until we shut down in hopelessness and parallel lives, and possibly the end of the marriage. So what *do we do* to connect more positively around conflicts?

Connect/Manage

The third and best conflict strategy is when couples are able to stay emotionally connected and respectful and work as a team even when they disagree. Dr. Gottman talks about three choices in the face of marital conflict. He says we can "turn away" from conflict, which is destructive avoiding or withdrawing. We can "turn against" our partner in anger and hostility and attack them. We have discussed these two damaging choices above. The third and preferable method is to "turn toward" our partner, responding to our differences in an attitude of acceptance and cooperation.[18]

BECOMING STRONG AND COURAGEOUS IN TURNING TOWARD OUR PARTNER

The best place to start is to align ourselves with our spouse against our negative conflict patterns. The patterns are the enemy, not the spouse. Of course, Satan is another enemy that we need to align against, as he exists to confuse and destroy us.[19] So, how do we learn to "turn toward" our spouse and stay connected in conflict?

First, as we discuss skills for effective conflict management, it is very important for us to accept that there is no right or wrong when it comes to conflict, just two different realities (of course, unless there is a moral wrong involved). I like that statement

"You can either be right or you can be married." With this basic premise in place, we then need some safety rules or boundaries for conflicts.

- *Timing is a very important safety measure.* We need to pick discussion times that are good for both people. As a stay at home mom, I remember by Friday evening I was busting a gusset to "discuss" my laundry list of weekly issues with my husband. As I have said before, being a slow learner, it took me years to realize that for him, Friday night was the absolute worst time for him to discuss serious concerns.
- We also need to *be willing to stop any interactions that get negative*, are going nowhere, bring in "the kitchen sink," or overwhelm either person. We only do more and more damage as we go on and on in negativity. An important aspect of these "time-outs" is that another time for continuing has to be set up and stuck to, so the time out does not become an escape route for avoidance.
- After we have those rules in place, it is helpful to *identify and define some areas of conflict.* The most common topics of conflict are communication, children, money, and sex. Dr. Gottman helps us identify which conflicts are more solvable and which are more complicated, perpetual issues and how to manage both.[20] Dr. Scott Stanley has a list of problem issues, to help us get started addressing them.[21]
- In addition to women practicing a softened startup and men being more willing to be influenced by their spouse, it is helpful for couples to *learn a good basic communication skill.* One of my favorites was developed by Dr. Stanley, called "the speaker-listener technique."[22] This technique emphasizes separating "feeling" discussions from "solution" discussions. It also has very clear rules for the discussion: to allow for safety and clarity of the speaker and listener rules. These rules encourage hearing and understanding our spouse's position on any given topic before we move to further discussion for compromise. This technique has

been life-changing for me as a pursuer and my husband as a withdrawer, because it levels the playing field and gives both parties an equal voice. Having and following rules works.

- I am excited to share with you Dr. Gottman's recommendations on *how to be a good complainer*. He specifies the differences between complaining and criticizing.[23] A good complaint focuses on the specific behavior or problem, not on judging or critiquing the person. When we complain we should use "I" language as we describe our position as a perception, not the truth. Learning to complain more effectively will help our conflicts be less negative and defensive.

THE IMPORTANCE OF FRIENDSHIP

Many marriage researchers and educators agree that successful conflict resolution is not the key to successful marriage. We will *always* be different and we will *always* have conflict. As we are able to improve and maintain the quality of our friendship with mutual respect, we will be protected from having such adversarial marriages.[24] Thus as we reduce negativity and build deeper friendship, making positive deposits in our spouse's love tank, our needs will be met, our anger reduced, and our conflicts managed more respectfully.[25] Seventy percent of men and women rate the quality of their friendship as primary to marital satisfaction. Dr. Harley found that our lack of feeling loved is a primary cause of marital hopelessness.

In this time of busy two-career and child-centered families, it is hard to make enough time for deep spousal connection. When marriages don't receive enough attention, they suffer. When we spend time together, we are saying, "You matter to me," "I like to be with you." We need to schedule time for dates and fun that do not involve children. Even regular short times to be together is helpful, as are weekly couple meetings. It is important to know each other intimately, including our differing love needs and preferences. We need to express appreciation of each other and take steps to connect. As we know each other better and kindle or rekindle the friendship that brought us together, we will increase our positive regard of each other. Within this respectful atmosphere we will be able to learn to manage conflict more positively as well.

A major conclusion of Dr. Gottman's extensive study of marriages is termed "the Sound Marital House." He found that as couples built a strong foundation of friendship through knowing each other, sharing interests, and turning toward each other, they were then able to move to more complicated tasks, such as conflict management, in a respectful way. When couples learn more effective skills for managing conflict, they are able to continue to build on the positives by creating shared dreams and meaning in life. The Sound Marital House is the model of the emotionally mature marriage.

Are you ready to let God guide you in becoming a powerful peacemaker in your family?

NOTES

1. John M. Gottman and Nan Silver, *The Seven Principles for Making Marriage Work* (New York: Three Rivers Press, 1999), 2.
2. Gottman and Silver, *The Seven Principles for Making Marriage Work*, 23.
3. John Gottman, *The Relationship Cure* (New York: Crown, 2001), 16.
4. Diane Sollee, http://www.smartmarriages.com.

5. Sollee, http://www.smartmarriages.com.
6. Gottman and Silver, *The Seven Principles for Making Marriage Work*, 2.
7. Gottman and Silver, *The Seven Principles for Making Marriage Work*, 26.
8. Gottman and Silver, *The Seven Principles for Making Marriage Work*, 105.
9. Gottman and Silver, *The Seven Principles for Making Marriage Work*, 27-34.
10. Gottman and Silver, *The Seven Principles for Making Marriage Work*, 26.
11. Sue Johnson, *Hold Me Tight* (New York: Little, Brown and Company, 2008), 67.
12. Terrence Real, *How Can I Get Through to You?* (New York: Fireside, 2002).
13. Matthew McKay, M. Davis, P. Fanning, *Messages* (Oakland, CA: New Harbinger, 1995), 144.
14. Lori Heyman Gordon, *PAIRS Professional Training Handbook*, (Reston, VA: Pairs Foundation, 1999)140.
15. Michael Agnes, editor, *Webster's New World Dictionary*, (New York: Pocket Books, 2003) 140.
16. H. Norman Wright, *The Pillars of Marriage* (Ventura, CA: G. L. Publications, 1979), 137.
17. Scott Stanley, *A Lasting Promise* (San Francisco: Jossey-Bass, 2002), 28.
18. Gottman, *The Relationship Cure*, 16.
19. 1 Peter 5:8
20. Gottman and Silver, *The Seven Principles for Making Marriage Work*, 129.
21. Stanley, *A Lasting Promise*, 92.
22. Stanley, *A Lasting Promise*, 59.
23. Gottman and Silver, *The Seven Principles for Making Marriage Work*, 164
24. Willard F. Harley Jr., *His Needs, Her Needs* (Grand Rapids: Revell, 2001), 117; and John Gottman, *The Relationship Cure*, 223, 235.
25. http://www.marriagebuilders.com.

CHAPTER 14

THE FACES OF FORGIVENESS

For if you forgive men when they sin against you, your heavenly
Father will also forgive you. But if you do not forgive men their
sins, your Father will not forgive your sins.
—Matthew 6:14-15

Forgiving means to pardon the unpardonable,
or it is no virtue at all.
—G. K. Chesterton

*T*HE KITE RUNNER[1] *tells of two little boys who grow up being inseparable buddies across class lines in Afghanistan. The rich man's son, Amir, is befriended by Hassan, the son of their servant. In a magical way they surmount the barriers to form a bond of a lifetime.*

They were a famous kite flying pair around Kabul. Amir flew and shrewdly cut other kites down, and Hassan was the kite runner with uncanny insight in finding and returning with the last fallen kite. Hassan told his beloved Amir that he would run kites for him "a thousand times over." When the boys were twelve years old, an egregious act occurred. As the scene unfolded I kept saying to myself, "No, don't do that," and, "No, no, don't, leave him alone." Amir abandoned his friend. He was fully aware that he was about to be raped by some young thugs. He saved himself at the expense of the one who loved him most. He ran away as if he didn't know Hassan.

Later, the betrayal haunted him with unbearable guilt, insomnia, and headaches. The boys' relationship was never the same again. After the betrayal Hassan worked and slept, eyes always to the ground. Unable to live with daily guilt, Amir set it up to appear that Hassan stole from him. This resulted in the breakup of two generations of friends, and their lives parted forever.

Time went on as Amir and his father escaped to Pakistan from the war, and then later to America. Amir got an education and married. He saw his and his wife's infertility as just another deserved punishment for his unforgivable childhood betrayal.

As difficult as it was to read and get pulled into the plot of the betrayal in *The Kite Runner*, the betrayals that occur in marriage are equally hard. *What makes it so hard?* For me, it's that they keep happening over and over. There is no other way to maintain love in a marriage, except to forgive over and over, seventy-seven times. I struggle with making sense of why we, who supposedly love each other, keep hurting each other so, necessitating forgiveness over and over.

The biblical mandate for forgiveness is very clear. There are many theories and methods for forgiving, which unfortunately don't make it any easier. We are called as believers to forgive over and over and over again. The cost of not forgiving is huge, in risking loss God, self or love.

Of course, even as I write this chapter, I am wrestling with personal forgiveness once again. Because our initial relationship centered around physical intimacy, it is not surprising that this is the "last holdout" for healing in our relationship. It has been an area of ongoing hurt and struggle for us. There has been much healing and forgiveness surrounding intimacy, but it remains a sensitive topic. I will always be sensitive to rejection, and I will probably always desire physical intimacy more than my husband. These parameters contribute to our ongoing struggle in this area. So here I am, once again struggling with forgiveness and searching for insight and personal growth in the area I am writing about. Doesn't God have an interesting sense of humor?

Walter Wangerin vividly describes marital forgiveness in his book, *As For Me and My House:*[2]

> Forgiving seems almost unnatural. Our sense of fairness tells us people should pay for the wrong they do. But forgiving is love's power to break nature's rule. Forgiving will not immediately soothe your pain; instead, it introduces a different pain, a much more hopeful pain, because it is redeeming. You do "deny yourself" and die a little in order to forgive. Pride dies. Fairness dies. Rights die, as do self-pity and the sweetness of a pout, or the satisfaction of a little righteous wrath. You take leave of the center of the marriage and of your own existence. You die a little, that the marriage might rise alive.

FORGIVENESS DEFINED

In this chapter I am using the terms *betrayal* and *offense* interchangeably. *Webster's New World Dictionary* definition of *betrayal* is "to fail to uphold, to deceive, to seduce then desert." *Offense* is defined as "a sin or a crime, creating resentment, to hurt the feelings of."[3] Following are more facts about what forgiveness is and what it is not.

Forgiveness is:

- Difficult and unfair.
- An act of obedience to the Lord.
- Giving up resentment and the right to get even toward someone who has wronged us.[4]
- Allowing the Lord to punish. Romans 12:19 says we are not to avenge ourselves, "but leave room for God's wrath, for it is written: 'It is mine to avenge; I will repay,' says the Lord."
- Laying down of strong feelings and our rights.
- Merciful, bringing freedom and peace.
- More than just saying "I forgive you."

Forgiveness is not:

- Excusing the person who hurt us.
- Forgetting the offense or tolerating the wrong.
- Just kissing and making up.
- An automatic ticket back into our lives.
- Guaranteed reconciliation with license to hurt again.
- Surrendering our right to justice.

Results of failure to forgive can be:

- Bitterness that eats us alive.
- The death of love.
- Not being forgiven by God.
- Lack of freedom from our betrayers.

The natural human response to betrayals and wounding is to experience our hurt through anger, bitterness, and resentment. We instinctively want to defend ourselves and get even for wrongs done to us. We somehow think withholding forgiveness will make them pay. Anne Lamott said that not forgiving is like us drinking rat poison and then waiting for the rat to die.[5] When we follow our human retaliation response to hurts, *we* are the ones who pay consequences spiritually, emotionally, and relationally. Blame and resentment toward another person lock us in negative relationship as well as locking ourselves out of a solution. We cannot feel joy, and we are motivated by anger and making the other person pay. One of the women I interviewed regarding forgiveness was honest in saying, "I am not a very pretty bitter person." I know that is true of me as well. We make ourselves miserable and are imprisoned by ugliness when we do not forgive.

Not forgiving affects our relationship with God and shows ingratitude for Jesus's sacrifice for our sins. Forgiveness is commanded by God. There is absolutely no way to misread Matthew 6:14-15, which says, "For if you forgive men when they sin against you, your heavenly Father will also forgive you. But if you do not forgive men their sins, your Father will not forgive your sins."

We cannot be both disobedient and close to God. It is common to blame God for our hurts and suffering. Scripture corrects this perception in 1 Peter 5:8 by telling us that Satan is the one who causes pain and suffering and every kind of evil. Our caustic emotions influence our behavior and damage our bodies as well as our hearts. God warns us about the effects of bitterness in James 3:14-16, saying it leads to defiance, confusion, and evil practices. Hebrews 12:15 says a bitter root can cause torment and defile many.

Unforgiveness kills love. It is confusing and strange that we repeatedly hurt the ones we love the most. Refusal to repair these marital betrayals wounds us more. Henri Nouwen says that we wound those we love because we look to them to fulfill our deep needs for love that only God can fill. He follows by saying our human love relationships are the source of our greatest wounds as well as our greatest joys.[6] The fact is, we cannot both refuse forgiveness and give and receive love.

Peggy regrets not working on forgiving her husband more when he was alive, but she has been able to grow in forgiving him even since his death. She had allowed her alcoholic husband to become a controlling dictator in their marriage. She was a self-described "fake person" whose job it was to keep the peace, so of course she did not confront any issues. She was not "allowed" to be angry, and her unspoken bitterness led to mistrust and living separate lives. After she became a believer, she claimed to have forgiven her husband. She sees in hindsight that she was just being overly spiritual to continue to deny and avoid conflict. No longer able to play the games of pretend, she checked herself into an inpatient program at age forty-five.

Although she was able to begin to forgive her husband after she was in treatment, she has forgiven him even more in the eighteen years since his death. Peggy now sees that the issues they struggled with were due much more to her dysfunction than she had realized. She is remorseful that their ability to connect and love was affected by their lack of forgiveness. She praises God that forgiveness can continue even after death, and she thanks Him for her growing sense of peace and freedom.

Application Questions:

1. What consequences have you experienced due to not forgiving your spouse?

2. Have you received God's forgiveness, and also forgiven yourself?

LIVING STRONG BY FORGIVING OURSELVES

Because God forgave us, we are also called to forgive others and we are able to give back to others what God has granted us, undeserved mercy. We not only have to extend this forgiveness to others, but to ourselves as well. In fact, it is imperative that we receive God's mercy before we are able to extend the same to others. What do we need to forgive ourselves for? We need to accept that we are sinners and have wronged God and others. We need to grieve what we have done and have failed to do in our lives. We need to own up to our mistakes and how we have disappointed God and others. We need to apologize for our lukewarm faith and for not always honoring and fully trusting God. We need to honestly and fully confess and grieve any mistakes and misjudgments.

Jane found that she had to forgive herself first before she was able to experience marital forgiveness. She grew up in a home where she was forced to apologize, but at the same time not taught to truly forgive. She remembered being told that she shouldn't get mad because "only dogs get mad." Early on in their alcoholic- and illness-based marriage she kept a scorecard of her husband's wrongs for future ammunition. As an active enabler and codependent, she needed to first pursue her own spiritual recovery for strength to eventually be able to work on relational recovery. God was so good in allowing her time and space to focus on her own recovery and knowing Him deeply. Although she feared forgiving her husband might open up a can of worms from her scorecard, she made the choice to move ahead in forgiving. She needed to open up herself from self-protection and take proactive but difficult steps to love and trust her husband. She sees now that she had not fully trusted God as her protector. Because she had the courage to forgive herself first, she has seen tremendous growth in marital trust and forgiveness.

Forgiveness is a gift to ourselves as we are then able to live in peace and joy without anger. Lack of forgiveness is a prison that keeps us disconnected from others and burdened by disappointment. It is a self-inflicted poison that dooms us to a life of discord and anger. Remembering our own sin and our great need for forgiveness and how we don't deserve it is the great equalizer in holding anything against another. Jane is a great example of a woman who found freedom in forgiveness.

> Deep and complete forgiveness is a process.

FORGIVING IN MARRIAGE

Although not impossible, when we begin to think about forgiving in marriage, it is preferable that we have already begun to forgive our childhood hurts and have forgiven ourselves. If we have not dealt with these past and personal issues, they will block our path to forgiveness. They will also continue to brew negative emotions that will interfere with marital forgiving. There are other issues to consider that also affect our ability to forgive in marriage.

- *Expectation setups.* We sometimes set ourselves up for difficulty in forgiving because of unrealistic expectations. My childhood hurts make me super-sensitive to marital hurts. There were a lot of betrayals, big and small, that I blew out of proportion, overreacted to, made myself a martyr over, and generally set myself up for. Past unresolved issues will affect our expectations in marriages and set us up for difficulty in forgiving.

  We live in an age of selfish entitlement. We hear messages such as "You deserve to be happy," "You don't deserve to be hurt," "You deserve to be loved by someone who always has your interest first." *Not!* We set ourselves up for a deeper and more difficult process of forgiveness when we have these and other unrealistic (sometimes godlike) expectations of any human being. After all, we are still two fallen sinners trying to live together. I am not saying we should accept abuse on any level, or turn a blind eye to betrayals or offenses. When we have not healed from our childhood issues and have an entitlement mentality, our marital hurts are more frequent, deeper, and more challenging to overcome and forgive.

- *Complications of love and trust.* Forgiveness is one of the most important and most difficult tasks in marriage. We desperately desire love, but also protect and fear from being hurt by it. This balancing act complicates our behaviors around forgiveness. The stakes are high, our ability to sustain lifetime marriages depend on it, but the tendency we have to repeat hurts undermines the trust we also need to maintain. The love and trust we need to sustain a decent marriage depend on being able to forgive.

- *The challenge of repetitive marital forgiveness.* Matthew 18:21-22 tells of Peter asking Jesus how many times we have to forgive our brother. Jesus replies in verse 22, "I tell you, not seven times, but seventy-seven times." From my vast experience, that isn't really enough to express how much we need to forgive each other as spouses. We have to forgive a *lot!* It takes a lot of grace to forgive that much. This level of repetitive forgiveness requires that we be indwelled with the resurrection power of Jesus!

It is hard! Over and over and over and over again, betrayal, forgiveness.

You get the idea. Luckily, *we can* access the deep and enduring and perfect love of God and His great and unfathomable love and forgiveness of us. This provides the grace and motivation we need to be able to forgive repeatedly. The tricky part comes when we have to balance our command from God to forgive with the boundaries we need not to allow or enable abuse to go on. Check out the chapters on assertiveness, boundaries and conflict for more guidance in how to do this. Remember, we *can* forgive without condoning repetition of abusive and addiction-driven hurts to continue. Reconciliation should not be an automatic outcome of forgiveness, but needs to be carefully considered depending on our individual situation.

Physical betrayals, in particular, are challenging to forgive. When we share our physical body with our husbands, we are giving them something sacred, our very selves. We don't share our physical selves to that depth with anyone else. Our ability to be vulnerable and share our bodies with our spouse depends on many factors. They include our self-esteem, past experiences in and outside of marriage, and body image. Women who have experienced rape or sexual abuse will have significant obstacles to trust regarding physical intimacy. Betrayals such as sexual addictions, adultery, and other addictions also greatly impact our marital intimacy. Maintaining physical intimacy is challenging and complicated, but is much more difficult when forgiveness is not a regular part of it.

Being Strong and Courageous in Forgiving Others

First Peter 2:22 tells us that Jesus "committed no sin." Verse 23 goes on to say he still did not retaliate when he suffered insults. "Instead, he entrusted himself to him who judges justly." Jesus did not threaten, did not entrust himself to man but to God alone. He knew what was in man, and we need to do the same. We need to entrust ourselves fully to God when our husbands wrong us. But we are also called to love, forgive, and call them to the truth while still not enabling abuses.

Forgiveness should not be given too quickly or too cheaply. Sometimes it is preached that we obediently need to forgive and we will instantly be healed of our hurt; that is, if we have enough faith. Certainly God *can* allow a miraculous forgiveness to happen, but this model typically is just a superficial lip service and does not respect the pain of the one betrayed. We need to separate the wrongdoer from the wrong. Then we need to allow them to suffer the natural consequences of their sin. This might mean relational, legal, financial, or moral consequences.

We need to get healthy in not enabling a person's sin by drawing boundaries around our relationship until trust and respect grow. We need to assess individually the wisdom and safety factors in terms of reconciliation with the one who wronged us. This is particularly important when dealing with any addictions, abuse of any kind, violence, or adultery. People who wronged us need to earn their way back into a trusting relationship by consistently showing a change of behavior and heart.

Marsha Means discusses this in detail in her book, *Living with Your Husband's Secret Wars,* regarding a woman's recovery from her husband's sexual addiction. She discusses that honesty is the price that needs to be paid for reunion after sexual betrayals. There has to be a rebuilding of trust through consistent truth telling with no more pretense.[7] Smedes, in *Forgive and Forget*, discusses the reality that a relationship that has suffered a deep hurt may never be able to return to its former state. He says we need to have a reunion that is within the bounds of our individual reality. This is more easily determined when a child is sexually abused than when a wife experiences deep emotional hurt in a marriage. The desire to move on can motivate a person to forgive too quickly and shallowly. This results in incomplete forgiving with continued anger and lack of connection. Deep and complete forgiveness is a process that hurts and takes time. Generally, deeper wounds take a longer time to forgive deeply.

Everett L. Worthington Jr. describes a simple forgiveness model in two difficult steps:[8]

1. *Decisional forgiveness* is the first step of obediently choosing to forgive. We may not feel like it, it may be very difficult, and it may seem unfair. We know that God forgave us, and we ourselves will not be forgiven unless we take this step. If we do not want to stay bitter and angry, we obediently decide to forgive. It is our conscious choice not to seek revenge on our partner. We decide to release them from making up for the hurt they have caused, and we commit to rebuilding the relationship and growing in trust. This first step merely opens the door to address the complexity of emotions surrounding offenses. It is normal to be reluctant to take this first step. A good place to start is to say to God, "I'm willing to be willing." Then be open to Him guiding us to be courageous past our fears.

2. *Emotional forgiveness* is the second step Dr. Worthington discusses, where we deal with the hurt, anger, bitterness, and distrust that are also a part of forgiving. Walter Wangerin calls this stage "heart forgiveness."[9] They are both referring to our need to heal from our hurt and replace the negative emotions of unforgiveness. This process takes work and time but is imperative for marital healing to take place on a deeper level.

Joan allows these steps to take place in her hurtful marriage by first making the decision, usually while on her knees, to forgive her husband each day. Joan has had a plethora of hurts in her twenty-seven-year marriage, including verbal abuse, emotional disconnection, and the fallout from her husband's sexual addictions. When she is able to stay submitted to God through reading the Bible and helpful books, praying, listening to songs and sermons, and discussing her struggles with others, she is open to see what area of her marital hurt God wants her to forgive. Over time, she becomes aware of an area that needs healing. She then goes to God individually, expressing her pain, loss, and anger. When she feels prepared with the right attitude and is less emotional, she is able to bring up the issue with her husband. She expresses her hurt until she is done. She is then able to release it to God, and her forgiveness in that area is complete. The good from Joan's difficult path of forgiveness is that she is becoming less bitter and is a godly encouragement to her family and other young women who seem to sense her wisdom in guiding them in their life struggles.

Mary was challenged to question the faith of her upbringing at age twenty-six. She feared finding her childhood beliefs inadequate, but her search caused her to fall in love with God's dependable Word. This new confidence in God would prove imperative to her marital survival in later years. She was on a spiritual high for years with her newfound personal faith.

Mary and her husband had always experienced difficult verbal fights with little resolution. His verbal abuse and working late resulted in a growing distance and no marital intimacy. Mary suspected her husband was having an affair after six to eight years of marriage. His denial plummeted their life into what Mary called "a living hell" for a few years. Mary's close relationship to the Lord and her prior Scripture memory were her lifesaving comforts. When her husband returned from six weeks away from home, he rededicated his life to the Lord. He finally admitted to the affair and broke it off.

Understandably, Mary's love and respect for her husband were gone. She asked herself, "What am I going to do?" She had fought to keep her husband in the home, but now that he was willing to do whatever it took to stay, she had to decide if she was *really* willing to forgive. Her first faltering step of obedience was when she told God she was willing to be a vessel. She was open to loving, accepting, and forgiving her husband. God led her to ask about the affairs, as she felt she needed to know what she was forgiving. She wrestled with the unfairness of it all. She said to herself, "Do I really, really believe all of the theology that I dearly love? Who am I that God loves even me?"

As she walked through the second step of forgiving, the process of dealing with the emotions, she determined that forgiveness is a hugely mental task, and she made several conclusions:

- We should not be surprised when trials come our way. (Matthew 6:34, John 16:33)
- We are challenged to take difficult circumstances, turn to God in them and then turn around and encourage others to rest in God's hands, as well. (2 Corinthians 1:3-4)
- It is a choice that we make *each day* to run our race, focusing on what is good, right, and pleasing to God. (Philippians 4:8)
- We need to remain motivated out of a desire to please God and desire to be kind and compassionate, not bitter. (Ephesians 4:31-32)

FINDING FREEDOM IN FORGIVING

It is not fair that we are the ones to humble ourselves and crawl back to reconnect with our spouse who hurt us. *They* hurt us; *they* should be responsible for reconnecting and making amends. This is very logical and human reasoning. God's economy differs. As believers we are called to a higher road of obedience in spite of our "fairness" logic. Jesus died for our sins. He was totally innocent. He did nothing wrong his whole life. His being mistreated, unaccepted, and mocked, and his tortured death were not fair. He was called to do something that did not make sense from a human viewpoint.

We are called to do the same in forgiving betrayals. Not only are we being obedient as we work at forgiving, but we are also avoiding the deadly consequences of not forgiving. It is comforting to know that God is in charge of the justice from our hurts. Romans 12:17-19 says:

> Do not repay anyone evil for evil. Be careful to do what is right in the eyes of everybody. If it is possible, as far as it depends on you, live at peace with everyone. Do not take revenge, my friends, but leave room for God's wrath, for it is written: "It is mine to avenge, I will repay," says the Lord.

Lewis Smedes says, "Forgiving is the only way we have a better fairness in our unfair world: it is love's unexpected revolution against unfair pain and it alone offers hope for healing the hurts we so unfairly feel."[10]

It is important to realize that it is not always wise or necessary to take our forgiving to our hoped-for place of reconciliation. In the case of sexual abuse, violence in relationships, and abusive and addictive circumstances, we can sometimes only accept God's forgiveness of us, forgive ourselves, and forgive those who betrayed us. For reasons of safety and our own mental health, sometimes forgiveness with boundaries around full reconciliation is the best outcome.

Living Strong

Sarah is a model of gracious forgiveness on many levels. Raised in a dangerous and chaotic dual alcoholic home, she learned early to care for herself as a tough little street kid. Violence in her home included guns, bloodshed, physical abuse, police, and being aroused from sleep with knife-wielding threats. There was ongoing sexual abuse from her mentally ill mother's boyfriends. What seemed like rescue by her father and stepmother became another chapter of abuse, because she never measured up to her idealized stepsister, and her crude survival personality no longer served her well. Her father gave her a week to straighten up or be sent to reform school.

She worked hard to be a perfect little eight year old, only for her father to die of a heart attack that week, before she could find out how he thought she had done. Assuming she had killed her father, she reasoned that if she were good enough, her father would return. Not only did he never return, the stepmother carried on the emotional abuse. She did her best at everything in school by excelling in athletics and academics.

At seventeen she met a boy who took her to a church retreat, where she became a believer. Sobbing as she came forward, she was unable to believe that she could be forgiven. A serious illness forced her to leave college and her promising Olympic career and return to her stepfamily to recover. When she went back to college she met Tom, who she was going to save from drugs and promiscuity. When they married and she got pregnant, he forced her to choose the baby or him.

When she returned home from her New York abortion, her overwhelming guilt led her to attempt suicide. She missed God's presence in her life during this time. She and Tom conceived again but separated shortly after their daughter was born, as he continued his promiscuous life. She feared another guilt-driven suicide attempt and was relieved to find a good Bible church. In spite of single parenting and empty promiscuity, she completed college. Another pregnancy seemed a direct punishment from God for her sin.

When Sarah approached church members in her pain, anger, and confusion, they loved and accepted her and convinced her God had also forgiven her. She was able to complete the pregnancy with joy. She laughed and cried as she accepted the child as a gift from God, and released her precious baby to a Christian adoption agency. She continued to live in the joy of God's grace and forgiveness for two years. Accepting her own forgiveness, she was able to begin to extend it to her mother, whom she had not seen since she was thirteen. Sarah forgave her stepmother as well, although she limited her exposure to her ongoing caustic ways. This is an example of forgiveness without full relational reconciliation due to dysfunction.

Sarah quickly attributes her ability to forgive others to her own undeserved forgiveness. She acknowledges that she is a terrible sinner saved by grace. She claims that the one who sins most understands our great need for forgiveness. Her forgiveness of herself began when she accepted that Jesus died for her personal sins and loved and accepted her. She was then able to receive her unborn child as a gift from God and lovingly pass her on to a Christian couple. She forgave her mother even though her mother had tried to abort Sarah and had a serious suicide attempt immediately after her birth. She has continued her tough road of forgiveness within her thirty-one-year marriage. There have been difficult issues of dishonesty and sexual addiction. She has continued to walk the line with her husband's sin issues, holding him accountable to honoring God, but struggling to do so in a way that does not feed her anger and resentment. She agrees with me that marital forgiveness is the hardest thing, in large part because of the repetitive nature of the betrayals in love.

> True forgiveness is an act of repentance and obedience.

Remember how I was wrestling with forgiving my intimacy injuries once again at the beginning of this chapter? That "story" has an ending. I wasn't eager to be the first one to break the ice of our growing coldness. It wasn't fair. But I could feel my anger slowly seething and growing, and heaven knows, I knew the ugly place where that would lead. So, I forgave the personal, and hurtful, and unfair, and tormenting repetitive betrayal. A "funny" thing happened after I wrestled with and gave up my need for fairness, my demand for equality, my all-too-common desire to be right. I experienced quickly fading intensity of my self-righteous attitudes. After a day or two, I could barely remember the details of the injuring event, much less that I "gave in." My human self still has to be careful not to tally up the event, lord it over my spouse, or hold on even just a little to self-righteousness over *my* letting go. I really don't do it primarily for myself, or my husband, but

I am motivated like my other sister-friends, out of obedience to the Lord, and it is sweet to return to being right with Him. Once again, the "rightness" of forgiving overcame the "wrongness" of the injury. This outcome of forgiving *is* a true miracle from God.

We women who have told our stories for this chapter have been greatly challenged to grant the undeserved mercy of marital forgiveness. The circumstances of our lives vary widely, but our faces of forgiveness are consistently similar:

- God has graciously granted us all the undeserved mercy of forgiveness of *our* sins.
- Difficult life experiences and being forgiven ourselves facilitate marital forgiveness.
- Bitterness reveals sinfulness.
- Jesus's sacrifice and death calls us out of our human desire to remain bitter or get even.
- The consequence of unforgiveness is too high a price to pay.
- When we say we love Jesus, we *have* to forgive.
- Jesus will provide the power and motivation we need to be able to forgive over and over again.
- Forgiveness is difficult, but it is the right thing to do.

What outcomes have we experienced from our obedience in forgiving?

- Satisfaction of obeying God and knowing we are forgiven.
- Maturing of our faith.
- Freedom from the power of the offender over us.
- Release of negative emotions.
- Realization that we are no longer victims.
- Freedom to love.
- Joy and peace.
- Renewed relationships.

In *The Kite Runner*, Amir's life did not end in a lifetime of unredeemed guilt. When Amir was thirty-eight years old, he was *summoned back to Pakistan by his father's best friend. The elder friend had known all along about Amir's betrayal of his dear childhood friend, Hassan. The friend also revealed another truth. Amir's father was also Hassan's father. Amir and Hassan were stepbrothers. After the initial shock and disbelief, the family friend told Amir that there was a "way to be good again." He informed Amir that although Hassan and his wife had been killed, their eight-year-old son was alive in an orphanage. Amir set out to rescue him from deplorable conditions and connect him with a couple who cared for orphans in Kabul.*

Long story short—the family friend dies. Amir almost loses his life freeing the son. A long hospital stay drags a two-week visit into a month. Slowly Amir sees the light and desires to adopt his blood nephew. In a letter Amir receives after the death of the family friend, he reads the friend's advice to him before he died, which was to:

- *Accept that God has forgiven him.*
- *Forgive himself.*
- *Allow his guilt to lead to good.*

The last scene in the book comes full circle as it describes Amir and his adopted son warming up to each other as they fly a kite together in San Francisco. Amir is the kite runner this time, and he tells his son, "I will run for you a thousand times over." Redemption is sweet.

Will you join Amir and sisters in this chapter in accepting God's forgiveness, forgiving yourself and others, and seeking good out of betrayals?

NOTES

1. Khaled Hosseini, *The Kite Runner* (Toronto: Penguin, 2003).

2. Walter Wangerin, *As For Me and My House* (Nashville: Thomas Nelson, 1990), 95

3. Michael Agnes, editor, *Webster's New World Dictionary*, (New York: Pocket Books, 2003), 63,448.

4. Charles Stanley, "Life Principle Notes," Part 4, *Anger and Forgiveness*, www.intouch.org., Accessed July 15, 2010

5. Anne Lamott, *Traveling Mercies: Some Thoughts on Faith* (New York: Anchor Books, 1999), 134.

6. Henri Nouwen, "Forgiveness: The Name of Love in a Wounded World," *Weavings,* vol. 7, no. 3 (Crossroads, 1992)16.

7. Marsha Means, *Living With Your Husband's Secret Wars* (Grand Rapids: Baker Books, 1999), 155.

8. Everett L. Worthington Jr., "Forgiveness in Marriage," *Christian Counseling Today*, Vol. 12 (2004), 60.

9. Wangerin, *As For Me and My House*, 102.

10. Lewis Smedes, *Forgive and Forget* (New York: Pocket Books, 1984), 124.

CHAPTER 15

INSIDE-OUT CALL

*A life lived listening to the decisive call of God is life lived before
one audience that trumps all others: the Audience of One.*
—Os Guinness

*Novem te, novem me
(May I know you, may I know myself)*
—St. Augustine

*T*HE QUIETLY POWERFUL *true story of Eric Liddell's path to Olympic Gold in the movie* Chariots of Fire *is inspiring. Eric was a Scottish lad attending prestigious Cambridge University post-World War I. His tremendous courage and convictions were veiled in a very kind and humble exterior. This made some say that they had never seen such drive or commitment, it was like an animal, and it unnerved them. His power and tremendous drive did not come from the mortal man, but from the presence of Jesus Christ within him. One of the arenas where this drive came out was in his running. Preaching on the race of life, he once told his wide-eyed audience that there was no formula for winning. But the power to see the race to the end comes from within. It comes when we truly seek the Lord and commit ourselves to his love. His father encouraged him to run in God's name and let the world stand back in wonder. The world did wonder when his convictions led him to refuse to run his Olympic heat on a Sunday.*

Harold Abramson's Olympic aspirations, training, and abilities paralleled Eric's. Their personalities and motivations couldn't have been more opposite. Abramson was visibly driven, nervously compelled, and admitting that he was addicted to running. He was arrogant yet insecure, as his value and worth depended on winning. He told his girlfriend at one point, "If I don't win, I won't run." He lived in frantic pursuit of winning with an even larger fear of losing. Abramson did win at the Olympics, but rather than satisfying him, it felt hollow. The man himself was strong, but his convictions and motivations were weak.

Liddell was able to run when his teammate switched heats with him. He ran like the wind, he ran for God. Prior to the Olympics his beloved sister in ministry expressed her fear about what all this running focus might do to him. She needn't have worried. He planned to finish school, run in the Olympics, and then carry on the work of his father on the mission field in China. He told her, "I believe God made me for a purpose, for China, but he also made me fast. When I run, I feel His pleasure. To give that up would be to hold Him in contempt. To win is to honor Him." And that he did. My hope for each of us is to be confident in saying:

"When I _____, I feel God's pleasure."

We can discover the purpose for our lives by following the path of the inside-out call. Our primary or inner call is our call to relationship with God. This involves fully surrendering and revealing our whole self to Him. We need to acknowledge our false self, our sinful, ugly, don't want to admit to anyone self, so that He can transform us into who He truly made us to be. Then and only then are we prepared to find out what He has called us to do. Inner self-surrender and transformation allow Him to lead and direct us to full revelation of our gifts in service to Him. Our inner call is to a person (God) and our outer call is to a task (specific service to Him). He wants us all to be able to confidently say, "This is what I was made to do."

So, you say, "Nice topic, but what does it have to do with me and my struggling marriage?" I'm glad you asked. By the time you have gotten this far into this book, you are realizing more than ever how changes in society and our thinking can distort our marriage expectations. Marriage was God's great idea, but it was never meant to make us complete or happy. We have each been made specifically by God for a much bigger purpose. When we are able to connect more deeply with God, receive His love for us, and seek and find how we can use the gifts He gave us in service to Him, then we will be fulfilled.

The more we look to be fulfilled by marriage or our spouses, the more disappointment we will experience. In *Man's Search for Meaning*, Viktor Frankl speaks about our happiness being fulfilled by being driven by a cause much larger than ourselves.[1] God's purpose will bring meaning and strength. It will allow happiness to ensue, as we grow in living well in spite of a less than ideal marital situation. We discover this overall purpose through both an inner and outer process.

INNER CALL

Our inner call to relationship with God is necessary groundwork to move forward in service to Him. Unless we are fully surrendered and spend effort listening and knowing God, we will never move beyond square one in finding or pursuing the passionate work

God created us for. Just as our human relationships, we can only develop a deep and intimate relationship with God by spending time with Him, learning about Him, and listening to Him. Check out the books on spiritual disciplines in the resources at the back of this book for a place to start. Other possibilities for growth include the local church, a spiritual mentor, pastors, and Bible study. Os Guiness clarifies what our focus needs to be when he discusses living for the "Audience of One." He speaks about this inner-directed call being the voice that will make the most difference in our lives. He describes our difficulty when we march to our own drummer due to outside influences. He also says, "A life lived listening to the decisive call of God is a life lived before one audience that trumps all others, the Audience of One."[2] Will you join me in learning to live decisively to your most important audience?

When we put God first in our lives, He will begin the not so pretty work of transforming us into our true selves. This begins by being honest about our false and sinful selves. David Benner discusses our true vs. false selves in great detail in *The Gift of Being Yourself*.[3] As children, it is automatic for us to develop the parts of ourselves that are encouraged by the big people in our lives. Our true selves can be inhibited further as we enter school and listen more to others' voices than our own voice. This happens to all children to some degree, but for little girls it is the beginning of losing our true voice in many other ways, as detailed in chapter 3 on identity. We learn to live for others' approval, acquiring stuff, and seeking success as measured by the world's standards.

We are confronted with a painful choice when faking it no longer works. We can decide to stay hidden behind the masks or take them off and excavate the real person underneath. *Second Calling* by Dale Hanson Bourke is all about finding our calling as midlife women. She tells how losing our false selves, or "idols" as she calls them, is a major task to rediscovering our true identity at midlife. Women have a different task at midlife than men. Midlife men move from success to significance, where women need to move from caring for others to caring for themselves.[4] Certainly many women are specialists at putting off their own calling, often having given up a big chunk of themselves for "the fam." We are certainly expert people pleasers, inauthentic livers, and wearers of fake smile masks. There comes a time in many of our lives when the selves we developed for the sake of anyone outside of God don't work anymore. It is scary to peek into this door of admitting our false selves, but as long as we deny them, our true selves cannot emerge. Kay Warren says that the biggest block to women surrendering is our addiction to running our own lives. She tells about how the "Kingdom of Me" becomes a selfish and safe place that prevents us from being fully who God desires.[5]

Parker Palmer discusses how our avoidance of the darkness of our limitations keeps us from growing our strengths. He says, "If we are to live our lives fully and well, we must learn to embrace opposites, to live in creative tension between our limits and our potentials."[6] Therefore, this full acceptance of our limitations and false selves, as well as our talents and gifts, is the first and necessary step toward self-transformation.

I remember when my husband and I were in college. He was taking organic chemistry and I had chemistry 101. I was trying to get some help from my straight-A chemistry husband when I couldn't understand the equations. In light of the blatant differences of our scientific brains, I concluded that I would never be a rocket scientist. It was hard for me to admit. I wanted to be good at chemistry, too. But through my admission of my limits, I felt a great relief and freedom and I was much closer to finding out what I was *really* good at.

When we live for others out of habit or hide behind false versions of us, we will never discover who God made us to be. We have to make a paradigm shift to live from the inside out instead of the outside in. Our "opportunity" to do this often comes because we are just plain tired of living an incongruous existence. Parker Palmer calls the courage to confront this discrepancy the "Rosa Parks decision." He describes the reason Rosa Parks sat down in the white section of the bus in the segregated South. She was not planning on becoming a hero; she was just plain tired of living a divided life. She was tired of living differently on the outside from

the contradictory truths that she held on the inside. She had come
to a point where "no punishment anyone could inflict on her could
be worse than the punishment that she was inflicting on herself in
conspiring for her own diminishment."[7] This is certainly a common
dilemma in the lives of Christian wives necessitating that we take
the following steps to live from the inside out.

- *Acknowledge the fake.* We are more able to become our true
  selves when we are authentic and live out congruent and
  undivided lives. After we acknowledge our fake, sinful,
  and "pleasing others" selves and surrender to God, our
  real self will be able to emerge. This process, centered in
  God, brings our inner and outer selves into congruence in
  preparation for authentic service. Parker Palmer's book,
  titled after an old Quaker saying, *Let Your Life Speak*,
  accurately expresses how this happens. He says, "Before
  I tell my life what I want to do, I need to listen to my life
  telling me who I am—listen for
  the truths and values at the heart
  of my identity."[8] *Acknowledge the
  fake so your real self can emerge.*
  This is a precarious proposition.
  God challenges us to step out in
  faith. He wants us to trust Him
  to guide us into new territory
  of authentic transformation and
  self-discovery.

  > "Before I tell my life what I want to do, I need to listen to my life telling me who I am."

- *Expect resistance.* Obstacles are common on the way to
  uncovering our calling. I began my recent journey in an
  atmosphere of hurt and anger at what the church did
  not provide for hurting women like myself. God forgave
  my less than ideal motives and guided me on in spite of
  myself. I had previously worked as a counselor, trainer, and
  women's program director. In the church I had volunteered
  as a women's Bible study teacher, missions trainer, and
  counselor. I believe that God has combined all of my past

experiences to prepare me to be a teacher and encourager to women in difficult marriages. I poured my heart out in my journal for two years before I stepped out in faith with my first class for women. At the time I began, my marriage was not a shining example. But by God's grace alone, I continued to follow His leading. I definitely felt the fear that both John Ortberg and Bruce Wilkinson talk about in their books about following our calling. The fear we experience as we step out of our comfort zone is normal. It can only be reduced as we move courageously forward through it. If we sit around waiting to feel fearless, we will be waiting a long time. I like how John Ortberg's book title, *If You Want to Walk on Water, You've Got to Get Out of the Boat*, expresses our dilemma so explicitly. We can't move into what God has for us if we stay where it is safe.

"Ordinary," the parable character in Wilkerson's *The Dream Giver*, finds that once he has left his comfort zone, he is not done with fears. He meets various bullies along the way.[9] Women face particular bullies due to spending much of our lives serving and pleasing others and denying ourselves. When we do step out to spend time and energy seeking God's plan for our gifts, those we have been serving may not exactly celebrate. As it is with Ordinary, we are often faced with resistance from those around us who are concerned for us, but also fear our changes nearly as much as we do. Some of my "bullies" were people who did not understand what I was trying to do. *Expect resistance and fear.*

- *Expect pain.* Another normal obstacle that we experience as we seek our calling is a time of storms and pain. As it was with Peter when he walked on the water, he was fine until the storm came and fear overtook him. The path to our fulfillment will not be without storms like Peter's. They will be used by God to strengthen us and prepare us for what is to follow. Ortberg talks extensively about how the storms and the fears are actually an indicator that we are on the right path.[10] It is normal to experience pain along the way. *Expect storms and pain.* Expect to be confronted with a decision to focus on fear of sinking, or trusting God to keep you up.

- *Expect to wait.* Oooooooh, I really don't like this last obstacle to finding our calling. Waiting. I think I can say with complete accuracy that my desired time frames for things happening in my life have *never* been the same as God's. Bummer. But wise, and purposeful, and all-knowing, after all He *is* God. Americans are not very good at delaying gratification to maturity, myself included. *Expect to wait for God's timing for change.*

Sue Monk Kidd has an excellent book on the necessity of waiting, called *When the Heart Waits.* She says we have all bought into the cultural myth that when we wait we are doing nothing. She claims instead that when we wait we are "waiting for our soul to grow up." And that it is only when we are still and waiting that we can become what God created us to be. She eloquently equates our process with the necessary waiting done as a cocoon evolves into a butterfly, and being rushed destroys the beautiful outcome.[11]

My path to writing this book has been laden with fear, doubt, waiting, bullies, storms, and pain, but in spite of all of these things God keeps bringing me back to what He wants me to do. Romans 11:29 confirms that, "God's gifts and call are irrevocable."

Outer Call

After we have surrendered ourselves fully to God and begun to know our true selves, we can embark on the great adventure of uncovering our outer call. This is the work that God has prepared and gifted us to do in service to Him.

Although there are spiritual gift inventories that help us uncover our gifts, there is no quick or secret formula. Ask your pastor for a gifts inventory that he would recommend. We need to be in prayer and consult those who know us as we do what John Ortberg calls "low cost probes" regarding discovery of our gifts.[12] We just begin to try things and be flexible to God's guidance in shutting and opening doors along the way. It reminds me of what Blackaby says in *Experiencing God*: Find where God is working and join Him.[13] Below are some things you can ask yourself to get started.

Application Questions:

1. What activities did I do as a child that I got lost in and felt fulfilled doing?
2. What do I love doing for its own sake despite the rewards?
3. What have others told me that I am good at?

LIVING STRONG

Jan had been married for eighteen years to a man who was much more interested in private time on his computer porn sites than with her. It seemed all they had in common was a mutual love and support of their daughter. Jan had worked before and after her daughter's birth, but sensed a rather vague urging for more as her daughter neared leaving for college.

Jan headed off to a short-term mission trip with the message "The spirit of the Sovereign Lord is upon you" ringing in her head from her Bible study. She wove her story of fears, inadequacy, and need for a Savior into children's craft times.

Her desire to serve the Lord with meaningful eternal work was ignited. Her former jobs paled in light of the kingdom work she was being drawn into. Our pastor commonly encouraged congregants to step out and do any jobs available in the church. He said with a smile, "Any job worth doing is worth doing badly." As we step out in faith and serve in any available area, the worst we can do is to do it badly, with the hope that along the way we will discover what God has designed us to do.

Jan experimented with numerous opportunities. She took a spiritual gifts inventory and did testing at the technical college. She began to experience the evolution of her urgings into her calling as she volunteered with a friend as a hospice activity assistant at a nursing home. A year later she got a part time job as an activity assistant. A few years later she was ready for more challenging work and became employed as the activity director for a Christian group home for mentally ill adults. Their daughter had been her life and joy and would be going away to college soon. Jan feared being alone with her husband, and was seeking an identity beyond wife and mother. This job was fulfilling, demanding, and completing. She had found the work she was made to do.

I asked Jan why this work was such a fit. With tears in her eyes, she calmly replied that she had experienced the same feelings of rejection and lack of acceptance as the men and women she ministered to. She did not need special training or education to know what they needed. They needed the same things that she had needed in her empty marriage. Her work helped her make sense of and redeemed some of the pain of her tough marriage.

She had a place where she fit and felt needed and appreciated. She blossomed in other areas by taking art classes, playing her beloved flute, and traveling with friends. She was proactive in seeking God and what He had made her to do. She has discovered fulfillment, joy, and peace, which she hadn't felt for a long time. Although her marriage is still hard after twenty-seven years, she has taken responsibility for her own happiness. Becoming stronger and more fulfilled with God's perfect love has reduced the hurt from her marriage. She has been surprised at some connections she and her husband are beginning to develop. She can see how their past friendship is gradually returning.

Jan found meaning in her suffering marriage and thus redeemed it to an extent. In *Man's Search for Meaning*, Viktor Frankl quotes Nietzsche's words: "He who has a why to live can bear with almost any how."[14] Frankl talks about our common existential problem that when we come to the end of ourselves through unchangeable circumstances, we are forced to be transformed. I am thankful that Jan allowed God to transform her within her unchangeable circumstances.

BECOMING STRONG AND COURAGEOUS

Jan struggled tremendously in her loveless marriage. She was a trooper, making the best of a bad situation as she was engaged in church, work, and raising her daughter. She felt an urging from the Lord to move toward work with more eternal value. She had no master plan on what that was or how to discover it. She was both dumbfounded and sure when she eventually ended up being a tremendous friend and encouragement to mentally ill adults.

I have seen similar outcomes over and over with hurting women. The pain of their circumstances brought them to their knees to connect with God on a deeper level. In the process of focusing on God instead of their difficult circumstances, they found a new and often surprising identity. They have then discovered with confident assurance the work God made them to do. Other examples are the mom who rediscovered her love of dance and went on to teach children. And the woman who was disappointed in what the church did not offer for hurting women and developed a program to bring hope to them, and to herself along the way as well. (It's me!) And the woman who identified that she had been sexually abused and used her righteous indignation to heal. She then learned how to facilitate the healing and empowerment of other abused women as encouraged in 2 Corinthians 1:3-5.

These stories exemplify what Viktor Frankl discovered in individuals who survived their concentration camp experience. He found that those who survived were able to find meaning in their suffering. The tension experienced between suffering and seeking a purpose is the motivating factor that draws us out of ourselves to a much larger cause. Frankl, a psychiatrist who survived a concentration camp himself, says that happiness cannot be pursued, but must ensue from getting outside of ourselves to a much larger meaning. He even goes so far to say that depression, aggression, and addictions are the result of our failure to find meaning in suffering.[15] That is very close to the message of this chapter—that we need to learn to live from the inside out.

John Maxwell has written an inspirational book bursting with accounts of individuals who refused to allow their many failures to defeat them. In his closing chapters he gives these simple but profound guidelines for change:

- See yourself clearly.
- Admit your flaws honestly.
- Discover your strengths joyfully.
- Build on those strengths passionately.[16]

The Covenant Prayer
(Adapted from John Wesley's original covenant prayer)

I am no longer my own, but yours.
Put me to what you will, rank me with whom you will;
Put me to doing, put me to suffering;
let me be employed for you or laid aside for you,
exalted for you or brought low for you;
let me be full, let me be empty;
let me have all things, let me have nothing;
I freely and heartily yield all things to your pleasure and disposal.
And now, O glorious and blessed God, Father, Son and Holy Spirit
You are mine, and I am yours.
So be it.
And the covenant which I have made on earth,
let it be ratified in heaven.
Amen.[17]

Will you pray to be transformed from the inside out?

NOTES

1. Viktor Frankl, *Man's Search for Meaning* (Boston: Beacon Press, 1959), 139.
2. Os Guiness, *The Call* (Nashville: Word, 1998), 71.
3. David Benner, *The Gift of Being Yourself* (Downers Grove, IL: InterVarsity, 2004), 75.
4. Dale Hanson Burke, *Second Calling* (Brentwood, TN: Integrity, 2006), 90.
5. Kay Warren, *Dangerous Surrender* (Grand Rapids: Zondervan, 2007), 37.
6. Parker Palmer, *Let Your Life Speak* (San Francisco: Jossey-Bass, 2000), 55.
7. Palmer, *Let Your Life Speak*, 32.
8. Palmer, *Let Your Life Speak*, 3.
9. Bruce Wilkinson, *The Dream Giver* (Sisters, OR: Multnomah, 2003), 27.
10. John Ortberg, *If You Want to Walk on Water, You've Got to Get Out of the Boat* (Grand Rapids: Zondervan, 2001), 111.
11. Sue Monk Kidd, *When the Heart Waits* (San Francisco: Harper, 1990), 22.
12. Ortberg, *If You Want to Walk on Water*, 69.
13. Henry Blackaby, *Experiencing God* (Nashville: LifeWay, 1990), 29.
14. Frankl, *Man's Search for Meaning*, 84.
15. Frankl, *Man's Search for Meaning*, 143.
16 John Maxwell, *Failing Forward* (Nashville: Thomas Nelson, 2000), 114.
17. John Wesley, "Convenant Prayer," http://en.wikipedia.org/wiki/Wesley_Covenant_Prayer, accessed October 10, 2009.

CHAPTER 16

WEAKNESS INTO STRENGTH BY FAITH

Life is not simply holding a good hand.
Life is playing a poor hand well.
—Danish proverb

We are free to determine what happens to what happens to us.
—Gerald Mann

- *He chose to live honorably even when rejected and discarded by his brothers.*
- *He chose a positive attitude under hardships of slavery.*
- *He chose to accept unjust imprisonment.*
- *He chose to succeed in prison.*
- *He chose to forgive unfairness.*
- *He chose to live a godly life, under ungodly circumstances.*

J OSEPH CHOSE ALL of these responses to his mostly unfair life circumstances. He is a major poster child for resilience in the Bible. Out of all of his difficult, unfair, unbelievable circumstances, he chose to persevere, have faith, and get stronger in spite of them. It is a promise after all that we will have trouble in this world, even in marriage.[1] We are told not to be surprised at the painful trials that we suffer, and we are to share also in the sufferings of Christ.[2] We are told to rejoice in our sufferings and expect them to produce perseverance, character, and hope.[3] Finally, when we identify with Christ and his sufferings, we can also share in the power of His resurrection.[4]

These statements all sound very spiritual and encouraging, but anyone who has been through trials and tragedies knows that victories don't come easily. So how *do we* bounce back and become resilient from the difficulties life brings? How *do we* make choices to transform the negatives of our lives into strengths and even praise the Lord for them? How *do we* develop hope from despair? As believers, the pain that brings us crashing to our knees can become the springboard to the hope and redemption that saves us. I hope that the pain of adversity and the glimmer of belief in the transformational power of the resurrected Jesus urges you on, to dare to believe your pain can be redeemed. I want to see us all choose to move from victim to victor in Him.

What Is Resilience?

Resilience is our ability to bounce back or recover from adversity. It relates to our interpretation of life events. When we choose to respond positively to life's challenges, we can develop lifelong strengths. Factors that influence our resilience include our personality, self-esteem, past experiences, family life, and our positive coping skills.

I appreciate the work of Steven and Sybil Wolin in the area of family and childhood resilience. Their research evolved from their observations of families. Steven is an M.D. and a psychiatrist working with families of disabled children. His wife, Sybil, is a child development specialist who does therapy with the same population. They both observed some striking differences in how families dealt with challenging situations. Some families got stronger, used all available resources, and thrived in spite of their difficulties. Other families shriveled up and died a slow death. Steve and Sybil set out to study why and how these families had such differing responses to similar issues, and reported their findings in their book, *The Resilient Self.*

The group that crumbled in adversity followed what the Wolins call the *damage model.* Our U.S. medical and psychological systems have traditionally focused on problems, illness, and weakness as the basis for treating individuals. Those who ascribe to this model have reduced ability to recover, and instead exhibit what we call "learned helplessness." These reactive victims are usually prone to dependence, unable and uninformed about helping themselves. People stuck here reap the "benefits" of blaming others for their problems, getting sympathy for their pain, and not taking responsibility for themselves or their reactions to challenging life events.

I have to admit, it is appealing at times to adopt this victim role. The trouble with a pity party is that it's boring and not many people come. This illness model has preceded the development of the positive, proactive, and strength-based approach of resilience.

Even though they experienced similar tragedies, the *challenge group* of families coped better and developed strengths from their adversity. They experienced pain and losses but were able to respond positively. Over time they were able to reframe and shift their views of the difficulties into opportunities to grow and get stronger. These families did what seemed miraculous. They fully felt and experienced the pain of family traumas, yet simultaneously rebounded with positive strength-building activities.[5] The resilience movement is one of learned optimism, with a focus on solutions and strength-building skills. God certainly repeatedly challenges believers to take responsibility and develop strength through struggles. When we seek God's purposes in our weakness and struggles, He promises to transform them, by faith[6]

The Wolins reminded me of an excellent example of resilience as expressed in the movie *City Slickers*. In one scene, the three adventure "cowboys" were riding their horses and sharing the best and worst days of their lives. Ed resisted sharing until last. He hesitatingly described witnessing another fight between his mom and dad. It was the day he realized that his father was not only cheating on his mother, but on the whole family. Ed gathered the courage out of his pain to tell his father, "You're bad to us. We don't love you."

His father left that day, and fourteen-year-old Ed took care of his mother and sister from that day forward. Ed told his cowboy friends that was his best day. Dumbfounded, they asked what his worst day was. He said, "Same day." The Wolins describe his experience as the paradox of *Survivor's Pride*,[7] the ability to transform adversity into strength. The Wolins' work involves assisting survivors to identify how they have been able to reframe their family traumas into strengths. Without exception, these individuals burst with relief and pride as they embrace their coping as survivors.

> We show survivors pride when we convert adversity into strength.

Application Questions:

1. Do you have a tendency to see your world as a glass half full, or half empty?

2. Do you know where you might have adopted this approach? Would you like to be more proactive in choosing to become more optimistic? Why or why not?

How Can Experiencing Adversity Be Beneficial?

Sounds a little silly even to say. Are there really benefits to the difficulties, traumas, and adversities that we experience? Yes, lots of them. None of us would ever ask for these heartrending tragedies in our lives, but the truth is "stuff happens" and we can get stronger as a result.

- We come to the end of thinking we are in control of anything, and fall to our knees in dependence on God. *Dependence is a benefit.*
- When He has our full and submitted attention, then the real work of growing us up begins. *Maturity is a benefit.*
- We are challenged to cope with difficulties of life in differing ways. This often results in developing more skills and building new strengths. *Skills and strength are benefits.*
- When the ways we have lived no longer work, we have to dig deep creatively in new and different ways. *Creativity and motivation are benefits.*
- Last, but not least, when tough circumstances find us hanging on by our fingernails we know we cannot do this thing called life alone. We are pushed to ask for help and support from others. *Relationships are a benefit.*

Trouble is, to receive any of these benefits we have to give up control, submit to God, look for truth, develop skills, get creative, and ask for help. This is hard to do, but the choice is ours.

Choosing Survival

Fred Epstein is a pediatric neurosurgeon who wrote a meaningful little book about resilient kids, called *If I Get to Five: What Children Can Teach Us About Resilience and Character.* He has seen many young patients show supernatural, life-changing resilience over and over again.

Naomi is the little girl who inspired the book and is a classic example of kids showing a resilience that shames many adults. Naomi was recovering her strength and awaiting her second, more dangerous brain surgery. She would excitedly say to Dr. Fred, "If I get to five, I'm going to beat my older brother at tic-tac-toe." "If I get to five, I'm going to ride a two wheeler." "If I get to five...." "If I get to five...." This little four year old knew she might not make it to five, but in spite of that, she lived fully in the present and held hope for the future.

Children's innocence allows them to not be sidetracked by the "I can't" or "I won't" of cynical adults. Children don't focus on past failures to predict the future. They are naturals at finding ways to redeem the suffering they experience, inspiring those around them to do the same. Dr. Epstein claims, "To the degree that we can continue to access our childhood strengths as adults, we will be more resilient, successful, and fulfilled."[8] Norman Wright says that crises lead us to be a yesterday person, or a tomorrow person.[9]

Dr. Epstein's observations became oh-so-personal when he experienced a serious head injury from a bike accident at sixty years of age. The very children he had saved became his heroes. They were role models for his long and painstaking recovery. We can learn a lot from suffering children. I don't know if this is exactly what Jesus meant when he said that we should be like little children, but I know that having their humility and their unpretentious and honest innocence would help me face my fears and difficulties more effectively than my "adult" pity party, denial, isolation, and do-it-myself approach.[10]

> Children don't focus on past failures to predict future success.

Examples of individuals who have persevered under difficult circumstances abound. I have benefited greatly from searching biographies of individuals who inspire me and draw me into more faithful living. We are often totally unaware that "famous" individuals have often had times of trial. Did you know:

- In a study of 413 gifted and famous people, 80 percent of them hated school.
- Seven out of ten of them came from very dysfunctional homes troubled by alcoholism, abuse, poverty, absent parents, and handicaps.[11]

- Dr. Steven Wolin discovered that two-thirds of abused children *do not* abuse others.[12]
- Seventy percent of kids from alcoholic families *do not* abuse alcohol.[13]

Obviously, these individuals made choices to be different from what their environment taught. For more inspiring real-life examples of popular and everyday individuals who refused to be stopped by failures on their way to success, I highly recommend Dr. Maxwell's book, *Failing Forward*. Maxwell expounds on his premise that the only way for us all to get ahead is to fail early, fail often, and fail forward.[14]

Biblical examples also abound. Job and Joseph are classic examples of faithful men who clung to God in spite of their never-ending traumatic circumstances. They certainly represent examples of resilience of biblical proportions. I tend to relate to the more obscure examples. I like the story of the woman at the well. She had a bad reputation, multiple husbands, and was not appropriate to talk to Jesus. Yet she came, thirsty for the living water that He offered. This woman was hesitant, ashamed, probably pretty beaten down by life. She was willing to grab a hope beyond her circumstances, allowing Jesus to touch and transform her.

The woman with the long-time bleeding issue was so ashamed and unworthy that she snuck up and touched just the bottom of Jesus's robe. She had great faith and was healed. Naomi was another woman who'd lost all she had. She was faithful and rose above her difficult circumstances, did what was right, and chose resilience. These individuals were able to reframe or redefine the meaning of their tragedies. Their future focus transformed their possible pity parties to a positive outcome and restored hope. They all exhibited Survivor's Pride.

Living Strong

Jane is another woman I admire who has shown remarkable faith and resilience throughout her lifetime. Both of her parents were alcoholic and abusive. She married her boyfriend after knowing him for thirty days. He left for Vietnam shortly and returned a year later a raging alcoholic with PTSD. Her husband was a responsible provider and a functional but disengaged alcoholic. The trials continued as Jane had back surgeries after each pregnancy, which involved body casts. She and their two young sons received loving care from a dear friend of hers who was a believer. Her friend taught Jane by example about a good and loving God, a description that was opposed to the critical and judgmental one she knew from her upbringing. Jane came to know the Lord personally through her friend, but she was hurt, angry, and resentful, because she was not able to bond with her babies or receive love from her husband.

Jane took her spiritual recovery seriously as she searched and prayed for a good Bible church in her area. She soon found a startup church, which she joined and in which she quickly became involved. She felt from day one that God had provided that church just for her. This also began her emotional and relational recovery, as she was referred to Al-Anon (families of alcoholics) and Adult Children of Alcoholics (ACOA) groups for education and recovery from the effects of alcohol in her life.

Today Jane sees that God was urging her to change herself before she began working on her marriage. She grew tremendously spiritually and discovered she was a controller, was overly responsible, and could not fix her husband. After attending Al-Anon for a few years, she was prepared to move to another level relationally.

She began by setting boundaries, including insisting that her husband and sons get help and go to counseling. When her husband relapsed in his AA efforts, she insisted he go into treatment, although he was also strongly motivated by the addictive habits of their teenage sons. Jane's husband grew tremendously as he continued treatment. Although their young-adult sons had struggles, she worked hard at staying out of the way. Jane and her husband both experienced much guilt and shame at the ongoing generational patterns of family struggle.

The next few times her husband had drinking relapses, she prayed for him and realized for the first time that God expected her to do more than just tolerate him. She actively worked at engaging with him on a deeper level. She trusted God and her husband more and more, by faith. She felt led to apologize to her husband for her former controlling, abusive, and dysfunctional ways. It was so difficult to do, she first whispered, "I'm sorry," into his ear when he was sleeping. Since then, she has been able to apologize sincerely, directly, and even when he has been awake!

Jane and her husband have experienced phenomenal relational recovery over their forty-five years together. The challenges of their lives have continued. In the last few years her mother, brother, and oldest grandson have all died. One of her sons was in prison for drinking and driving, and the other one had serious medical issues from an accident. Jane continues to struggle with arthritis and back issues, but that does not stop her from working, riding her custom Harley motorcycle, and serving the Lord. She has seen five of her rebellious family of ten come to the Lord. She has seen God do miracles of love and care in her family that she thought would never happen. Her philosophy as a natural pessimist is to bemoan the losses in her life, but she chooses to grieve honestly and remain closely connected to the Lord and other positive believers. Her faith leads her to seek the plans that God has for her, whatever trials come along. Sounds like a resilient survivor to me.

BE STRONG AND COURAGEOUS, AND FIND MEANING IN SUFFERING

Job and Joseph survived and found meaning, Jane survived with meaning, Naomi and the Samaritan woman survived and found meaning. What can we learn from them about surviving life's many struggles? "It is significant that our Lord presented no formula relative to the why and what of suffering. Instead, He presented a way of victory and triumphant living in the face of suffering.[15] Our primary mode to become survivors in our difficult marriages is acceptance of what God does and does not promise:

- God has a purpose in our suffering. (Romans 8:28)
- God is present in our suffering. (Deuteronomy 31:6)

- His grace is sufficient in our suffering. (2 Corinthians 12:9)
- His strength is made perfect in our weakness. (2 Corinthians 12:9)
- He brings peace through our suffering. (Philippians 4:7)
- He brings strength through our suffering, by faith. (Hebrews 11:34b)

What are we to do? Stuff happens. Life's not fair. The pain is deep, and it lasts too long. I include myself with these women who have done what Bill O'Hanlon calls "following their wounds." He claims that we need to accept our wounds to become stronger. We need to express our negative emotions, be upset, and be angry for a season, and then turn it into a contribution.[16] When we accept the thorns, like Paul did, we can develop a "new normal" and discover how God leads us to meaning out of our tragedy. When we deny or run from the hurt, we become reluctant warriors, disempowered, and unable to fight our foes and fears. Ben Franklin summed it up by saying: "The things which hurt, instruct." Scripture guides us in the same way as the apostle Paul encourages us to comfort others with the comfort we have received from God in our suffering.[17]

None of us asks for the trials we receive. Upon hearing that one of his adult children had cancer, Dr. Epstein said what we all think when adversity strikes: "This is the test of courage I never wanted to pass."[18] I know I never wished for a near-divorce in our marriage, which would lead me to develop a ministry to other hurting wives. I also know:

- Shari didn't choose to develop a ministry to other mothers grieving the death of a young-adult child.
- Kristi did not plan to develop a ministry to others who miscarried or lost infants.
- Karen did not strive to minister to other sexually abused women
- Sarah didn't dream of ministering to other wives with husbands into porn.

- Jan did not wish to be fulfilled by loving mentally ill adults with the love she never received in her difficult marriage.
- Mary did not dream of encouraging women who struggle with their husbands' serious sexual addictions.

Viktor Frankl survived and found meaning in suffering by following his horrific wounds from living in a concentration camp for three years. His entire family died in a camp. Prior to his forced stay in the camp he had been a psychiatrist, but he became "Number 119,104" in camp. Viktor came away from his near-death years with some powerful conclusions about human suffering and resilience:

- Even when every possible thing is taken away, a person still has a choice over his thoughts.
- Finding a meaning bigger than ourselves is imperative as a chosen response to suffering.
- Our search for meaning for our lives is a primary motivation for all people.
- Individuals who were not able to find meaning in the concentration camps died.
- It is normal and healthy to have tension about where we are and where we are to go in life.
- When suffering is unavoidable, we are forced look at ourselves and search for meaning in it.
- We can only be fully ourselves when we forget ourselves for a cause bigger than ourselves.
- *Tragic optimism* is our ability to make the most of a difficult situation through change and taking responsible action.[19]

In his book *Resilience*, Norman Wright listed things that survivors say. Even if the women above did not say these exact words, they certainly are examples of living them out. I recommend that you copy a few of them and stick them on your refrigerator until you believe them!

- "I will examine the future and let it guide what I do in the present."
- "No matter what happens, I will not allow myself to be defeated. I will keep trying and not give up."
- "I am a fortunate person, regardless of what I have experienced."
- "I will take advantage of every available opportunity."
- "I can accept my imperfections and learn to enjoy life and give to others."
- "I can find meaning in situations and events that involve suffering or great loss."
- "I will not allow myself to behave as a victim."
- "I'm determined to keep pushing ahead."
- "I am willing to grow and change and learn new roles."
- "I want to be involved with people who will build me up and help me grow."
- "I can face the challenge of life and handle the stresses and crises of life without denying their existence or giving up."[20]

So, friends, let us follow our wounds rather than fight them. Let us refuse to become victims and let us find meaning in our suffering. Let's become Wild Warrior Women. Let us put on the full armor of God to wage war against the enemy who would have us give up on our marriages and God's plan for our lives. Let us arm ourselves as warriors in this spiritual battle.[21] Let us be wild and strong about how we fight for our families and marriages. Let us radically challenge the views of the world, which would have us be victims stuck in pity parties who talk about how we "deserve" to be happy. Let us be empowered to take responsibility for our own happiness in God's power. Let us learn more about marriage so we can face its reality rather than its imagined enemies.

Let us follow the example of the earthy, everyday women of Lockerbie, Scotland. These warrior women lost homes and family and friends from the bombing of Pan Am Flight 103 as it flew over their rural community in 1988. They fought international red tape to turn their personal trauma into a passionate battle. They fought to be able to wash the tattered, bloodied clothing of crash victims. They fought to be able to return them to the shocked families as a final tribute to those who died. This compassionate response to others' struggling with the senseless loss of life began the healing of all. As a result of their actions, they were able to make meaning of their suffering and move everyone from the grieving of despair to the grieving of hope.[22]

Will you commit to becoming a Wild Warrior Woman with me?

NOTES

1. John 16:33, 1 Corinthians 7:28
2. 1 Peter 4:12, Romans 8:17.
3. Romans 5:3-5.
4. Romans 8:17.
5. "How to Survive (Practically) Anything," *Psychology Today* (January 1992): http://www.psychology today.com/print/20618, accessed March 10, 2010.
6. Hebrews 11:34b.
7. Steve Wolin and Sybil Wolin, *The Resilient Self* (New York: Villard Books, 1993), 12.
8. Fred Epstein, *If I Get to Five* (New York: Henry Holt, 2003), 136.
9. Norman H. Wright, *Resilience* (Ann Arbor: Servant, 1997), 200.
10. Matthew 18:3-4.
11. Wright, *Resilience*, 157.
12. Wolin and Wolin, *The Resilient Self*, 15.
13. Wolin and Wolin, *The Resilient Self*, 90.
14 John Maxwell, *Failing Forward* (Nashville: Thomas Nelson, 2000), 114.
15. Stephen Olford, *Sword of Suffering* (Chattanooga: AMG, 2001), 24.
16. Bill O'Hanlon, *Change 101* (New York: W. W. Norton & Company, 2006), 4.

17. 2 Corinthians 1:3-7.

18. Epstein, *If I Get to Five*, 126.

19. Viktor Frankl, *Man's Search for Meaning* (Boston: Beacon Press, 1959), 147.

20. Wright, *Resilience*, 191.

21. Ephesians 6:10-18.

22. Deborah Brevoort, "The Women of Lockerbie" (play at Festival of Faith and Writing, Calvin College, 2008).

CONCLUSION:
FARM FIELDS AND
CEMETERIES

*He is no fool who gives what he cannot
keep to gain what he cannot lose.*
—Jim Elliot

I HOPE AND pray that this story of courage and faith inspires you to move past fears of the known and unknown in your challenging marriage. It is about a "test of courage they never wanted to pass."[1]

When I turned fifty, I began to exercise more regularly, riding my bike and swimming and walking. Each spring when I returned outside from a long winter in the gym, I rediscovered some new aches and pains from the increased intensity of exercise. As I went huffing and puffing past the newly plowed farm fields on my garage sale bike, I often recalled my farmer friends Warren and Donna.

My husband had done their cow work as their veterinarian and he and Warren had many a good spiritual discussion amidst C-sections and downed cows. Our sons were in school and wrestled together, resulting in a lot of shared bleacher time as parents. With none of their children interested in continuing farming, Warren and Donna followed their call to the mission field in their early forties. They parted with their cows and equipment and furnishings and struggled with leaving their families. It was evident to all during furlough from Africa that they were where right where God wanted them to be. They were excited, challenged, and full of joy. It wasn't like it was easy. Their first few positions were much different from expected. They were sustained by their faith and knowledge that they were in the center of God's will and their hardworking, persevering farm mentality. They were compelled to go and persevere on the often hard path that the Lord had for them, and they did it with joy.

I also think of our dear friends when I pass by the country cemetery on my bike, because Warren and Donna were violently murdered about seven years into their missionary service in Uganda. They were finally getting settled into a ministry that fit them on a rural agricultural station and their stone house was being built. They gave their lives for the work they were called to do. They made the ultimate sacrifice. As I ride by those farm fields, with little green shoots of corn coming up in straight rows, and as I ride past the country cemetery, my memories of Warren and Donna give me strength beyond my burning muscles and my hurting heart.

As women in difficult marriages, we need to live in exactly the same place as my friends, not in Africa, but in the center of God's will for our lives. When we live there, we face our fears with His strength, knowing we will *never* be left alone. We persevere in much less than ideal circumstances as God leads. We live contentedly with strength and courage in spite of our difficulties. We do not profess to know the outcome of our faithful living. We put on the full armor of God as we become "Wild Warrior Women," hoping and praying for healthy marital reconciliation.

We *can* often influence the health of our marriage. Yet we are only half of the marriage equation and sometimes we have divorce done to us. One-third of struggling marriages suffer the damage and danger resulting from addictions, adultery, or abuse. Often these "Triple Threats" have taken too much of a toll, and staying is not even wise. So we press on in our faith, we persevere in doing what is right, we pray for marital well-being. But if it does not occur, we continue on, living in the truth and the path of faith that God has laid out for us.

Warren and Donna modeled a courageous and sacrificial faith and give me strength to carry on in my far from perfect marriage. They took the difficult path, obediently following what God called them to do, and they did it with all of their hearts. They were models to me of believers who lived by 1 Corinthians 9:24-26. They went into strict training to be able to run to get the prize that will last forever. They did not run aimlessly so as to be disqualified for the prize. They were compelled by their call to live and trust their God over the circumstances. They did not live for themselves, but for Him who died for them. And then they made the ultimate sacrifice and died for Him.

When I feel tired, rejected, frustrated, or alone, or when I don't want to forgive again and again, I often remember my friends. They persevered to the very end, making sacrifices for their faith. Can I not do the same? Can I be as faithful as they were to allow God to strengthen me as I follow the harder path? Will I be able to persevere, no matter what happens, with the joy that they showed?

Will I hear God say to me when I enter His presence, "Well done, my good and faithful servant"[2]?

Will you?

NOTES

1. Fred Epstein, *If I Get to Five* (New York: Henry Holt, 2003), 126.
2. Matthew 25:21.

APPENDIX A:

KNOWING GOD

"YOU'RE NOT THE BOSS OF ME!"

W HEN MY SON was about three years old he was quite angry that I pulled him away from the busy street. I still remember his tearful, pouty face and his arms crossed across his chest as he confidently announced, "You're not the boss of me!"

As they say, "The apple does not fall far from the tree." I also did not want to have anyone be the boss of my life. At thirty-two years of age, I was an angry, depressed, lonely, unloved woman and I was searching for answers. My marriage was falling apart and I had run out of human options. Most of us come to a point in our self-managed lives where we realize we need help. We need a boss, and it is God. When we are broken and searching, this is what we need to do:

1. Admit we've failed in managing our own lives. (Romans 3:23: "All have sinned and fallen short of the glory of God.")

2. Ask Jesus to come into our life and forgive us. (1 John 1:9: "If we confess our sins, he is faithful and just and will forgive us our sins and purify us from all unrighteousness.")

3. Live in the peace and fullness He will give us. (Romans 5:1: "We have peace with God through our Lord Jesus Christ," and John 10:10: "'I have come that they may have life, and have it to the full.'")

4. Join a local church and grow within your new family. He will be the best Boss we have ever had. He will love us, accept us, guide us, and correct us. The payment for connecting with this Eternal Boss is also great. We will receive the peace and security that we will never be alone and will spend eternity with Him in heaven.

Will you join me in asking God to be your forever Boss?

Appendix B:
The Image of Me

Your word is a lamp to my feet and a light for my path.
—Psalm 119:105

THE TOPIC OF self-esteem can be confusing. God certainly wants us to be wholly who He made us to be. But in our self-centered society today, the way we care for ourselves needs to be balanced with a healthy dose of humility. Selfishness in marriage is a particularly difficult trait to deal with. We need to develop ourselves, but not at the constant expense of our family. We need to love and serve and sacrifice for our families, but not totally at our own expense.

We have all been influenced regarding how we view ourselves by the people and experiences in our upbringing. No matter what our experience has been, we will function our best as we fully embrace who God says we are. Our image of ourselves needs to be based on God's truths regarding His love, acceptance, and empowerment of us!

Truth #1: God loves me.

> But God demonstrates his own love for us in this: While we were still sinners, Christ died for us.
>
> —Romans 5:8

No, in all these things we are more than conquerors through him who loved us. For I am convinced that neither death nor life, neither angels nor demons, neither the present nor the future, nor any powers, neither height nor depth, nor anything else in all creation, will be able to separate us from the love of God that is in Christ Jesus our Lord.

—Romans 8:37-39

This is how God showed his love among us: He sent his one and only Son into the world that we might live through him. This is love: not that we loved God, but that he loved us and sent his Son as an atoning sacrifice for our sins. Dear friends, since God so loved us, we also ought to love one another. No one has ever seen God; but if we love one another, God lives in us and his love is made complete in us.

—1 John 4:9-12

TRUTH #2: GOD MADE ME AND CHOSE ME.

For you created my inmost being; you knit me together in my mother's womb. I praise you because I am fearfully and wonderfully made; your works are wonderful, I know that full well. My frame was not hidden from you when I was made in the secret place. When I was woven together in the depths of the earth, your eyes saw my unformed body. All the days ordained for me were written in your book before one of them came to be.

—Psalm 139:13-16

For we are God's workmanship, created in Christ Jesus to do good works, which God prepared in advance for us to do.

—Ephesians 2:10

For he chose us in him before the creation of the world to be holy and blameless in his sight. In love he predestined us to be adopted as his sons through Jesus Christ, in accordance with his pleasure and will.

—Ephesians 1:4-5

But you are a chosen people, a royal priesthood, a holy nation, a people belonging to God, that you may declare the praises of him who called you out of darkness into his wonderful light.

—1 Peter 2:9

TRUTH #3: GOD WILL NEVER LEAVE ME OR FORSAKE ME.

For the LORD loves the just and will not forsake his faithful ones. They will be protected forever, but the offspring of the wicked will be cut off.

—Psalm 37:28

The LORD is with me; I will not be afraid. What can man do to me?

—Psalm 118:6

The LORD will keep you from all harm— he will watch over your life; the LORD will watch over your coming and going both now and forevermore.

—Psalm 121:7-8

My sheep listen to my voice; I know them, and they follow me. I give them eternal life, and they shall never perish; no one can snatch them out of my hand.

—John 10:27-28

TRUTH #4: GOD STRENGTHENS AND EMPOWERS ME.

I pray that out of his glorious riches he may strengthen you with power through his Spirit in your inner being.

—Ephesians 3:16

Now to him who is able to do immeasurably more than all we ask or imagine, according to his power that is at work within us.

—Ephesians 3:20

But he said to me, "My grace is sufficient for you, for my power is made perfect in weakness." Therefore I will boast all the more gladly about my weaknesses, so that Christ's power may rest on me.

—2 Corinthians 12:9

We are hard pressed on every side, but not crushed; perplexed, but not in despair; persecuted, but not abandoned; struck down, but not destroyed. We always carry around in our body the death of Jesus, so that the life of Jesus may also be revealed in our body.

—2 Corinthians 4:8-10

No, in all these things we are more than conquerors through him who loved us. For I am convinced that neither death nor life, neither angels nor demons, neither the present nor the future, nor any powers, neither height nor depth, nor anything else in all creation, will be able to separate us from the love of God that is in Christ Jesus our Lord.

—Romans 8:37-39

Let's grow in God's image of us with His word as our lamp, to become strong and courageous warrior women.

APPENDIX C:

TRIPLE THREATS

ABUSE, ADDICTIONS, AND adultery are what I call "Triple Threats" to marriages. They are occurring in record numbers today, and they present their own unique and difficult challenges to the preservation of marriages. I have mentioned before that in marriages that struggle and end up divorcing, two-thirds are low to medium conflict situations, and these are the marriages that would be more likely to respond positively to at least one spouse applying the principles from this book.

The other one-third of the struggling and divorcing couples are in very difficult, abusive, resistant, sometimes dangerous marital situations. That does not mean it is not worth your while to grow and become healthy if you are in the one-third category, but it is important that you be informed of the special dynamics of these especially challenging circumstances.

Terry Real says there is *no* chance of learning intimacy skills for couples who are currently in an affair, drinking excessively, are in financial crisis, have sexual acting out, are experiencing threat of emotional or physical harm, or if one or both are suffering from depression, anxiety, or an eating disorder. His experience has shown that as long as any of these issues are going on, *no* amount of coaching or good intentions will bring success.[1] Any professional worth their salt would wholeheartedly agree. In these situations we need to learn about the particular issue and get strong enough to address them in the model that has been found to be most effective for personal and relational healing. The first step is to accept that our spouse's choices are not our fault, and we need to pull away and allow them to suffer the natural consequences of their actions.

Abuse

I am combining verbal, emotional, and physical abuses in this section. All abusive situations are wrong and not honoring of ourselves or what God intends for marriage. Most situations of abuse involve two individuals that have low self-esteem and express their inadequacy through acting out (the abuser), or accepting abusive treatment (the victim). It is estimated that one-fourth of all relationships will experience some form of domestic abuse in their lifetime, with three million women being physically abused per year.[2] Domestic violence is defined as a pattern of coercive behavior aimed at gaining and then maintaining power and control over the behavior of an intimate partner. Domestic abuse is not linked to age, race, socioeconomic status, religious, or educational level. Abuse is greatly underreported due to shame, fear, and threat of death. Warning signs of abuse include jealousy, controlling behavior, hypersensitivity, volatility, cruelty to animals, hostile language, isolation, breaking objects, threats of violence.

Physical abuse is often preceded by verbal abuse, but the longer either goes on, the more difficult it is to change or stop. The habits of a couple get entrenched. In the typical pattern, the man who is abusing becomes more controlling and the woman's plummeting self-esteem and feelings of "I caused it" or "I deserved it" both keep the couple locked into this cycle.

Patricia Evans has written an excellent resource for anyone experiencing a verbal component to their abuse, *The Verbally Abusive Relationship*. It is full of information on patterns of abuse, power, and how to respond to abuse.

Gary Chapman delineates a three-part cycle of physical abuse in his book *Desperate Marriages*. The first phase is a tension-building phase where the abuser is getting irritated and he begins to express his anger. When he is not appeased by her efforts of soothing, they move into phase two, the explosion phase, where the aggressive physical violence takes place. The "honeymoon" phase is calm and usually involves sincere-sounding expressions of deep remorse from the abuser. There are guilt-reducing apologies, kindnesses, and promises made out of fear of losing the relationship.[3] Unless the deeper issues fueling the abuse are addressed, this deadly cycle of abuse will continue to repeat.

Abuse also continues because the woman is embarrassed to admit it is going on, as if ignoring it will make it go away. It doesn't go away. As time goes on the woman becomes overwhelmed and helpless, blames herself, and becomes isolated, dependent, and more controlled by the abuser, and even begins to think that she really is as stupid and unworthy as he says. All of these dynamics allow for the downward spiral of abuse, and the longer it goes on, the more difficult it is to crawl out of.

When a woman admits to herself that she is in an abusive relationship, her next step is to tell a trusted friend about the suspicion or presence of abuse. This will be a tremendous help for her to begin to get assistance and grow stronger. It is so important to have support and stop the typical secrecy of abuse.

To anyone who suspects that they are in an abusive relationship of any kind, I highly recommend that you contact your local organization that supports women who are abused. Each situation is unique, and there is no wiggle room for taking the wrong approach when violence is involved. Even with my strong belief in the techniques in this book, *I would not recommend that anyone in a physically abusive relationship apply them without counsel from experienced professionals.* Women get killed when they are not informed of the best way to remain safe as they become strong and healthy, and they need to learn from an informed professional how to stop or get away from the abusive situation. A few places to start would be the National Coalition against Domestic Violence at ncadv. org, or the National Domestic Violence hotline: 1-800-799-7233.

Steven Stosney has revolutionized the treatment of abusive spouses. Previously the majority of treatment of abusers who claim to want to heal has been mostly ineffective anger management classes, typically ordered by the court system. Having come from an abusive background, Stosney went deeper into the backgrounds and sources of the abusers' actions. He has a phenomenal 87 percent success rate in treating abusers with his method called "Compassion Power." He has learned that many times, abusers' anger gets out of control as a defense against the hurt that they have experienced. He sees the majority of abusers as not having experienced compassion in their upbringing, and therefore, they continue to act out on their anger with no compassion toward their victim. His successful methods of rehabilitation include teaching about anger and self-esteem as well as emotional regulation and reconnection with core values that have been buried under the anger and hurt. It sounds rather "out there," I know, but the results speak for themselves, and you can check out his successful boot camp experience, research, and methods further at www.compassionpower.com.

ADDICTIONS

This is a jam-packed topic area and I will do my best to give a good overview of it. *Addictions* are defined in Google as "being abnormally tolerant to and dependent on something that is psychologically and physically habit forming." Addictions are a dysfunctional coping mechanism for unresolved pain and issues in our lives. Any addiction that we are involved in medicates or numbs the pain we fear looking at, so it really serves a self-protective purpose in the life of the addict. The most common form of addiction include drugs (including illegal and prescription) and alcohol; sexual addictions such as pornography, sex, compulsive masturbation, adultery (which will be covered in the next section); food, gambling, spending, work, performance, and controlling.

Addictions are scary and confusing. The partner of a person with an addiction often struggles with how to love the person without accepting his or her destructive behaviors. My mother chose the common pattern of enabling, or allowing my dad's alcoholism and workaholism to dominate and damage our family's life. Enabling any addiction is refusal to face the addiction, and includes denying it is a problem, covering up for the problem, lying about the problem, tolerating the problem, turning a blind eye to the proverbial "elephant in the living room." The first step of recovery from addictions is that the addict accepts their disease and acknowledges its consequences. Therefore, anyone who also fails to admit and point out the problem is complicit in its continuation and is not being loving.

Al-Anon is a group that parallels Alcoholics Anonymous, but it is for families that have been affected by alcohol. They have programs for spouses, children, teens, and other family of alcoholics. They have a great online site that gives locations of meetings and simple quizzes to determine if alcohol is an issue in your family. The organization recently published a book for families called *Discovering Choices*. The book includes many stories of individuals who have been affected by alcoholism and how various tools from Al-Anon have helped them. Check out Al-Anon's vast resources at http://www.al-anon.alateen.org/english.html. Once we acknowledge that we cannot change anyone else, this site would be a good place to start to strengthen ourselves.

Sexual Addiction is defined as a sickness involving uncontrollable sexual activity including pornography, repeated affairs, habitual lust, voyeurism, incest, compulsive masturbation, and child molestation. Many of these sexual addictions start early in a young man's life as he waits deep into his twenties to marry and his sexual habits are seared into his visual and sensual brain.

Marsha Means gives a helpful protocol for women for healing in her book, *Living With Your Husband's Secret Wars*. She discusses common reactions to finding out about a sexual addiction and how to confront and hold a spouse accountable without making it our problem. She talks about the effects on our self-esteem, grieving, forgiving, and living again. No small tasks, but much more possible as we seek resources from other women who have walked this torturous road of healing from a husband's sexual addiction.

Every Heart Restored is another book based on a wife's healing from a husband's sexual sin. This resource is also full of personal stories to elucidate the differences between male and female sexuality, and what is normal for a wife's response to her spouse's betrayal.[4] Due to the prevalence of sexual addiction, most marriage Web sites today have many resources and articles on recovering from sexual addictions. Some good places to start for general information are:

http://www.smartmarriages.com
http://www.laughyourway.com
http://www.dnaofrelationships.com

Specific resources for sexual addictions, most of which include on line help:

http://www.faithfulandtrueministries.com
http://www.bethesdaworkshops.org
http://www.sexaddict.com
http://www.sexualwholeness.com
http://www.pureintimacy.com

ADULTERY

Adultery is rampant today, unfortunately as much in the church as in the community. We live in such a fast-paced, pressured society, it is difficult to find the time and energy to get educated and do the work it takes to maintain a long-term marriage. Paired with the "I deserve to be happy" mantra and the fact that many more women are "available" in the workforce, times are ripe for looking outside of marriage for emotional and sexual connections. The good news is, there is a trend toward accepting that the occurrence of an affair no longer means the automatic end of a marriage.

As women in difficult marriages we are vulnerable to seeking love and connection outside of our marriages. We all want to be loved and desired. The enticement of infatuation fools us to believe we will be fulfilled in the arms of another man. I hope that the information in this book convinces that unless we heal ourselves and learn relational skills, we will only repeat our dysfunctional habits in any other relationship we seek. The content of this appendix will address the dilemma we face when our husbands seek fulfillment in another relationship.

The first thing we need to do as women is not accept responsibility for our husband's affair(s). No matter what we have been or not been in our marriage, no matter what difficulties we have both contributed to, he is the one fully responsible for making the wrong choice of responding to another woman.

Our chosen reactions to an affair can greatly affect the aftermath. Our reaction to the betrayal of our marriage vows understandably often includes expressing our anger and hurt by crying, begging, or pleading with our husbands to end the affair and return to the family. This response is very natural under the circumstances, but as much as it is possible, we would benefit from toning down a highly dependent and emotional response. The more neediness and drama we express, the more "material" an already straying husband has to continue to walk away. The more chasing we do, the more running they do. It really is an exaggerated version of the pursual-withdrawal pattern discussed previously. Please read the much more thorough discussion and guidelines from Michele Weiner Davis in her book, *Divorce Remedy*. Check out her website for more details on how to have an attitude of self-respect and dignity with honesty and accountability as you read her articles "Healing from Infidelity," "While Your Spouse Decides," and "Is Your Spouse Having an Affair?" at www.divorcebusting.com.

Another website for great support on this topic is from a woman who spearheaded a movement to not automatically divorce when her husband had an affair many years ago. Her site is www.dearpeggy.com. She started a network of support groups for affair recovery across the country called Beyond Affairs Network, or BAN. You can find much helpful recovery information and possibly a local support group at www.beyondaffairs.com.

A classic work on affair recovery is documented in the book *Not "Just Friends"* by Shirley Glass. Her "walls and windows" analogy is very helpful to keep in mind regarding protecting ourselves from affairs in our marriages. Glass says that we can have intimacy in our marriages only as we are honest and open about the significant issues in our lives. When we withhold information, we put up walls that are barriers to intimacy. When we open up, we are opening up windows to connection once again. Affairs happen when the unfaithful person puts up a wall against their spouse and opens up a window to let the affair partner in. Affair recovery involves reconstructing our walls and windows to provide secure and trusting intimacy within the marriage.[5] This is a difficult and painful path, but recovery is possible.

Conclusion

The saddest situations for me to see regarding the Triple Threats are Christian women who believe that what they have to do within their hurtful marriages is to be more submissive and more accepting of their husbands' damaging, sinful behaviors. They also pray more for them and live the sacrificial, "don't make waves" Christian life. I am certainly not saying there is anything wrong with submitting, praying, and accepting—and God can certainly come in and redeem any situation with these methods. But in the areas of the triple threats, these methods alone are very unlikely to be helpful in turning the situations around.

These deep-seated and addictive habits do not tend to turn around without the firm and informed actions of tough love. I have seen women go on and on for years, praying, tolerating, and enabling abusive, addictive, and destructive behaviors of their husbands. The women have the best of intentions to be obedient and faithful women of God. Unfortunately their form of obedience is enabling and perpetuating abusive and ungodly behaviors, and they are usually the last to know. They struggle with setting boundaries and holding their spouses accountable and speaking the truth in love.

Women facing any of these Triple Threat situations need to move out of the enabling role into one of tough love and strength. They usually realize the error of their ways when decades of this form of "acceptance" results in escalation and entrenchment of addictive habits along with their own growing bitterness and anger. So sad, so unnecessary, so disappointing and maddening. In his

Love Must Be Tough classic, Dr. Dobson has said that he has seen this form of tolerance and longsuffering prove fatal to a marriage, and that loving toughness is the best response to blatant rebellion and sin.[6] I agree.

I have made a commitment to do as much as I can to change my family's pattern of generational sin. It has been a difficult and at times overwhelming ideal. My shoulders are not that big. I have done a lot wrong, I have set us back, and I have dropped the load at times. Sometimes I feel like I have one foot in each world, one in the life and patterns and dysfunctions of my past and the other in the new life of freedom and peace and healthy relationships. This doesn't sound too bad until I tell you that at times I don't know where I am living, and it seems like the chasm between where I have each foot planted is slowly spreading apart and I am being forced to do the splits. It is hard. The bottom line is that none of us can do this alone; this is a spiritual battle. First Peter 5:8-9 tells us to be self-controlled and alert. Our enemy prowls around like a roaring lion, looking for someone to devour. We are to resist him, stand firm in our faith.

A soft and passive approach does not work when we are warring against a lion. For *this* battle we need protective armor and power. When we are armed, we need to take our troubles, especially in the areas of the Triple Threats, out of the dark place of denial and secrecy. We need to stop enabling the sin of our spouses and allow them to suffer the natural consequences of their choices. Stop protecting, stop excusing, and bring the darkness into the light, which is the only way it will be eradicated. After all, if negative patterns are not healed in our generation, they will be sure to be repeated in the next…and the next. This not a battle for the faint of heart. This is a spiritual battle for Wild Warrior Women.

Will you commit to learning about and battling against any Triple Threats in your marriage?

NOTES

1. Terrence Real, *How Can I Get Through to You?* (New York: Fireside, 2002), 199.
2. http://www.dvrc-or.org/domestic
3. Gary Chapman, *Desperate Marriages* (Chicago: Northfield, 2008), 136.
4. Stephen Arterburn, Fred Stoeker, and Brenda Stoeker, *Every Heart Restored* (Colorado Springs: Waterbrook, 2004).
5. Shirley Glass, *Not "Just Friends"* (New York: The Free Press, 2004), 12.
6. James Dobson, *Love Must Be Tough* (Dallas: Word, 1996), 6, 60.

APPENDIX D:

IF IT HAS TO END

I AM PSYCHOTICALLY optimistic, so have to make one more plug for saving marriages. Please, friends, make sure you have done all you can to save your marriage. Once again, that means being healthy, and not enabling abusive behaviors. Professional or pastoral counseling that would address any physical, spiritual, or psychological issues is a good first place to start. If you are overwhelmed with the struggle, to the point where you can't even think straight, I would recommend that you consider a legal separation. The purpose of a separation in this case would be to reduce the tension and emotional volatility and confusion that is often part of a difficult marriage. The separation should have guidelines and rules as laid out in Lee Raffel's book, *Should I Stay or Go*. This book is specifically designed to break a marital impasse.

I suggest you also check into Retrouvaille, which is a Catholic, but nondenominational weekend for troubled marriages. It is often the last-ditch effort for couples who might even be separated when they go. My husband dragged me there many years ago when I had already died and given up on us. It was the turnaround that we needed at the time. These weekends occur around the country, are reasonably priced, and have a great format and success rate on reconciliation of very difficult situations. You can find the information you need at www.retrouvaille.org.

If divorce is being done to you, there is still much you can do. The reactions we have when confronted with being the "dumpee" will greatly affect the outcome. There is a video series called *Choosing Wisely Before You Divorce*, which is an excellent resource for knowing the dynamics of going down this path. You can find more information at www.beforeyoudivorce.org.

I also recommend *Divorce Remedy* by Michele Weiner Davis, which has a great section called "The Last Resort Technique." Davis clearly lays out the reasoning for controlling our response to a spouse's leaving. Her basic premise is that when we respond with pleading and desperation, we participate in chasing our spouse away. Our spouse's annoyance and anger at our response can be used as justification for leaving. To do her model justice, I recommend you read more about it in her book.

In addition, check out the Smartmarriages.com website for articles on "Before You Think About Divorce" and "Unwanted Divorce, How to Stop." Gary Chapman's classic book, *Hope for the Separated*, is excellent for staying spiritually centered in a bad situation. One of the best Christian resources for seriously struggling marriages is Dr. Tim Clinton's *Before a Bad Goodbye*. I like this book because it is realistic about the struggles of a dying marriage and informative about healthy, spiritually-based considerations.

You may be reading this appendix because it is already too late for your marriage. Either your husband has chosen divorce, or you have. I am assuming you have not come to this decision lightly. In fact, I am sure you have prayed your heart out and have been tormented by this decision. No matter how you have arrived at this point, and no matter how necessary it is, it is a very difficult and painful place in which to live. It may very well be a very appropriate choice, it still may result in your feeling disappointed, shamed, guilty, feeling like a failure and like you have been rejected and dumped. Did I get it pretty right?

I am so sorry for your pain and the circumstances that led you to this place. I want to encourage you to go from where you are, and continue to grow into the special woman whom God made you to be in spite of the difficult adjustments ahead. I have been disappointed at times at the church's response to divorced women. I have seen them be further injured by feeling judged and blamed for the divorce. I think it is just lack of understanding of the soul-killing circumstances of a dangerously difficult marriage, and not always knowing what to provide for a woman's healing. If this is your situation, I want to encourage you to be proactive at growing a thick skin for those who do not understand, so that you do not take on unnecessary guilt or shame. I also want to encourage you to be honest with your feelings as you process your grief and loss, and find those around you who will be supportive of your healing.

It is hard to write guidelines for all circumstances, but here are some general recommendations for recovery from divorce.

- Do your own work. Go to counseling, a support group, Al-Anon, Bible study, and any other resources you can find, to make your own emotional and spiritual healing a priority. If you do not grow out of your unhealthy patterns of relating, you will have another "opportunity" in your next relationship, to learn it again, the harder way.
- P.S.: Wait a good long time, at least a year, before you do any dating.
- Take care of yourself, eat well, exercise, stay in God's Word, and find a supportive network to help you do that. Work to have a balanced life. Be honest about any unhealthy coping you might turn to, including alcohol, drugs, promiscuity, spending, denial of pain, or others, and address them.
- Get educated about the issues related to your breakup, whether it be alcohol, sexual addiction, abuse, depression, mental illness, or other reasons. Your purpose is not to fix up your ex, but to learn about yourself and any roles you might have played in the problems so that you do not repeat this dysfunction down the road.
- A good Christian group to look for is Divorce Care (Divorcecare.org). Consider starting a chapter if it's not already active in your area.

REFERENCES

COMMUNICATION

Alberti, Robert, and Michael Emmons. *Your Perfect Right: Assertiveness and Equality in Your Life and Relationships*, 1st ed. San Luis Obispo, CA: Impact, 1970.

Alberti, Robert, and Michael Emmons. *Your Perfect Right: Assertiveness and Equality in Your Life and Relationships*, 8th ed. Atascadero, CA: Impact, 2008.

McKay, Matthew, Martha Davis, an345d Patrick Fanning. *Messages: The Communication Skills Book*. Oakland, CA: New Harbinger, 1995.

Tannen, Deborah. *You Just Don't Understand: Women and Men in Conversation*. New York: Ballantine Books, 1990.

COUPLES' BOOKS*

(*These books are most helpful if both spouses are interested.)

Eggerichs, Emerson. *Love & Respect: The Love She Most Desires; The Respect He Desperately Needs*. Nashville: Integrity, 2004.

Gardner, Tim. *Sacred Sex: A Spiritual Celebration of Oneness in Marriage*. Colorado Springs: WaterBrook, 2002.

Gray, John. *Mars and Venus, Together Forever*. New York: Harper Paperbacks, 1994, 1996.

Smalley, Gary. *The DNA of Relationships*. Wheaton, IL: Tyndale House, 2004.

GENERAL MARRIAGE
(*These can be helpful when read alone or with your spouse.)

Benner, David G. *Surrender to Love: Discovering the Heart of Christian Spirituality*. Downers Grove, IL: IVP Books, 2003.

Clinton, Tim, and Gary Sibcy. *Attachments: Why You Love, Feel, and Act the Way You Do*. Brentwood, TN: Integrity, 2002.

Cloud, Henry, and John Townsend. *Boundaries: When to Say Yes, When to Say No—To Take Control of Your Life*. Grand Rapids: Zondervan, 1992.

Cloud, Henry, and John Townsend. *Boundaries in Marriage*. Grand Rapids: Zondervan, 1999.

Colbert, Don. *Deadly Emotions: Understand the Mind-Body-Spirit Connection That Can Heal or Destroy You*. Nashville: Thomas Nelson, 2003.

Davis, Michele Weiner. *The Divorce Remedy: The Proven 7-Step Program for Saving Your Marriage*. New York: Simon & Schuster, 2001.

Davis, Michele Weiner. *Divorce Busting: A Step-by-Step Approach to Making Your Marriage Loving Again*. New York: Simon & Schuster, 1992.

Davis, Michele Weiner. *The Sex-Starved Marriage: Boosting Your Marriage Libido: A Couple's Guide*. New York: Simon & Schuster, 2003.

Gordon, Lori, and Jon Frandsen. *Passages to Intimacy*. New York: Fireside, 2000.

Gottman, John. *The Relationship Cure: A 5 Step Guide to Strengthening Your Marriage, Family, and Friendships*. New York: Crown, 2001.

Gottman, John. *Seven Principles For Making Marriage Work*. New York: Three Rivers Press, 1999.

Harley, Willard. *His Needs, Her Needs*. Grand Rapids: Revell, 2001.

Hendrix, Harville. *Getting the Love You Want*. New York: Henry Holt, 1988.

Johnson, Sue. *Hold Me Tight: Seven Conversations for a Lifetime of Love*. New York: Little, Brown and Company, 2008.

Jacobs, John. *All You Need Is Love And Other Lies About Marriage.* New York: HarperCollins, 2004.

Kane, Ray, and Nancy Kane. *From Fear to Love: Overcoming the Barriers to Healthy Relationships.* Chicago: Moody, 2002.

Love, Pat. *The Truth About Love: The Highs, the Lows, and How You Can Make It Last Forever.* New York: Simon & Schuster, 2001.

Real, Terrence. *How Can I Get Through to You?: Closing the Intimacy Gap Between Men and Women.* New York: Fireside, 2002.

Satir, Virginia. *Peoplemaking.* Palo Alto, CA: Science and Behavior Books, 1972.

Seamands, David A. *Healing for Damaged Emotions.* Wheaton, IL: Victor Books, 1981.

Stanley, Scott. *A Lasting Promise: A Christian Guide to Fighting for Your Marriage.* San Francisco: Jossey-Bass, 2002.

Townsend, John. *Loving People: How to Love and Be Loved.* Nashville: Thomas Nelson, 2007.

Thurman, Chris. *The Lies We Believe.* Nashville: Thomas Nelson, 1989.

Wright, H. Norman. *The Pillars of Marriage.* Ventura, CA: G. L. Publications, 1979.

HURTING MARRIAGES

Augsburger, David. *When Enough is Enough.* Ventura, CA: Regal Books, 1984.

Augsburger, David. *Caring Enough to Confront.* Ventura, CA: Regal Books, 1981.

Chapman, Gary. *Desperate Marriages: Moving Toward Hope and Healing in Your Relationship.* Chicago: Northfield, 1998, 2008.

Chapman, Gary. *Hope for the Separated: Wounded Marriages Can Be Healed.* Chicago: Moody, 1982.

Clinton, Tim. *Before a Bad Goodbye: How to Turn Your Marriage Around.* Nashville: W Publishing Group, 1999.

Cloud, Henry, and John Townsend. *Rescue Your Love Life: Changing the 8 Dumb Attitudes & Behaviors That Will Sink Your Marriage.* Nashville: Thomas Nelson, 2005.

Dobson, James. *Love Must Be Tough: New Hope for Marriages in Crisis*. Dallas: Word, 1996.

Downing, Karla. *10 Lifesaving Principles for Women in Difficult Marriages*. Kansas City, MO: Beacon Hill Press of Kansas City, 2003.

Engelmann, Kim. *Running in Circles: How False Spirituality Traps Us in Unhealthy Relationships*. Madison: InterVarsity, 2007.

Frank, Jan. *Door of Hope: Recognizing and Resolving the Pains of Your Past*. Nashville: Thomas Nelson, 1995.

Glass, Shirley. *Not "Just Friends": Rebuilding Trust and Recovering Your Sanity After Infidelity*. New York: The Free Press, 2003.

Hemfelt, Robert, Frank Minirth, and Paul D. Meier. *Love Is a Choice: The Definitive Book on Letting Go of Unhealthy Relationships*. Nashville: Thomas Nelson, 1989.

Missler, Chuck, and Nancy Missler. *Why Should I Be the First to Change?: The Key to a Loving Marriage*. Coeur d'Alene: Koinonia House, 1991.

Smedes, Lewis B. *Forgive and Forget: Healing the Hurts We Don't Deserve*. New York: Pocket Books, 1984.

Whiteman, Thomas, and Thomas Bartlett. *Marriage Mender: A Couple's Guide for Staying Together*. Colorado Springs: NavPress, 1996.

Williams, Joe, and Michelle Williams. *Yes, Your Marriage Can Be Saved: 12 Truths for Rescuing Your Relationship*. Carol Stream, IL: Tyndale House, 2007.

Identity

Benner, David G. *The Gift of Being Yourself: The Sacred Call to Self-Discovery*. Downers Grove, IL: IVP Books, 2004.

McGee, Robert S. *Search for Significance: Seeing Your True Worth Through God's Eyes*. Nashville: Thomas Nelson, 1998, 2003.

Meyer, Joyce. *The Confident Woman: Start Today Living Boldly and Without Fear*. New York: Warner Faith, 2006.

Meyer, Joyce. *Approval Addiction: Overcoming Your Need to Please Everyone*. New York: Warner Faith, 2005.

Palmer, Parker J. *Let Your Life Speak: Listening for the Voice of Vocation.* San Francisco: Jossey-Bass, 2000.

MARRIAGE AND DIVORCE

Fischer, Bruce. *Rebuilding, When Your Relationship Ends.* San Luis Obispo, CA: Impact, 1981, 1992.

Fowlke, Lorie. *Thinking Divorce? Think Again.* Orem, UT: Fowlken Press, 2004.

McManus, Mike. *How to Cut the Divorce Rate in Half.* Potomac, MD: Marriage Savers, 2008.

Raffel, Lee. *Should I Stay or Go?: How Controlled Separation Can Save Your Marriage.* Chicago: Contemporary Books, 1999.

Marquardt, Elizabeth. *Between Two Worlds, The Inner Lives of Children of Divorce.* New York: Crown, 2005.

Popenoe, David. *War Over the Family.* New Brunswick, NJ: Transaction, 2005.

Smoke, Jim. *Growing Through Divorce.* Eugene: Harvest House, 1976.

Waite, Linda, and Maggie Gallagher. *The Case for Marriage: Why Married People Are Happier, Healthier, and Better Off Financially.* New York: Broadway Books, 2000.

Wallerstein, Judith, S. *The Unexpected Legacy of Divorce: The 25 Year Landmark Study.* New York: Hyperion, 2000.

Wallerstein, Judith, S. , Blakeslee, Sandra, *Second Chances.* New York, Houghton Mifflin, 1996.

SPIRITUAL DEVELOPMENT

Barton, Ruth Haley. *Sacred Rhythms: Arranging Our Lives for Spiritual Transformation.* Downers Grove, IL: IVP Books, 2006.

Blackaby, Henry T., and Claude V. King. *Experiencing God: Knowing and Doing the Will of God.* Nashville: LifeWay, 1990.

Bourke, Dale Hanson. *Second Calling: Passion and Purpose for the Rest of Your Life.* Brentwood, TN: Integrity, 2006.

Calhoun, Adele Ahlberg. *Spiritual Disciplines Handbook: Practices That Transform Us.* Downers Grove, IL: IVP Books, 2005.

Chambers, Oswald. *My Utmost for His Highest*. Grand Rapids: Discovery House, 1992.

Foster, Richard, J. *Celebration of Discipline: The Path to Spiritual Growth*. New York: HarperCollins, 1979, 1988, 1998.

Guiness, Os. *The Call: Finding and Fulfilling the Central Purposes in Your Life*. Nashville: Word, 1998.

Kidd, Sue Monk. *When the Heart Waits: Spiritual Direction for Life's Sacred Questions*. San Francisco: Harper & Row, 1990.

Lucado, Max. *A Love Worth Giving: Living in the Overflow of God's Love*. Nashville: W Publishing Group, 2002.

Maxwell, John C. *Failing Forward: Turning Mistakes into Stepping Stones for Success*. Nashville: Thomas Nelson, 1979.

Moore, Beth. *Praying God's Word Day by Day*. Nashville: Broadman and Holman, 2000.

Olford, Stephen. *The Sword of Suffering: Enduring Words of Hope, Inspiration, and Healing in the Midst of Despair*. Chattanooga: AMG, 2001.

Ortberg, John. *If You Want to Walk on Water, You've Got to Get Out of the Boat*. Grand Rapid: Zondervan, 2001.

Palmer, Parker J. *A Hidden Wholeness: The Journey Toward an Undivided Life*. San Francisco: Jossey-Bass, 2004.

Volf, Miroslav. *Free of Charge: Giving and Forgiving in a Culture Stripped of Grace*. Grand Rapids: Zondervan, 2005.

Wilkinson, Bruce, and Heather Kopp. *The Dream Giver*. Sisters, OR: Multnomah, 2003.

FOR WOMEN

Anderson, Joan. *A Year by the Sea: Thoughts of an Unfinished Woman*. New York: Broadway Books, 1999.

Arterburn, Stephen , Fred Stoeker, and Mike Yorkey. *Every Heart Restored Workbook: A Wife's Guide to Healing in the Wake of Every Man's Battle*. Colorado Springs: Waterbrook, 2004.

Davis, Michele Weiner. *The Sex-Starved Wife: What to Do When He's Lost Desire*. New York: Simon & Schuster, 2008.

Evans, Patricia. *The Verbally Abusive Relationship*. Holbrook, MA: Adams Media, 1992, 1996.

Frank, Jan. *Door of Hope: Recognizing and Resolving the Pains of Your Past.* Nashville: Thomas Nelson, 1995.

Gilligan, Carol. *In a Different Voice: Psychological Theory and Women's Development.* Cambridge: Harvard University Press, 1982.

Gottlieb, Laurie. *Marry Him: The Case for Settling for Mr. Good Enough.* New York: Penguin, 2010.

Heyn, Dalma. *Marriage Shock: The Transformation of Women Into Wives.* New York: Random House, 1997.

Hybels, Lynne. *Nice Girls Don't Change the World.* Grand Rapids: Zondervan, 2005.

Jarvis, Cheryl. *The Marriage Sabbatical: The Journey That Brings You Home.* New York: Broadway Books, 2001.

Krasnow, Iris. *Surrendering to Marriage.* New York: Hyperion, 2002.

Lerner, Harriet Goldhor. *The Dance of Anger: A Woman's Guide to Changing the Patterns of Intimate Relationships.* New York: Harper & Row, 1985.

Means, Marsha. *Living With Your Husband's Secret Wars.* Grand Rapids: Revell, 1999.

Munson, Laura. *This Is Not The Story You Think It Is: A Season of Unlikely Happiness.* New York: Penguin, 2010.

Oliver, Gary, and Norman Wright. *Good Women Get Angry: A Woman's Guide to Handling Her Anger, Depression, Anxiety, and Stress.* Ann Arbor: Servant Publications, 1995.

Warren, Kay. *Dangerous Surrender: What Happens When You Say Yes to God.* Grand Rapids: Zondervan, 2007.

MOTIVATION

Epstein, Fred. *If I Get to Five.* New York: Henry Holt and Co. 2003.

Frankl, Viktor, E. *Man's Search for Meaning.* Boston: Beacon Press, 1959.

Maxwell, John. *Failing Forward.* Nashville: Thomas Nelson, 2000.

Wolin, Steven J. and Sybil Wolin. *The Resilient Self.* New York: Villard Books, 1993.

Wright, H. Norman. *Resilience.* Ann Arbor: Servant Publishing, 1997.

FOR MORE INFORMATION

Check out my website for more information on marital healing and announcement for upcoming workbook and web-based teaching at: www.iwanttostaymarriedbuthow.com.

CPSIA information can be obtained at www.ICGtesting.com
Printed in the USA
LVOW04s1852250813

349506LV00002B/437/P